211 Things A Bright Boy Can Do

Tom Cutler

A PERIGEE BOOK

A PERIGEE BOOK
Published by the Penguin Group
Penguin Group (USA) Inc.
375 Hudson Street, New York, New York 10014, USA
Penguin Group (Canada), 90 Eglinton Avenue East, Suite 700, Toronto, Ontario M4P 2Y3, Canada (a division of Pearson Penguin Canada Inc.) • Penguin Books Ltd., 80 Strand, London WC2R 0RL, England • Penguin Group Ireland, 25 St. Stephen's Green, Dublin 2, Ireland (a division of Penguin Books Ltd.) • Penguin Group (Australia), 250 Camberwell Road, Camberwell, Victoria 3124, Australia (a division of Pearson Australia Group Pty. Ltd.) • Penguin Books India Pvt. Ltd., 11 Community Centre, Panchsheel Park, New Delhi—110 017, India • Penguin Group (NZ), 67 Apollo Drive, Rosedale, North Shore 0632, New Zealand (a division of Pearson New Zealand Ltd.) • Penguin Books (South Africa) (Pty.) Ltd., 24 Sturdee Avenue, Rosebank, Johannesburg 2196, South Africa

Penguin Books Ltd., Registered Offices: 80 Strand, London WC2R 0RL, England

211 THINGS A BRIGHT BOY CAN DO

Cover image of boy by Bryan Landsberg
Cover design by designbydavid.co.uk

First American edition: October 2007
Originally published in Great Britain in 2006 by HarperCollins Entertainment.

Perigee trade paperback ISBN: 978-0-399-53415-7

PRINTED IN THE UNITED STATES OF AMERICA

10 9 8 7 6 5 4 3 2

211 Things A Bright Boy Can Do

This book is dedicated to the memory of Fred Banting and Charles Best, without whose imagination and dogged persistence it could never have been written.

TIRED TIM

Poor tired Tim! It's sad for him.
He lags the long bright morning through,
Ever so tired of nothing to do;
He moons and mopes the livelong day,
Nothing to think about, nothing to say;
Up to bed with his candle to creep,
Too tired to yawn; too tired to sleep:
Poor tired Tim! It's sad for him.

Walter de la Mare

CONTENTS

ACKNOWLEDGMENTS

Any bright boy who stops to think about it will realize that he is dependent much of the time on girls and women. The following are a few of those who kept an eye on me while I was working on this volume. First, my startled mother, Pauline Cutler, who thinks I need my head examined; second, my charming editor at HarperCollins, Kate Latham, who was never less than enthusiastic; also my editor at Perigee, Marian Lizzi, who kept on laughing, and her delightful assistant, Katie Wasilewski; next, my endlessly cheerful agent, Laura Morris, who deserves a medal for supererogatory patience; then Nicolette Caven whose smashing illustrations illuminate the text; not forgetting my good friend Jo Uttley, who went to some plays with me as a sort of heroic therapy; and, finally, my incredulous, indulgent, happy, normal (and cute) wife, Marianne, who always made sure I had my bus money and that my hair was combed. She is my favorite of all.

HOW TO USE THIS BOOK

This book is aimed chiefly at boys, guys, geezers, blokes, and fellows between the ages of about 16 and 106 who find themselves at a loose end on a wet Wednesday afternoon. Probably the best way to use it is to lower yourself in somewhere and, after a nervous look around like a man in search of a breach in the wall of a nuclear reactor, get the hell out for decontamination.

Here you will find—along with the usual stuff about how to lay bricks and how to use your watch as a compass—many of those activities you have heard about but always imagined were impossible, such as how to weigh your head, how to win money in a casino, and how to take your underpants off without removing your pants: in other words, all those fundamental life skills they don't teach at school.

Unlike the activity books of yesteryear, which often called for esoteric items such as permanganate of potash, orpiment, aqua fortis, or litharge of lead, this volume demands only those props and ingredients that will be lying around. I admit that if you are going to spit-roast a suckling pig, there will be a few unusual articles required, but for the most part you shouldn't have to go far in search of equipment.

The "how to" books of my youth often contained instructions so complex and boring that one simply fell asleep reading them. I have therefore taken pains to ensure that no procedure in this volume is made up of more than a few steps, and that the directions are as transparent as an angel's tear.

I have also personally tried and tested nearly everything that follows, though I confess I didn't get the opportunity to do any actual fire walking or make a citizen's arrest. But I *did* pickle my own eggs and play the bagpipes—though not at the same time. In those cases where I couldn't actually try something, I quizzed the most expert experts I could find.

To simplify matters, I have assumed throughout that you are right handed. If you are not, please don't send letters to the government, just reverse the directions and everything will be OK. In fact, I refer to your hands quite a bit in the following pages and the drawing below shows how I've named the digits.

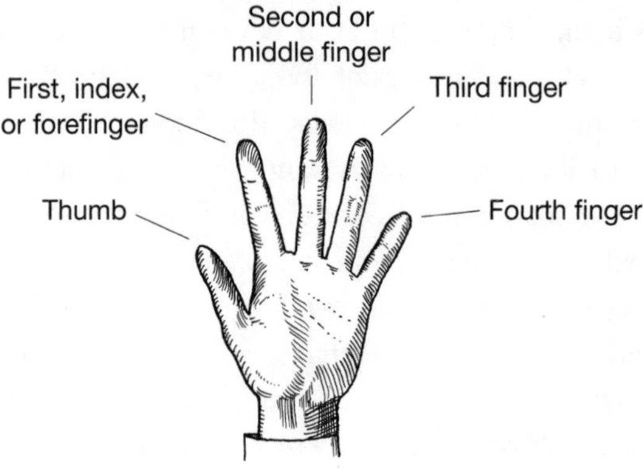

With hankies, napkins, and sheets of paper, I refer to the corners in the following way. The top left I always call A, top right B, bottom left C, and bottom right D.

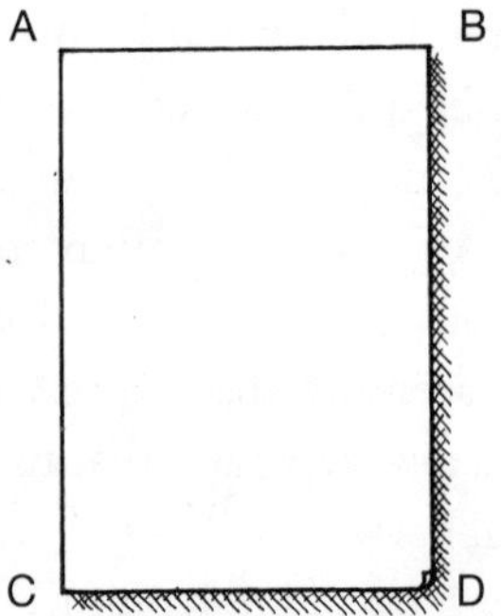

Occasionally I have referred to women as "girls." If this should upset your girl, I hope you will discourage her from organizing a book burning and point out that wherever it seemed more appropriate to write "she" than "he" I did. So at least I've been inclusive.

With proper practice and presentation, even the simplest of the tricks in this volume can be turned into a showstopper. Many have been dredged from the sludge of my memory and most I have been doing since I was a schoolboy. I admit, though, a debt of gratitude to Martin Gardner, author of numerous books of tomfoolery, puzzles, and gags that occupy the fuzzy no-man's-land between science, math, and magic. His comprehensive collections occasionally reminded me of something I'd forgotten. I must also thank Ben Dunn, whose idea this book was and who first approached me to write it. He put me on to a couple of crazy things I'd never heard of—which takes some doing. I apologize to him for burning the hair off his arm during one trick that got a bit too exciting.

I order you not to try anything dangerous that you read about here. Walking over a bed of hot coals is hazardous even for a professional hot coals man. Instead, treat these items as curiosities: mere ruminations on what one might try in an ideal world.

I have included a few tricks and gags requiring cigarettes, ashtrays, and matches although I realize that it can now be difficult to do stunts with these items for the simple reason that the government has banned smoking in many places. You'll just have to use your imagination.

You are welcome to adapt instructions and recipes according to what's in your cupboard, but if the instructions say *sharp* scissors, that is what you need, and if they say glue, then you'd better not use tape. Certainly don't blame me if you do something differently and it all goes afoul.

Finally, I know what's still troubling you: how come this book is called *211 Things A Bright Boy Can Do* instead of something more sensible like 200 things? The reason's simple really, and it's this: round numbers are difficult. Just imagine if Joseph Heller's *Catch-22*, John Buchan's *The 39 Steps*, and Federico Fellini's *8½* had instead been called *Catch-20*, *The 40 Steps*, and *8*. A bit of a letdown, I think you'll agree—much tastier the other way.

Look, we're wasting time; let's get cracking!

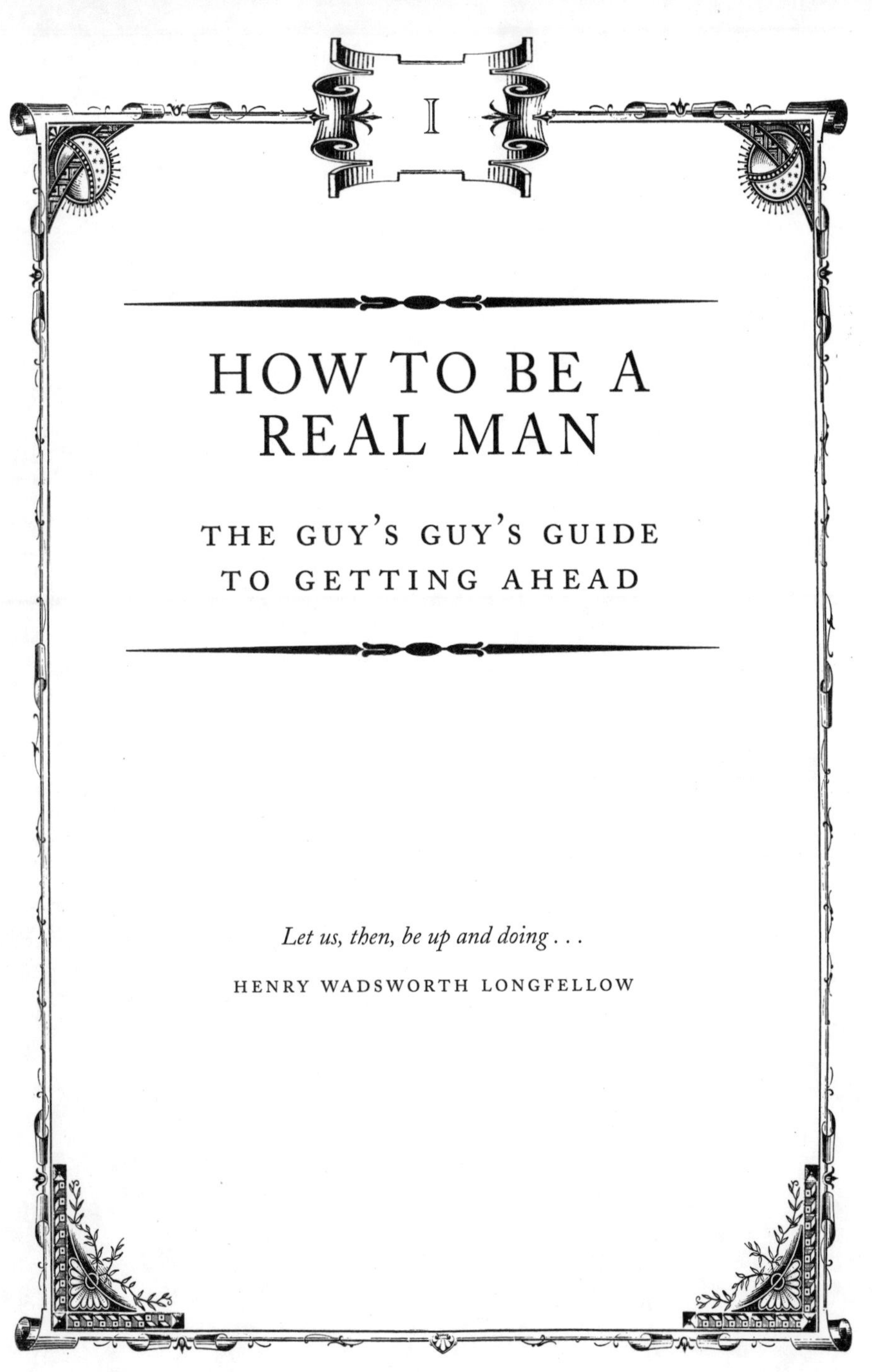

I

HOW TO BE A REAL MAN

THE GUY'S GUY'S GUIDE TO GETTING AHEAD

Let us, then, be up and doing . . .

HENRY WADSWORTH LONGFELLOW

HOW TO
USE YOUR WATCH AS A COMPASS

Suppose your Jeep has broken down in the desert. You know that there is an oasis 5 miles to the east of where you are, but a wilderness stretching for 50 miles in every other direction. The trouble is you have lost your compass, so how are you going to find the water? The answer's simple, as it always is in these utterly unlikely scenarios. You are going to use your watch as a compass. Here's the way to do it.

Method

1 Remove your watch, and point the hour hand at the sun.

2 Lay a match across the radius of the dial, halfway between the hour hand and 12 o'clock. The match will be pointing south (in the northern hemisphere—north in the southern hemisphere). That's all there is to it.

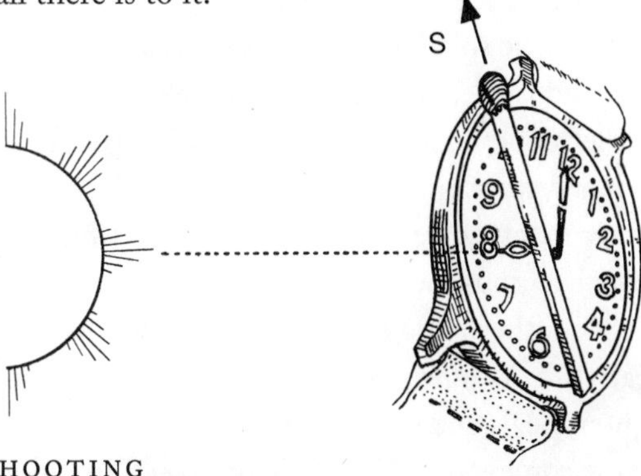

Troubleshooting

Suppose, instead of the desert, you are in the jungle and mist has obscured the sun. If you take a pencil, a stick or even your finger, and hold it upright on a pale stone or something, it will cast a fairly clear shadow even on a dim day, showing you the direction of the sun. You can now align your watch correctly.

What if you wear a digital watch? Simply note the time, draw an imaginary clock on your palm with your finger, and make your calculations in the same way.

◎ *1 million seconds is 11 days; 1 billion seconds is 31.7 years.* ◎

HOW TO
ORDER WINE IN A RESTAURANT

Should you be dining in a low-end restaurant you'll probably know more about wine than the person serving you. But in posh places an expert wine waiter called a "sommelier" will be on hand to guide you. Unfortunately, in a few restaurants—and not always the cheaper ones—the wine waiter is a snooty impostor, or an ignorant jerk, or *both*. Your best defense against idiots like this is to know a bit about the subject in advance. Here's a survival guide for the ordinary fella.

Choosing from the Wine List

1 The bulk of wine sold in the US comes from France, Italy, Spain, Australia, and Chile, with California making a strong showing as well. But let's talk European, as this is what you'll most likely encounter in a restaurant.

As a very rough guide to what to have with what, red Burgundies go well with serious meat and hearty French cooking. Beaujolais, which is a southern Burgundy region, is good with lighter food and meaty fish. Whites, including Champagne, tend to be better with lighter meals and other seafood.

When it comes to Italy and Spain, you'll find that Riojas and tapas go well together, while Chiantis and Orvietos are good with pasta and pizza and other Italian dishes. Obvious really: match regional food with appropriate regional wine and you'll be sitting pretty. On the other hand, if you're looking for a good wine at a more sensible price, you'll often find some wonderful uncelebrated options tucked away on the list.

2 Restaurants generally put enormous markups on booze, as you can sometimes see from the $5.99 supermarket labels depressingly left on the bottle. They also know that diners are often too self-conscious to pick the cheapest wine, opting instead for the one *second from the bottom*. That's where they'll put some horrible hooch with a gigantic profit margin. Best to aim for wines in the middle of the range.

3 Sometimes the cornucopia of choice can be a bit overwhelming but don't be daunted. A good bet is something you haven't heard of or can't pronounce. Shun the Chardonnays, Merlots, Pinot Grigios, Frascatis, Valpolicellas, and other "factory" wines, and watch out for Bordeaux because second-rate vintages abound and margins can be high. Chilean, Spanish, Argentine, Croat, Portuguese and Greek wines are often a much better value, especially the reds.

4 Many house wines taste as if they've been piped from a tanker and are best avoided if you're having a proper meal. But if it's a cheapo gut-filler, or you've got a heavy cold, there's no point in ordering something fancy, so go for the house wine without shame. Don't bother tasting it though (see below). A quick sniff will do.

5 If you are ordering Champagne, hold on to your hat—the prices can kill you. It's often better to buy a really good non-sparkling white instead. Whites (including bubbly) are served cold and reds generally at a warmer temperature, though Beaujolais Nouveau is excellent chilled. Ask for an ice bucket if you want to keep your wine cold. But if it's mainly water in there and not much ice, that won't do.

All that rigmarole with the bottle

There's really no need for all the pretentious "tasting" of ordinary house wine that goes on in so many restaurants. Nonetheless, you should certainly take the trouble to check that a bottle of expensive wine that you are about to buy has not gone bad. Don't allow yourself to be rushed during this process. The first thing the waiter will do before opening the bottle is show it to you. He's not doing this for his health, he wants you to confirm a couple of things.

1 First of all, see that it's unopened. If it's open, send it back (hardly ever happens, now).
2 Next, have a look at the label. If you are confused, you're in good company: 72 percent of French wine drinkers say they don't really understand the information on wine labels. The main things to check are that it's the right vineyard and the right vintage (year). If not, ask for the proper one or choose an alternative. The differences in price and quality between one vintage and another from the same vineyard can be huge.
3 Once he's opened the bottle, don't let the waiter fill your glass more than halfway, unless it's Champagne. Good ones know you need room to swirl the wine a bit.
4 Look at the wine: it should be clear and bright. If it's cloudy or full of bits, send it back. Now, with your first and second fingers on the foot of the glass gently make a small circle on the tabletop, gradually building up some speed. Swirling it like this unlocks the wine's smells (the bouquet).
5 Sniff it to check it hasn't gone bad in the bottle. Modern production techniques mean that with recent vintages this is about as unlikely as a bad egg. Nonetheless, if it smells of wet cardboard or the musty area under the railway arches it's probably "corked," having reacted with the stopper and gone bad. *Corked wine is not wine with bits of cork in it.* If you detect the perfume of cheese, or sauerkraut, it's no good; send it back. If the "nose" is vinegary you'll all have been knocked sideways the moment it was opened. If it smells funny but you are a bit unsure ask the sommelier. Just say: "You're the expert, so please have a look at this and take a whiff. Is it meant to be all murky like that, with the nauseating odor of damp dogs in a grimy old stable?" And don't allow him to persuade you it's OK. Stick to your guns; the nostrils never lie. In

a reputable place, your waiter will replace a rejected wine, without demur.

6 If you are handed the cork just ignore it. Once upon a time diners would check that the vineyard and vintage that appeared on the cork were the same as those on the label so as to prevent unscrupulous restaurants putting posh labels on crappy wine, but this doesn't happen now. Sniffing the cork is like kicking the tires on a secondhand car. There's absolutely no point to it and you'll look a fool—especially if it's plastic! I once saw a chap sniffing a screw top. Not sure what was going on in *his* head.

7 You can now taste the wine, but if it's passed the test so far it's almost certainly OK. By the way, never say: "Yes, that's delicious." The waiter wants you to verify that the wine is in good condition and that you are happy to buy it. He's not trying to find out if you like the flavor. If restaurants did that, waiters would be opening bottles all night and taking half of them away again.

8 Only a sommelier who didn't understand his craft would offer you a sparkling wine to taste. If it's bubbling, it's fine.

◎ *You are more likely to be killed by a Champagne cork than by a tarantula.* ◎

HOW TO
TELL WHEN A GIRL LIKES YOU

When it comes to recognizing the cornucopia of courtship signals that a woman uses to show a guy that she likes him, a man is about as clever as a savage at a kabuki drama. Women, who have a worldly understanding of this language, and who consciously use it all the time to attract mates, often find themselves singing their Siren song, as it were, to the deaf. So here, for Cro-Magnon man, is a no-nonsense list of the signs to look out for.

On the beach or in the street

- *Backward glance over her shoulder*: this signal means "follow me." So *follow her.*
- *Hair touching*: if she touches or plays with her hair, you're on her radar.
- *Head toss*: often accompanied by the hair flick—you've got runway clearance.

Across the room

- *Smoothing or checking clothing*: in a bundle of signals this is often her first move.
- *Displaying the inside of the wrists*: frequently combined with hair touching, it's a green light.
- *Thumb in belt*: this "pointing" gesture is sexually assertive—maybe you like that.
- *Sideways glance through partly closed eyelids*: if she looks away as you catch her eye, it's a blatant come-on.

Closer together

- *Hand/s on hips, with body pointing toward you*: things are warming up.
- *Slowly crossing and uncrossing the legs*: rather like the trader setting out his barrow.
- *Mouth open*: an all-purpose sexual signal, the polar opposite of the spinster's pursed lips.
- *Widened eyes and eyebrows raised*: fleetingly brief, this is one of the subtlest subconscious signals and is often missed. It says, "I fancy you something rotten!" Be on the lookout for it.
- *The shoe flop*: flopping her heel in and out of her shoe is an openly erotic gesture.
- *Stroking her thigh*: come on, old boy, you're cleared for takeoff.
- *Closeness*: has she moved close enough to breathe on? What are you waiting for?

- *Knee touching*: did her knee lightly touch yours? No, it wasn't an accident.
- *Hand touching*: might be very brief, but you are in the home stretch.
- *The long intimate gaze with dilated pupils*: serious "trouser disturbance" time.
- *Stroking of a long object, such as a bottle, bread stick or pepperpot*: oh, *come on.*
- *Finger sucking*: for crying out loud! If she finds some reason to ask you to suck her finger, or sucks yours, you're wasting valuable time. Get upstairs.

Lady-moth pheromones can excite males who are more than 6 miles away.

HOW TO ANALYZE A HANDSHAKE

You don't need a degree in psychology to gain a bit of valuable insight into others when flesh meets flesh—I'm referring to the good old-fashioned handshake, of course. A ritual of greeting as old as the hills, the handshake is a package of primeval signals that help us to make quick subconscious decisions about the person we've just met. So, whether dealing with a prospective employee, your congressman, or a new friend, you'll be off to a head start if you know how to analyze this prehistoric nonverbal salutation.

The manner of a handshake can vary greatly but there are three overriding styles: the coequal, the compliant, and the controlling. All handshakes can be classified under these main headings, with hand posture being the chief indicator of intent.

1 THE COEQUAL HANDSHAKE

The most common handshake is the coequal, in which the open palm is presented in a vertical position, with thumb uppermost. If you are offered a hand like this, you can assume that the other person sees you as an equal so shake in the usual way. The standard number of shakes is between two and three.

2 The compliant handshake

Shaking hands with your palm up is a way of surrendering authority. The palm-up shake can be a useful one to offer someone who feels threatened by you but there are some revolting versions that make the flesh creep when you are on the receiving end. The "wet squid" or "vicar's fingers" is probably the best known of the obsequious shakes. It is horrid to have to take hold of four clammy white fingers, slackly dangled in your direction, the limp hand reflecting a limp personality. An even more passive-aggressive version of this one is the flaccid "two-fingered widow." This is like being offered a couple of cow's udders to shake. These passive shakes contain strong "keep-away" body language—and they work.

3 (a) The controlling handshake

The controlling handshake is usually done to you by a pushy boss or another person in authority who will, in all likelihood, also have initiated the shake. A downward-facing palm is the signal that they intend to dominate you, and the angle of the palm relative to the floor reflects their level of aggression and dominance.

If you are at a job interview, or about to be given instructions by your boss, you may choose to return the shake in the only polite way possible: with your palm facing the ceiling. But if it's your girlfriend's old beau trying to shake hands in this way, you will surely have to reclaim control. You do this by stepping forward with your left foot as you reach for his hand, taking it in the only way you can, with your palm up, underneath his. Now bring your right foot forward and, at the same time, turn his hand over so that yours is on top. You have assertively neutered his dominant shake and are now standing right in the middle of his personal zone so he'll be feeling horribly uncomfortable. Then say something like: "Do you realize that haircut makes you look like a girl?" Problem solved.

The most aggressive handshake of this kind is the stiff-arm, thumb-out, palm-down shake. Don't submit to this bullying gesture unless you are looking forward to the knuckle grinding follow-on. The only way to counter this one is not to take the hand but to come into the attack from above, firmly encircling the guy's wrist, and shaking his arm hard. This will humiliate him and, when combined with the bold step forward into his intimate space, it is hard to beat.

3 (B) The double-handed controlling shake

Sometimes called the "politician's shake," this assertive shake comes in various levels. In the start position, the shaker cups the recipient's right hand and displays a huge cheesy grin. The next four levels are all favorites of salesmen whereby they hold on to your right hand as normal and use the left for (a) the wrist-hold, moving on to (b) the elbow clutch, (c) the biceps squeeze, and, finally, (d) the shoulder grip. There is one further complex shake, not often seen, whereby the shoulder grip is maintained while the salesman—usually smiling or laughing broadly—collapses his left cheek on to your shoulder, as if sharing some long-forgotten hilarious family memory. These shakes are all meant to show various degrees of chumminess but are usually met by a sickly grin on the face of the victim.

The Mason's handshake

It is well known that the Masons have a secret handshake, although nobody I spoke to was prepared to confirm any of the following. Feared by some as a sign of conspiratorial wickedness, the Masons' shake is actually more like the handshake of the Boy Scouts, signaling little beyond membership of a congenial club. The Masons are a hierarchical bunch with a strict pecking order of different shakes that has its own jolly Biblical nomenclature. Handshake names include "Shibboleth," "Giblim," "Boaz," and one that sounds like a sort of bamboo-metal chair, "Tubalcain."

The shakes go from the subtle and ordinary looking, right up to the full-blown "real grip" of a Master Mason: "Ma-Ha-Bone," which resembles a pair of copulating cephalopods. Below is a description of the Master Mason's "pass grip" for you to practice.

TUBALCAIN—THE "PASS GRIP" OF THE MASTER MASON

To an onlooker, this seems pretty much like any other handshake, but if you're shaking hands with a Mason he will feel the difference. It's much the same as the lower-ranking "Shibboleth" shake, in which you press your thumb into the space between the other fellow's first and second knuckles, and the "Jachin" shake, which comes between "Shibboleth" and "Tubalcain," and in which you press your thumb on to his second knuckle.

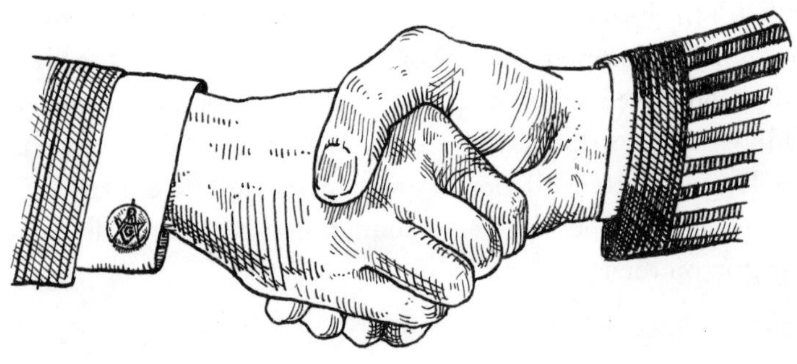

"Tubalcain" requires you to press your thumb firmly *between the other man's second and third knuckles* as in the illustration. If he's a Mason, he'll do the same. What you get up to next is entirely your own affair.

◎ *The largest "golden handshake" on record is reported to be $53 million.* ◎

HOW TO
BE A SURFER DUDE, LIKE TOTALLY

Should you be an inhabitant of Colorado rather than Californi-a, you probably don't get much local surfing action. But that doesn't mean you can't become a real cool surfer dude. What does it take, after all? Some baggies, a pair of Huarache sandals, a bushy bushy blond hairdo, and a bronzed rippling six-pack.

OK, so you're in your garage waxing down your surfboard, looking cool and beachoid—but there's something missing. Of course: *Surfspeak.* All surfer dudes are fluent in Surfspeak: a distinctive patois rooted in Hawaiian. You should be aware, however, if you are a beginner, that Surfspeak is like off the wall to the max, like totally dude. So don't be surprised if, on encountering a native speaker, you're like, "No way!" and they're like "Way!" Here's a typical dialogue in Surfspeak, with translation into English.

Howzit, brah?
How do you do, sir?

The surf is epic, fully macking double overhead corduroy to the horizon.
The sea conditions are currently favorable.

Latronic, dude.
Until next time then, sir.

Hawaiian surfing was first recorded during the 1780s in the journals of Captain Cook, the Hawaiian chiefs apparently taking special pleasure in showing off on their boards. Captain Cook must have scratched his wig a bit at the sight of this and wished he was back home in Upper Shadwell, having a nice cup of tea. This was all before the locals stabbed him to death in an argument over some tongs.

Basic surfing technique involves paddling out on your board and then paddling back toward the shore until you are able to catch a suitable wave. (The sharp part goes at the front and that little rudder thing goes in the water.) I'm afraid this paddling business is not very cool looking, but you will be fairly unobtrusive so don't worry about the babes jeering at you from the beach. The topography of the seafloor determines good surfing waves, so go to the places where you know the waves are surfable: not Long Island, for example. Tidal differences can have a significant effect on wave quality. In Hawaii the difference between high and low tide tends to be only two or three feet, which is good. In Bali and Panama the difference can be two or three times this. Anyway, once a big enough wave has collected you and your board, stand up on the thing and begin looking totally dudeish as it carries you toward the shore. That's all there is to it, really. Couldn't be simpler.

Don't be tempted to improvise with ironing boards or the top off your mom's old breakfront; you'll look about as cool as Buzz Aldrin driving an ice cream truck.

◎ *Dennis Wilson, the only Beach Boy who could surf, drowned in 1983.* ◎

HOW TO
MOW THE PERFECT LAWN

There's an old country saying: "It's either a lawn or a life, you can't have both." Like many others, this one is completely untrue. Providing you take a little care, there's no reason you can't have an impressive yard *and* time to enjoy it. But neglect it, and your beautiful grass will soon be fighting a tangle of unwelcome growth underfoot. So feed and water regularly, and tackle weeds, worms, and other pests as soon as you can. Mowing a well-looked-after lawn will not only make it look its best, but will also stimulate growth. Here is the mower's bible in a nutshell.

- Get a really good mower and look after it.

- Mow from March to October—twice a week in summer, once a week at other times—when the lawn is dry. Regular trims are good. Infrequent short-back-and-sides are bad.
- Optimum grass height is between 1 inch and 1¼ inches. Make sure you've brushed off stones, tennis balls, and beer cans before you mow.
- Don't allow grass cuttings to stay on the lawn: they are unsightly and do more harm than good.
- To avoid ripples in your grass ("washboarding"), vary the direction of successive cuts by 90 degrees. Left–right, followed by up–down, and back to left–right.
- *Stripes*—for goodness' sake do these properly. To start with, you need a roller on your mower. It's the roller that makes the stripes.

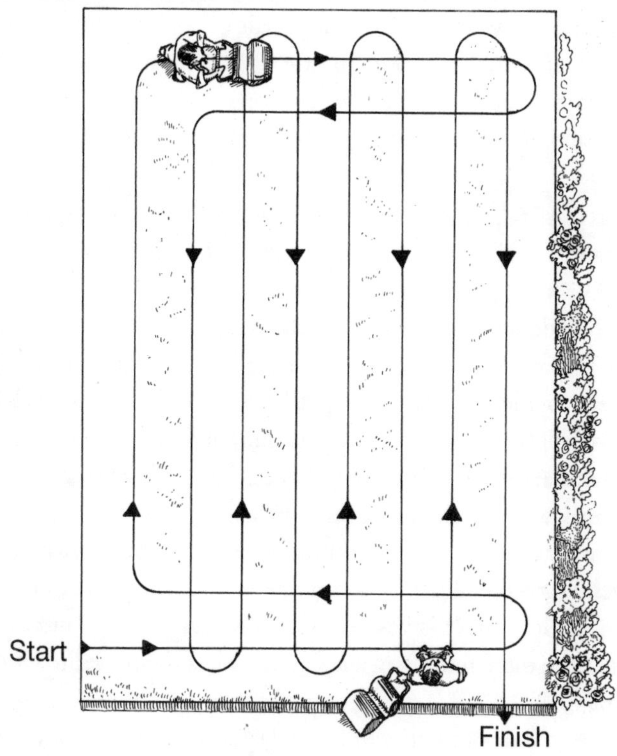

The effect is produced by taking your mower for a walk all over the lawn, without stopping, like an aged parent in a wheelchair. If you consult the diagram on page 15, you'll see how it should be done.

◎ *Americans spend an estimated $29 billion on lawn care each year.* ◎

HOW TO
SURVIVE FOR A WEEK WITH JUST ONE SET OF CLOTHES

Suppose you are stranded in a foreign hotel. Maybe a hurricane has destroyed the airport and shops, or perhaps you have absentmindedly packed only enough clothes for one day: a shirt, a sweater, one pair of pants, a pair of underpants, and a pair of socks. Even the most lackadaisical man would cringe at the thought of going seven days in the same threads, especially if he had a roving eye and was in holiday mood. Fear not, here's how to survive this minor emergency.

1 Every night, take a shower in the hotel—wearing your socks. Give them a really good soaping. After a thorough rinse, remove your socks, wring them out and hang them over the radiator.
2 British broadcaster Johnny Morris claimed to travel the world with just three shirts: the one he was wearing, one "washing" in the sink and one dripping dry. My technique, however, dispenses with all but one shirt. Fill the bath, and wash your shirt and underpants with the complimentary soap, giving the collar a good scrub. Wring out your underpants and hang them over the radiator. Put the shirt on a hanger and allow it to drip dry into the bath, or over the heater. For persistently wrinkly shirts try hanging them in a steamy shower. The wrinkles melt away. It is wishful thinking of the worst kind to believe that the mere folding of a soiled shirt has the power to cleanse it overnight.
3 With care, a pair of pants can easily last a week. If they are jeans,

or otherwise informal, you're in luck. Just drape them over a chair. If they are fancier, lay them out under the blanket and sleep on top of them. The creases will come up nice 'n' crisp. Don't put them under the mattress; it leaves spring marks. A sweater will remain presentable for ages, so long as you don't dribble soup down it or scrunch it up.

4 In the morning, everything will be clean and dry. What more could you ask?

◎ *Naphthalene mothballs are highly poisonous if swallowed.* ◎

HOW TO
IMPRESS A GIRL ON A BUDGET

For most women, power is an aphrodisiac, the symbols of which are objects such as sports cars, expensive clothes, and smart watches. These can all be hard to come by when you are a young guy so if you don't have access to them you must give girls the impression that you do. Let us suppose that you have arranged to spend a day in town with a woman. Here are a few ideas.

- First, you must dress the part. Make regular trips to a fancy town or neighborhood nearby, where many fine second-hand items, including almost new linen suits and silk ties, can be picked up from charity shops for a song.
- The night before your meeting, knock on the door of a house with a garden of beautiful flowers. Tell the little old lady that your mother is dying but that a few of her blooms would cheer her final hours. She will clip you a handsome bunch. Wrap them in fancy paper (cost, about $2).
- On the day of your meeting, stop into a shop selling expensive gentlemen's toiletries. Try some classy aftershave and then rush out, saying it's annoying your hay fever.

- The car problem is tricky. Taxis cost a fortune and you can hardly cram your girl into a bashed up jalopy, so insist on walking. A short stroll to an elegant (free) art gallery is the thing. Bone up beforehand, and you can come out with things like: "Of course, after *The Laughing Cavalier,* Frans Hals finished up a poverty stricken old man in the poorhouse." It will lend you the air of a connoisseur without costing you a penny.
- If you don't have a flashy watch, don't wear one at all. Should the subject come up, just comment: "I never wear a watch. As Goethe said, 'The present moment is a powerful goddess.'" Your erudition will score you points that even a Rolex can't.
- As lunchtime rolls around, say: "It's such a lovely day, why don't we picnic by the river?" The idea will strike your girl as utterly charming. (It will strike you as fantastically *cheap* compared to a restaurant.) As you settle yourself under a willow tree, whip out your pièce de résistance: a bottle of French Champagne. This will be one of the two bottles given to you by your parents when you graduated from something or other—you don't mention this. If you leave it in the freezer until it's about to solidify, it will still be cold at lunchtime. After a glass of Champagne, produce the picnic. This will consist of some crusty bread, a jar of fine French paté (your loss leader), some homemade pickled eggs (see recipe, page 269), a good lettuce, fresh arugula, and so forth. For dessert, you'll find doughnuts cheap and filling; lollipops look great, last ages, and are a bargain at 50¢ each.
- If you manage it properly, 80 percent of the Champagne should end up inside your lady friend, so she will probably just want to doze beneath the trees after lunch. That's fine, it's free. If you like, you can do a few tricks with a blade of grass (instructions on page 123).
- For the evening's entertainment avoid the cripplingly expensive opera and instead get hold of some free tickets to a funny TV show. After the performance, invite her back to your place for "supper."
- On to dinner—at your abode, of course. Pasta rapida (see page

289), is cheap, delicious, looks and smells fantastic, and is impossible to screw up (just don't overcook it). Another bottle of the industrial Champagne will smooth things along nicely.

Excluding travel, the whole day should have come in well under thirty bucks, and the rest of the evening ought to be entirely free of charge . . .

◎ *Some 22,000 checks are deducted from the wrong bank accounts every hour.* ◎

HOW TO
PAINT A DOOR

There is something primeval about painting a door and, like barbecuing, it is the province of the male. There are different approaches to the job nonetheless, from the carefree, via the workmanlike, to the punctilious, but however it is done, a well painted door is a lovely thing to look at, and many a happy hour can be spent admiring a guy's well-painted entryway.

This is the old-fashioned method. To make washing easier, coat your hands in Vaseline before you begin, or wear surgical gloves.

Required

- *Paint*
- *Brushes*
- *Turpentine*
- *Pumice stone*
- *Sandpaper*
- *Radio*
- *Snack-making equipment*

Method

First scrub the door thoroughly with a weak solution of soapy water, using the stump of an old broom. Smooth the whole surface by rubbing down with a pumice stone and plenty of water, especially if the washing has raised the grain. Rinse the door thoroughly and allow it to dry (a couple of days is wise).

Stir your paint with a stick and pour what you require into a smaller pot for convenience. Let's say you are painting a four-panel door. The first job is to paint the moldings, beads, recessed crannies and grooves, using a 1 inch flat brush. Put a rubber band around the bristles to keep your strokes neat and tidy. It is now time for a snack. To stop your brush drying off while you leave it, wrap it in a bit of cling wrap. It will easily last overnight.

Having painted the moldings, it is now time to do the panels. Following the directions of the arrows in the drawing, paint *across* the grain with a two inch or three inch brush and once the panels are covered, "lay off" in the direction of the grain. To do this, wipe the brush clean of surplus paint and put the bristle tips at the top of the panel. Now draw the brush down to the panel foot, using a light stroke, and continue in this way, overlapping each stroke slightly as you proceed to the right, until all the panels are done.

Next, paint your muntings (the upright middle rails). Follow these with the top, middle, and bottom horizontal rails, and finish with the stiles (the vertical side rails). Your coats of paint should be alternately "sharp" (diluted with turpentine) and "round" (undiluted, for a glossy finish). Each should be allowed to dry properly, and sanded with fine sandpaper, before repainting.

◎ *TV painter Bob Ross's favorite activity was cleaning his brushes.* ◎

HOW TO DEFEND YOURSELF WITH NOTHING BUT AN UMBRELLA

Every young man should acquaint himself with the basics of self-defense with an umbrella, walking stick, or lady's parasol, if only to pick up a few ideas for an entertaining after-dinner speech or video installation.

Properly handled, a tightly rolled umbrella can be a singularly effective defensive weapon, although it makes a sorry club. Do not be tempted to hit your assailant with it—all that will happen is that he will become wet, since a closed umbrella absorbs much of the energy that the ill-armed defendant would intend to transmit straight into an aggressor's head, and an open one is a hopeless weapon, especially in high wind. I have heard it said that the sudden opening of a self-expanding umbrella in an assassin's face is momentarily startling, giving you an edge of surprise, but you then have the problem of collapsing and furling it again. No, the best thing to do is to use the point, the spike-jab being the umbrella's deadly secret weapon. Hold the instrument in front of you like a rapier and give your opponent a swift, sharp poke in the face, abdomen, or privates. That should curb his enthusiasm pretty quickly.

Cousin of the umbrella is the walking stick, and the same jabbing move with the stick's blunt tip has an equally persuasive effect on a ruffian. Once he is on the ground, you will find you can hold him there till the cows come home, with your stick planted resolutely in his middle. Occasional downward pressure is a convincing reminder that he is in a weak negotiating position. You can now chat to him about the inadvisability of swearing, the expected arrival of the cops, and other points of interest.

Whereas an umbrella makes a poor bludgeon, the walking stick is the connoisseur's weapon of choice. The ability to deliver a hearty wallop with a rapidly swung walking stick puts even the most palsied grandpa into a position of power. Practice whistling your stick through the air in enormous circles while strolling in the countryside. You will find it possible to get up enough momentum to knock the side-view mirrors off cars.

Faced with an attacker, swing the stick like a helicopter blade, suddenly bringing it down on him from above, in a slicing action. This makes it difficult to grab, enhances its potential to hurt, and leaves your other arm free to effect a nose grip or ear twist, or to maintain a protective guard. Aim especially for the forearm or the inside of the knee, or for the bony bits: collarbone, shin, elbow, and hand. Avoid an assailant's head—unless you are trying to kill.

◎ *Kung fu star Bruce Lee was a philosophy major.* ◎

HOW TO APPEAR MORE INTELLIGENT THAN YOU ARE

Mark Twain was famously of the opinion that it is better to keep your mouth shut and be thought a fool than to open it and remove all doubt. Witty though this remark is, it is false, according to new research that shows that people judge strangers' IQs in some odd ways. Here are a few recommendations based on the findings.

- *Speak quickly.* Speaking fast is a true indicator of intelligence but it can also be a sign that you've been at the cooking sherry so watch out.
- *Use a large vocabulary.* Having a lot of words at your command is a reliable mark of intelligence. Dullards are unlikely to bother faking it because it's such hard work.
- *Be clear.* Clarity is another pretty obvious indicator of mental capacity. It's a tough one to fake, though.
- *Interrupt people.* It may seem rude, but interrupters are viewed as more intelligent.
- *Talk loudly.* This is believed—falsely—to be a sign of intellectual capacity. It is, in fact, just a sign that you talk loudly.
- *Avoid a halting speaking style.* It is erroneously believed that hesitancy, and a speaking style larded with "ums" and "ers," indicates low brain power, even though many brainy people are shaky mumblers.
- *Don't use slang.* Although bright people often use slang, it is assumed (wrongly) to be a mark of dimness.
- *Be tall.* There are plenty of brainy midgets. But taller appears smarter.
- *Wear glasses.* It has long been known that glasses are believed to indicate brains. They don't, but it doesn't stop people thinking they do.
- *Look neat and clean.* Like being tall this has little to do with intelligence but people think it does.
- *Be slim.* Although it is obviously crazy to believe that fat people are less intelligent, this is what people *do* believe.

◎ *"Those who enter the country illegally violate the law."—George W. Bush.* ◎

HOW TO
DEAL WITH CROWDED TRAINS AND LONG LINES

Once, I was on an underground train in London and we were packed nose to nose. After a minute the situation began to bother one fellow, who shouted out: "Can you move down please!" People shifted from one foot to the other but didn't really move. The man—clearly a genius in this department—then called out: *"Look, this lady is going to be sick."* I have never seen people shrink back with more alacrity, and I now use the technique myself. It works every time.

This encouraged me to investigate that other bane of modern life: how to choose the shortest line at the supermarket.

Even with a graduate-level mathematical analysis of a small three-line setup it's easy to see that from a purely probabilistic angle the odds are already two to one that one of the lines you didn't choose is likely to be quicker than the one you did. But it's worse than that because Real People and their age-related behaviors contaminate the math.

A good way to overcome this difficulty is to work out the average age of each line by adding up everybody's (estimated) age and dividing the total by the number of people in their line. Imagine two lines: line A, containing three people, aged, 45, 20, and 60, with an ALA (average line age) of 41.6, and line B, containing three people, aged 11, 65, and 85, with an ALA of 53.6. Smaller numbers are what you're after throughout this whole exercise and line A gets a youth advantage of 12.0 in this example.

Next you must multiply the ALA by the estimated number of cart items in that line, divide the total by 1,000, and round off, to give yourself a useable number. Let's suppose line A has some 60 items and line B about 35. (The general principle is that older people tend to have less stuff in their carts.) Your rounded sums give a score of 2.5 for line A ($41.6 \times 60 \div 1{,}000 = 2.496$), and 1.9 for line B

(53.6 × 35 ÷ 1,000 = 1.876). Looks like line B, the older line, is now your best bet.

But wait; you have yet to take account of the LOLQ (little old lady quotient), and, let's face it, LOLs are never in a hurry. Furthermore, every 30 seconds extra an LOL spends chatting to the checkout girl about Werther's Originals must be multiplied by the number of people behind her. If there are 10 other people in the line, then that's 10 times 30 seconds, or 300 seconds, or 5 *valuable total-man-minutes* of unnecessary heart-attack-inducing stress. That old lady's 30-second gossip is a life-threatening health problem.

To arrive at your LOLQ you must divide the number of LOLs by the number of people in the line and multiply this by 5 to make it sensible. The lower the LOL quotient, the faster the line. So if it's 5 LOLs in a line of 10 your LOLQ is 0.5. In line A it's an LOLQ of 0, and in line B its 0.7 (rounded up). You now multiply this by 5 to get an adjusted LOLQ for line A of 0, and for line B of 3.5.

By adding your adjusted LOLQ to your previous figure you arrive at an FLS (final line score). So in line A (younger) you add 0 to 2.5 to get a final line score of 2.5. In line B, (older), you add your LOLQ of 3.5 to 1.9 to give you an FLS of 5.4. This gives line B, your older line, a line disadvantage of 2.9. Even though they have done less shopping, they will take longer.

If you don't fancy all that arithmetic, try a quick averaging round-up. Old and lots of shopping, bad. Younger and less shopping, good.

Or you could just go to the line with the cute checkout girl.

◎ *The shopping cart was invented in 1937 by Sylvan Goldman.* ◎

HOW TO
LAY BRICKS

During idle moments, Winston Churchill enjoyed nothing more than a bit of recreational bricklaying. If you'd like to be a British prime minister or overthrow a fascist regime, laying bricks could be just the thing to get you started.

REQUIRED

- *Trowel (a cake cutter will do in an emergency)*
- *Mortar*
- *A straight edge of some sort*
- *A concrete foundation*
- *Mortarboard (not the sort with a tassel, obviously)*
- *Some bricks*
- *A potato on a string*

INSTRUCTIONS

Before you begin, mark a straight line along your foundation. To bed in the first bricks, take a dollop of mortar and spread it with your trowel or cake cutter along the line. On one side of your bricks you'll see a sort of hole, the so-called "frog." Lay your bricks, frog facing upward.

After the first brick, lay the second a few feet along, and bridge the gap with your level to check they are the same height. When you're happy, fill the intervening space with more bricks. For the joints between the bricks, scrape a little mortar on to the edge. Cutting bricks is a frightful nuisance, so wiggle them instead to even up the gaps. Carry on until you reach the end of your wall.

Unless you're making a corner (more advanced) you'll need to start your second layer with a half-brick, otherwise all your joints will line up, weakening the wall. As mentioned, cutting a brick is a pest. It is best done by laying it on the floor and whacking it hard with a stemmed blade, such as a brick "bolster."

Spread some mortar on top of the lower course and make a valley all the way down the middle with your trowel. As you push the bricks on top, the mortar will fill the valley. Trim off any that squishes out the sides. A length of stretched string will help keep your second and subsequent rows in line.

Remember to make these periodic checks:

- *Stick check.* Use a marked stick to verify that your layers are at the right height.
- *Level check.* Don't try to level individual bricks or you'll go crazy.

Lay your level along a whole row. Tap recalcitrant bricks into place.

- *Potato-on-a-string check.* This improvised plumb line (use a *small* potato) will ensure that the wall is perpendicular.
- *Straight-edge check.* Use on the face of the wall to ensure it's flat. Your trowel handle is ideal for dealing with naughty bricks that are out of place.

Remember: When laying bricks, your pants should always be loose enough to expose the crack in your behind.

◎ *At age 13 Sean Connery worked as a bricklayer.* ◎

HOW TO BE HAPPY

Animals are happy as long as they are healthy and well fed, but people often aren't. If you are one of the unhappy people who doesn't enjoy life, then this page is for you.

"Happiness scientists" have discovered that cheerfulness is genetically programmed and is fairly impervious to life's ups and downs. A group of millionaires is likely to be about as happy or miserable as a group of paraplegics. But this doesn't mean you can't train yourself to be generally happier than you currently are.

The "how happy are you already?" test

Happy people share some character traits. For example, they tend to have realistically modest aims. They are not eaten up by envy, shame, guilt, boredom, or fear, but are full of zest, affection, and zeal, warming both hands before the fire of life. They judge themselves against their own standards rather than those of others and aren't constantly looking over their shoulders at the Joneses or relentlessly pursuing material things, a habit described by one psychologist as "toxic to happiness."

To discover whether you are one of these happy bunnies, or a miserable swine, fill in the following boxes from 1, if the description is utterly wrong, to 5, if it is utterly right. If it's a "don't know," mark it 3.

- ☐ I am optimistic and outgoing.
- ☐ I forgive and forget.
- ☐ I like myself.
- ☐ I always see the best in others.
- ☐ I have close friendships.
- ☐ I get great satisfaction from my daily activities.
- ☐ I occupy myself in an absorbing job or hobby that sometimes causes me to lose all track of time (e.g., zither playing, stamp collecting, or brain surgery).

To score your test, just add up the numbers. Scores from 7–14 indicate that you are in utter misery; from 15–28 that you are somewhere in the middle but, at the lower end, could be happier; and from 29–35 that you are insufferably cheerful.

How to be happier today

Instead of sitting every night polishing your Unhappiest Person of the Year medal, the best way to become happier is to focus on your strengths and talents—those things you are really good at and enjoy (don't say "being miserable"). Happy people tend to use their strengths a lot.

In addition, you should begin to *behave* happy. The following is a list of staggeringly simple behaviors that have been found to change the brain's chemistry, producing feelings of happiness.

- Greet a stranger.
- Do somebody a good turn.
- Secretly cancel a grudge.
- Call an old friend and arrange to meet up.
- Volunteer for something of absolutely no benefit to yourself.

- Get some exercise.
- Start growing a plant (see page 172).
- Watch a film, or read something, that really makes you laugh.
- Turn the TV off and spend an hour on a hobby.

It's simple really.

The world's happiest countries: (1) Nigeria, (2) Mexico, and (3) Venezuela.

HOW TO
CURE A HANGOVER

The short answer to the question, "Doctor, what's the best cure for a hangover?" is, "There isn't one, so don't get drunk." But that is unhelpful, so here are a few things you can do to *treat a hangover's horrid symptoms.*

WHAT IT'S DOING TO YOU

When you drink a pint of beer, glass of wine, or tumbler of scotch, the alcohol is absorbed in the small intestine and taken in the bloodstream to the liver where it is metabolized by two enzymes: alcohol dehydrogenase and aldehyde dehydrogenase. The first of these converts the drink into a highly poisonous volatile compound called acetaldehyde, about which we will learn more later.

The body does its best to excrete spare sauce in the urine and on the breath, but you can drink it faster than your liver can process it, so it ends up doing all kinds of crazy things to your brain. These pre-hangover or so-called "drunk" symptoms include various delusions, such as that you are a frightfully interesting guy and God's gift to women.

As the evening wears on, the booze begins to mess up your brain's world-interpreting apparatus, causing wobbly staggers and vertiginous dizzy spells that send the room around in circles until you feel wretchedly sick. This lovely effect is helped along by the nauseatingly toxic acetaldehyde I just mentioned. At this point your body assumes (correctly) that it has been poisoned by something that went in your mouth, and often decides to return the contents of your stomach to the outside world. Hence Saturday-night-pavement-pizza syndrome.

Hangover symptoms

Interesting though the science of getting utterly bladdered is, however, we are more interested in your condition the next morning, when you wake in a strange room, with a tongue like sandpaper, and the sensation that a sumo wrestler has been squeezing your head all night, his thumbs pressing down on your eyes. If you're lucky you'll also be enjoying zooming vertigo, prize-winning queasiness, and the urgent desire to be unconscious once more.

By-products of alcohol metabolism are the main cause of your foul-tasting mouth, while your dry tongue is the result of dehydration, since the vehicle used to get the poisons out of your body is urine, which you've been making a lot more of than usual. Your throbulating headache may be due to dilated blood vessels in the brain or to a low blood-glucose level—a complication of processing the booze.

Congeners, substances incidental to fermentation and distillation, are answerable for a lot of your "I wish I was dead" symptoms. This list shows in order the congener-viciousness of various drinks, from mild to formidable.

1. Vodka (best for hangover reduction)
2. White wine, and gin
3. Beer
4. Scotch whisky
5. Sherry
6. Red wine
7. Brandy (very vicious)

Mixing drinks is as unwise as the good fairy always said it was because the body has to deal with congeners of different types, and it's not really up to the job. Beer is a good bet all around because it fills you up, is generally weaker than wine or spirits, and is at the lower end of the congener-viciousness scale.

The cure

Huge fried breakfasts, hostile mixtures of raw eggs and Worcester sauce, or violent exercise are just so many old wives' recipes. A sweet drink will bump up your blood sugar if it's low, and one containing caffeine may help your headache by constricting blood vessels in the brain (as may a bag of frozen peas on your head). A thin broth will taste nice, be hot, and supply a sort of moral nourishment at the same time. B vitamins are said to aid alcohol metabolism, as is an amino acid called cysteine, found in sprouts and garlic. But unless you feel like having a bowl of garlicy sprouts, your best bet is to find some cysteine supplies from a speciality food shop. There's certainly no doubt that marmalade is good if you are feeling sick, being the only food that tastes the same coming up as it does going down.

Maybe the most cheerful remedy ever suggested is the one attributed to Eddie Condon: "For a bad hangover, take the juice of two quarts of whisky." It's true that more booze (hair of the dog that bit you) can temporarily relieve the withdrawal symptoms of a heavy user such as W. C. Fields, but for the rest of us the best remedy is the intake of very large volumes of water, a couple of fizzy indigestion tablets every four hours (if you can stand the noise), and plenty of rest or, indeed, sleep. Fresh air can make you feel better, as can a hot shower or bath, but it's those boring ones that really do the trick.

◎ *The world's headache-sufferers swallow some 50 billion aspirin each year.* ◎

HOW TO
JUDGE A WOMAN'S BRA SIZE AT A GLANCE

Trickier than it sounds, this pastime is more science than art and it has many practical advantages. It is not something many men are able to do and, at the same time, is enormous fun to practice. You'd be amazed how accommodating women can be when you explain what you are up to, and they love letting you guess. What's more, it's an excellent spatial-thinking exercise if you are considering a career in civil engineering.

Much of the skill lies in the ability to estimate the circumference of a body. This is notoriously difficult to do. To test your own powers try guessing the circumference of a tall glass. You'll find if you now measure it that the distance around its mouth is *almost always greater than its height*. Very deceptive—you've got to keep your wits about you.

Down to business

The bust size is the measurement around the fullest part of a woman's breasts and you must get used to guessing this. After a bit of trial and error with a few game ladies and a tape measure, you should start getting the hang of things. Anyway, let's suppose, for practice, that you've guessed a bust size of 38 inches. *Remember this.*

Next, estimate the thoracic circumference *under* the hooters. If you guess an even number, add four; if odd, add five. Your final figure is the lady's hypothetical band size. Suppose you guess 32 (even) and add four, you arrive at a band size of 36.

To get the cup size, compare the band size with the bust size. If the numbers are the same, then she's an A cup. Otherwise, each inch of difference equals one cup size: if the bust is an inch larger than the band, then she is a B cup; two inches larger, a C; and so forth, spasmodically through the alphabet. In our example the bust size (38) is two inches larger than the band (36), so she is a C cup. Funny cup sizes like DD at the Mae West end of the scale can throw the novice, but whatever happens you'll have a lot of fun weighing the evidence and working it all out. It's better than TV anyway.

◎ *The world's biggest watermelon weighed in at a staggering 268.8 pounds.* ◎

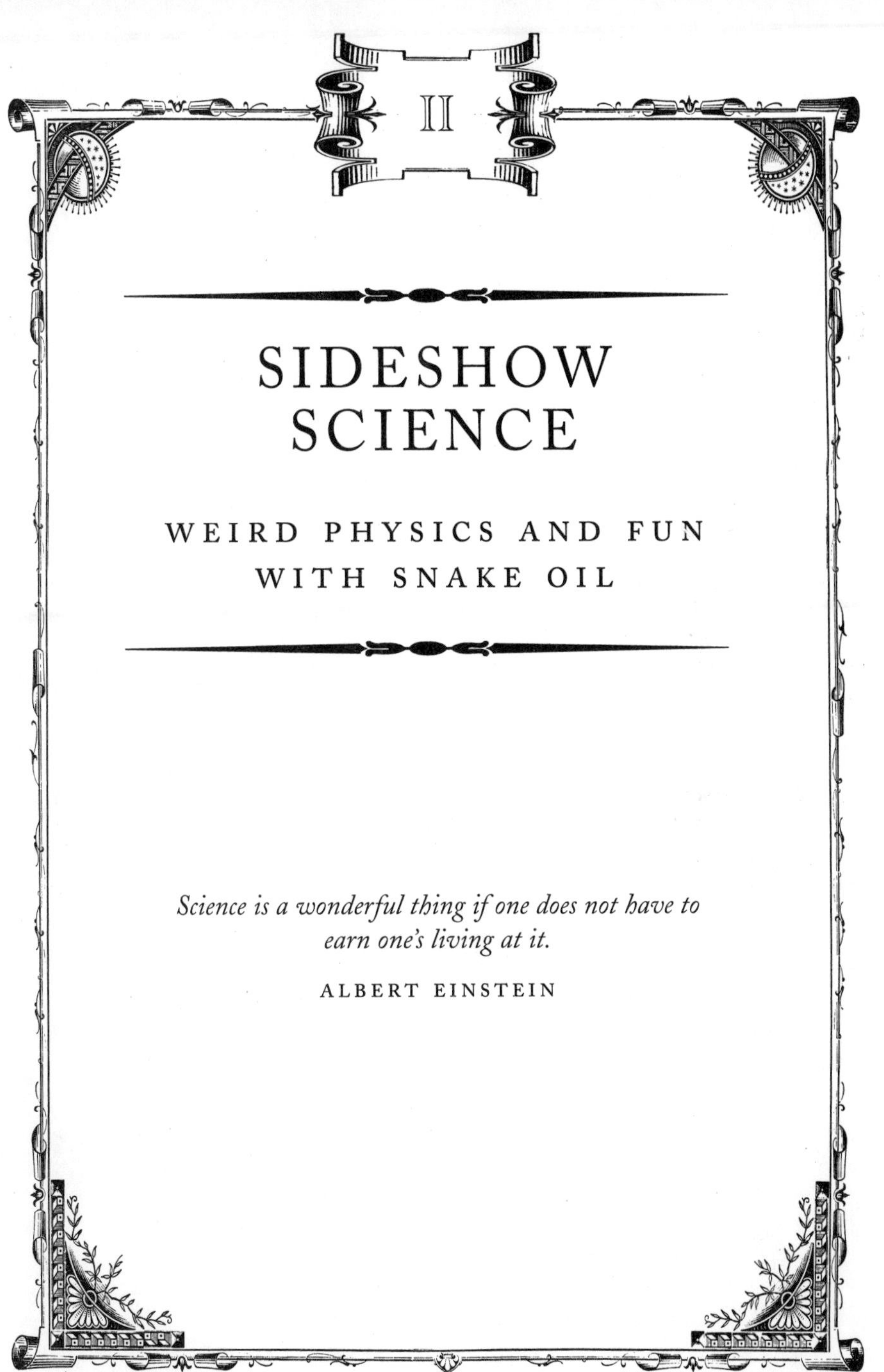

II

SIDESHOW SCIENCE

WEIRD PHYSICS AND FUN WITH SNAKE OIL

Science is a wonderful thing if one does not have to earn one's living at it.

ALBERT EINSTEIN

HOW TO
LEVITATE YOUR BALLS

The faster a stream of air is traveling, the lower is its pressure. This is called the Bernoulli effect, after Daniel Bernoulli, the Swiss scientist who first worked it out. The principle is usually understood in relation to an airplane's wing, where the air moves faster over the characteristically curved upper side than it does underneath. The air pressure is therefore lower on top than it is below, and it is this that, together with the wing's attitude, pushes the plane up off the ground. The job of the engines is to move the wing forward with sufficient thrust to create the required lift. If it slows down enough a plane will just drop out of the sky. Remember this the next time the stewardess is explaining where the life jackets are hidden.

We are used to the funny properties of airplane wings, but the Bernoulli effect can produce some weird results in other situations, where the principle is not so obvious. Here are a few surprising tricks you can do with it.

Bernoulli's balls

Find a hair dryer, the kind with a cylindrical pipe on the end. Turn it on and put a ping-pong ball into the air stream. It will spin in the air, held in place by the higher pressure outside the moving air column. This is exactly the same principle as the pea levitation on page 262.

The trick can be demonstrated on a grander scale with a leaf blower and a plastic soccer ball, though you will need to experiment. If you tilt the blower and hide behind the shed door, the ball seems to be spinning in midair, all by itself (if you ignore the incredible noise).

Non-fatal attraction

Close the windows and attach a ping-pong ball to each end of a two-foot length of string. Dangle the string over a ruler, so that the balls are level, about an inch apart. Blow hard between the balls and, instead of separating, as you might imagine, they will be pushed together because of the lower pressure of your moving breath.

Balloons and empty beer cans are also suitable for this trick—and a great excuse for a party.

Funnel fun

Drop a ping-pong ball into a funnel and challenge a friend to blow it out. You can improvise with the cut-off half of a plastic bottle.

Get your victim to blow up through the tube as hard as he likes. The ball will stay put and he will end up puffed out, red-faced, and with a crick in his neck. Offer him a different funnel and tell him he is blowing too hard. You have previously wiped very hot chili sauce round the end of this funnel. This has nothing to do with the Bernoulli effect, but it is fun.

◎ *Another name for air rushing from high-pressure areas into low is "wind."* ◎

HOW TO
WALK THROUGH A POSTCARD

How annoying it is to return home from a washed-out camping trip just to be greeted by take-out menus, a reminder from the dentist, and a postcard showing the tropical island paradise where your buddy is on vacation with his leggy girlfriend. The following cathartic exercise is a good one for venting your spleen, and works well with junk mail, but is perhaps most impressive with a simple postcard.

The effect can be performed almost anywhere, and the apparatus is cheap and easy to come by. What's more, it can be carried around in your pocket until you are ready to do the maneuver in front of an audience.

Required

- *A postcard*
- *A pair of sharp scissors or a craft knife*
- *A ruler (if you want to be neat)*

Method

Explain that you are going to cut some slits in the card, which will enable you to walk right through it. This usually provokes comments along the lines of: "Get out of here, you joker!" So just watch their faces as they realize they'll have to eat humble pie.

1. Fold the postcard in half lengthwise.
2. Open it out flat again and cut a slit along the fold, finishing just short of the edge at each end.

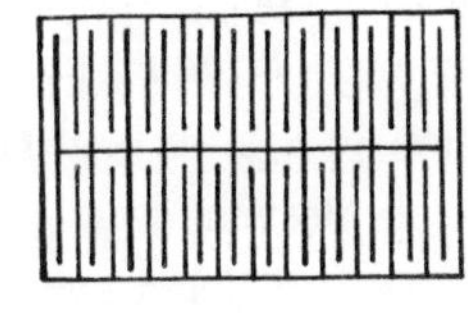

3. Double it over again and cut slits at right angles to the fold. The first of these should begin at the fold and finish just short of the card's long edge. The next should start at the edge and finish just short of the centerfold. Proceed along the card, alternating the cuts, as shown in fig. a, right.

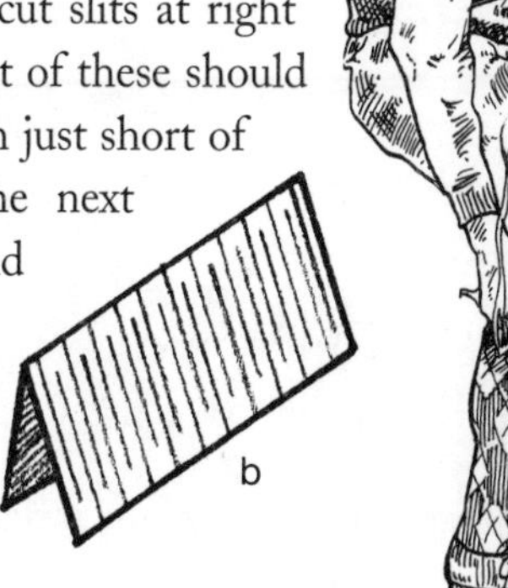

4. Delicately pull the card open and stretch it into a zigzag loop (fig. c). This is quite large enough to step into, so draw it up and take it over your head with a final flourish, asking: "Whose round is it?"

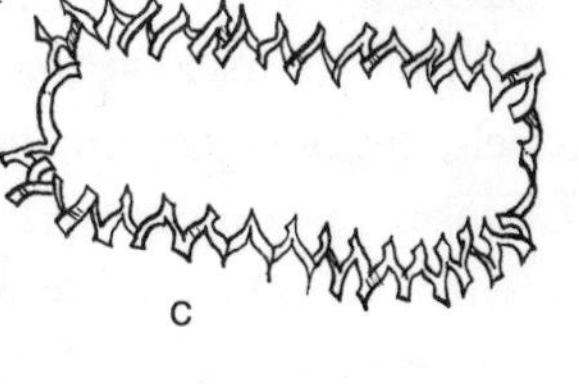

◎ *Deltiology is the study and collection of postcards.* ◎

HOW TO
LIFT A MAN OVERHEAD WITH ONE ARM

This genuine demonstration makes a great bet in the pub because it sounds so very unlikely, especially if you are not all that muscular or tall. For goodness sake, choose lighter men to do this with during the first few performances or you'll find yourself on the waiting list for hernia surgery. When you issue your challenge you should nominate a particular person, to prevent some smart aleck asking you to lift his 300-pound uncle. Just say: "I bet everyone I can lift Bill over my head with one arm."

Required

- *A chair*
- *A man's belt*
- *A man*

Method

1. Ask your subject to stand on the chair.
2. Fasten the belt around his chest. It should go under his arms and buckle up at the back.
3. Position yourself in front of him and slide your hand under the belt, knuckles against the middle of his chest.
4. Close your fingers over the belt and bend your legs at the knee (where else?) straightening your arm as you do so and locking it into position.
5. Turn your back on your subject and slowly straighten your legs, keeping your arm stiff at shoulder and elbow, because any bending now will spell ruination. As you slowly stand, your subject will be lifted clean off his chair. If you allow his weight to be supported on your back, you'll find that you can actually carry the fellow a short distance. Once the audience's applause has died down,

lower your subject to the ground, put your belt back on, and pocket your winnings.

Remember, do not bend your arm at any time or all will be lost. Should you, despite your best efforts, collapse under your subject—or fail to lift him at all—don't worry, you'll score points just for trying. With practice you'll find you can carry heavier men. Tall men often appear bigger than short men of the same weight, and with a fellow in a top hat the whole thing looks funny as well as difficult. There's nothing to stop you from doing a little jig across the room if you like.

◎ *Attila the Hun was only 4' 6" tall.* ◎

EIGHT WAYS TO CONFUSE YOUR BRAIN

The brain is a very clever instrument and it can work perfectly well upside down or underwater. But it is also quite easy to fool even when it knows you are trying to fool it. The following games and illusions all rely on the brain's capacity to get things a bit wrong.

1 THE FLOATING SAUSAGE

Touch your index fingertips together and bring your hands toward you. Unfocus your eyes (look at the far wall) as your fingers get to within a few inches of your nose. If you now separate the fingers slightly a cocktail sausage will seem to be floating between them, as in the picture.

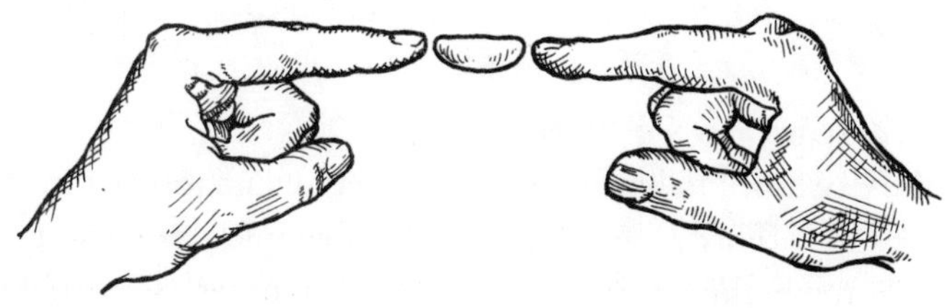

2 Put the burglar in jail

This game is as old as the hills and is a nifty demonstration that what you see with your two eyes can be misinterpreted by your brain. Bring this page toward your face while defocusing your eyes. As you do so, the burglar will "slide" sideways into his cell. Stop when the bottom of the broken line is about 1 inch from your nose. (OK, he's a bit out of focus but what do you expect—miracles?)

3 A hole in the hand

Hold up your left hand, open, with palm facing you, and position the cardboard inner tube from a kitchen roll against the side of your hand so you can see through it. By putting the tube to your right eye, keeping both eyes open, and sliding the hand to the middle of the tube, you can produce the effect of a large hole in your palm. Keep your focus on the far wall.

4 Make your own movies

Before the dawn of Hollywood there was the thaumatrope, Greek for "wonder turner." This is one of a number of simple 19th-century toys that rely on the brain's inability to forget for a moment something the eyes have just looked at. This is called "persistence of vision" and, in this case, it results in two rapidly alternating pictures becoming apparently superimposed.

The thaumatrope was the precursor of the mutoscope, or arcade moving-picture machine, which featured a minute's-worth of successive still pictures that appeared to move when cranked on a reel by the viewer. Typical scenes included mildly pornographic ones of scantily clad or naked ladies bathing, gyrating, or doing unlikely things with articles of kitchen equipment.

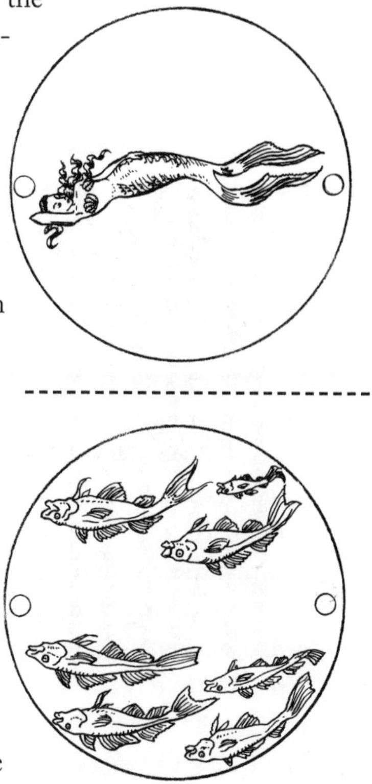

To make your own thaumatrope, trace or photocopy the illustrations right. Fold your image along the dotted line with illustrations on the outside. Next, sandwich a postcard between the leaves and glue them down securely.

When the paper is dry, cut around the circle and, with your granny's knitting needle, make two holes on opposite sides, as marked. Next, thread a thin rubber band through each hole and double them over on themselves. If you now wind the disk and then pull on the rubber bands, the card will spin, creating the impression that the mermaid is swimming among the fishes.

5 Goldilocks's hot-cold-warm water

Fill three bowls with water. Rather like The Three Bears story, the first bowl contains hot water; the second, cold water; and the third, tepid water. Plunge your left hand into the cold water and your right into the hot. After a minute or two, put them into the warm water. It will feel hot to your left hand and cold to your right.

6 The Yablonski fingers

This is just like strip poker, only quicker. Challenge your opponent (female, obviously) to touch her nose with the tip of her left middle finger and at the same time touch the tip of her right middle finger with her left thumb. When you say "Yablonski" she is to reverse the position quickly, putting her right middle finger on her nose and her left middle finger on her right thumb. This is furiously difficult, especially if you complicate things by making it a rule that she must change only on the word "Yablonski." You can then have fun calling out "Polanski," "Sikorsky," "Gesundheit!" and so on. Each mistake or slow response results in the compulsory removal of an item of clothing. You've practiced and she hasn't—the results are a foregone conclusion.

7 An extra nose in an instant

Who of us hasn't at some time cried out in despair: "If only I had two noses, life would be so much easier?" Probably nobody, come to think of it. Nevertheless, here's a way to create the feeling that you have exactly that.

Cross the first and second fingers of your dominant hand and stroke their tips gently against the end of your nose. It produces the weird sensation that you have two noses. This trick was first mentioned by Aristotle. Surely he had better things to do with his time.

8 Animate your own cartoon

To animate your own cartoon, take two pieces of paper about a quarter the size of a letter-size sheet. Tape these together at the top (short) edge.

Near the bottom of each sheet, draw a circle (trace around a quarter). The circles must be precisely superimposed (a window makes a good light box). On the bottom circle draw two simple eyes and a nose. Duplicate them exactly on the top sheet.

On the bottom face, draw a short straight line for a mouth. Now, on the top sheet, draw a curved smiley mouth. If you curl the upper sheet against the blade of a pair of scissors so that it rolls up, you can insert a pencil and rapidly superimpose the top sheet over the bottom. The effect is of a face alternately neutral and smiley. If you put dots in the eyes on the bottom sheet and change their positions on the top, you can make the eyes move too.

The effect is usually attributed to persistence of vision but it is surely more to do with humans having evolved the ability to perceive a change in position as indicating movement, which is what happens in the natural world, helping animals to hunt.

If you have ambitions to animate your own cartoons, the next step is to make your own flip book, using a notepad. Draw a stick man jumping up and down in the corner then flip the pages rapidly. You'll be amazed at the results.

◎ *A typical human brain is 5½ inches wide.* ◎

HOW TO
WALK ACROSS RED-HOT COALS

There's nothing more likely to make you wince with vicarious pain than watching a guy walk across a bed of red-hot coals in his bare feet. How on earth do they do it? The stunt is often presented by guru types who tell volunteers that walking over the glowing embers is a question of mind over matter. In fact, it's nothing of the sort; it is a mixture of basic science and good old-fashioned hokum. Nonetheless, I must emphasize that *it can be extremely dangerous to walk across hot coals, and you must never try it at home.* As if you would.

The illusion of danger

Temperature is a measure of the degree or intensity of heat, but in this fire-walking business it's not so much heat as *conduction* that we're worried about. For example, you can put your hand into the hot air of an oven without it hurting, but touch the metal rack and it will burn you something rotten even though it is the same temperature as the air. This is because air is a very poor conductor of heat—so poor, in fact, that it's used as an insulator. Metal, on the other hand, is an excellent conductor, which is why frying pans are made of it and why fire walking is never done over red-hot ball bearings.

Those "coals" are hardwood charcoal, another poor thermal conductor even when alight (charcoal is commonly used as an insulator). Added to this the surface of the coal is mainly ash, *another* excellent insulator—you can touch it quite comfortably with a fingertip. This is one reason you don't barbecue sausages on the charcoal itself, but at a distance.

Of course, given sufficient time, hot air and hot coals will conduct enough heat to burn you. That's why it's a bad idea to stop for a sandwich in the middle of the fire—just as it would be to leave your hand in a hot oven for an hour.

This is the key to fire walking: *you are insulated* from the heat. The coals are always allowed to acquire an ash-coating by burning for a while before anyone gets on to them, and the flames that would otherwise singe your leg hairs have had time to die down. A fellow walking across the fire in bare feet will be quite comfy as long as he doesn't dawdle.

Radiant heat and that glow

Have you ever wondered why fire walking is always demonstrated in the evening? It's because the coals glooooow a beautiful orange, an effect not nearly so visible in daylight. Together with the *radiant* heat (which makes you back away going "Phwoar!") the orange glow convinces you that the fire is tremendously hot—which it is. The temperature is likely to be well above 1,000 degrees. The illusion, though, is that the coals are going to burn your feet on contact, which isn't true, for the reasons I have mentioned.

As I say, this isn't something you want to try to disprove at home, but next time some blowhard tells you it's all about mind over matter you can set the record straight with your erudition.

◎ *The Eiffel Tower is 6 inches taller in the summer because it swells in the heat.* ◎

A FUNNY ROUTINE WITH A MÖBIUS LOOP

People say there are two sides to any argument, just as there are two sides to a piece of paper. The trouble is that some pieces of paper only have one side. You can demonstrate this quite plainly by making a Möbius loop, named after astronomer and mathematician August Ferdinand Möbius, who came up with the idea in 1858. Some weird-looking things are possible with this topological oddity, and the best of the effects appear below.

Required

- *Large sheet of paper*
- *Sticky tape*
- *Scissors*

Method

Cut a 2-inch strip from a length of brown parcel paper or plain wrapping paper. Give the strip a single twist and join its ends together with clear tape.

Weird effects

1. If you cut the loop in half all the way around you will get not two loops, but one very long one.
2. If you twist your strip twice before taping its ends, and cut it as described in effect number 1, you will get two identical linked loops.
3. If you cut the loop by starting a third of the way from the edge, you will finish with two loops linked together, one large and one small.

A little demonstration

A physics professor of my acquaintance used to illustrate the odd properties of the Möbius loop by performing a sneaky trick on two students. This is how to do it.

1 Prepare three strips, each about 6 inches wide, and 10 feet long. Loop them, twisting the first once, the second twice, and leaving the third untwisted. Make a clearly visible mark on the untwisted one.

2 Give two volunteers a prepared loop each, keeping the innocent (marked) one for yourself. Because of the length of these loops, the twists won't be noticed. Each person also gets a pair of sharp scissors.

3 Say: "This is not a test of skill, it's a test of speed. I am going to award a prize for the first of you to cut two separate loops, like this." Cut your loop in half and display the two new ones.

4 Warn your volunteers to watch their fingers, and, tell them to start snipping, on your command. Before long, your first victim finds he's got one enormous loop, while the other will have two loops, as requested, but interlinked.

◎ *August Ferdinand Möbius was a descendant of Martin Luther.* ◎

HOW TO
DRIVE A NAIL INTO A PLANK WITH YOUR BARE HAND

The effect here is that you take a serious-looking nail and, wrapping its head in a cloth, strike it into a wooden board with nothing but your bare hand. Like the ability to belch at will, this is one of those things with almost no practical application. But if you take the trouble to learn how to do it, you are always ready to wow people with a demonstration of your skill. The only problem is you have to carry a plank around with you all the time. (Unlike belching, it's more important here that you follow the instructions *precisely and with care*, otherwise you will hurt yourself.)

Required

- *An 8 or 10 inch nail*
- *A rag or large handkerchief*

- *A short wooden plank*
- *2 chairs*

There are two keys to success in this exercise. The first is to use the right plank. What you are looking for is one made of a wood that is not too dense. Clearly, nobody is going to be impressed if you use a piece of balsa, but a mahogany board will do you no favors either. Firs and some pines are good ones to look out for. The plank should be about a yard in length and the thinner it is, the easier your job will be.

The second key to success is how you wrap the nail. The main function of the wrapping is to absorb and diffuse the energy transmitted to your hand as the nail strikes the board, so that you hit it hard enough to go in, without nailing your hand to the plank at the same time. The larger the amount of cloth in your hand, the easier the task.

INSTRUCTIONS

1. Display the nail, holding it upright by its tip. This makes it look nice and long. Wrap your rag or hankie around the head so that it lies in the center of the cloth, which is balled up and held in your right palm, the nail protruding between the curled middle and third fingers, at a point between the first and second knuckles.
2. Ask two volunteers to place the board between two sturdy chairs and stand back.
3. Steady the plank with your left hand and raise your right hand slowly and dramatically, as high as you can reach.
4. Suddenly bring your hand down hard, absolutely perpendicular to the board. You must strike it with the nail perfectly straight or it will not penetrate.

5 Remove your hand and unwind the wrapper to reveal the nail in the wood.
6 Pass it around and ask a few young ladies to pull out the nail. They'll have their work cut out for them.

◎ *Until the end of the 18th century nails were made by hand.* ◎

PARANORMAL SPOON BENDING (THE EASY WAY)

Some years ago, a foreign gentleman, widely believed by the media to have supernatural powers, achieved international stardom by doing impossible looking things with metal objects. In fact he was nothing but a big fat liar who was using plain hoodwinkery to bamboozle his spectators. The self-styled "Spaniard with X-ray eyes" was exposed in the 1930s, when Harry Houdini peeked from behind, while he was being all paranormal with a watch, and caught him cheating.

Similar cases are recorded in Reginald Scot's 1584 bestseller *The Discoverie of Witchcraft*, and though I'm sure those who currently claim special powers are truly paranormal, I wonder why we are still waiting for the headline "Psychic wins lottery."

One of the most useless things these people claim to do is bend spoons and forks by stroking them. This seems a waste of extrasensory energy to me, as the same effects can be achieved with the pedestrian powers possessed by the rest of us. Here is one way to bend cutlery, which looks supernatural.

Preparation

Bend a fork backward and forward between your hands until it forms a fatigue fracture in the neck. You'll notice a little bump where it is about to break. Give two or three of these rigged forks to an accomplice.

Invite a few gullible friends to a paranormal evening, asking them to bring along some of their own silverware.

PERFORMANCE

Nominate a guardian of the cutlery and give her a tray on which to collect the utensils. Instruct her not to let them out of her sight. Your stooge dumps the rigged forks in with the rest and it's pure theatrics from there on.

Pick up one of the trick forks and hold it in your left hand at the tip of the handle with the tines toward your spectators. Place your right fingertips over the bump and begin to rub gently, using your left fingers to provide gentle opposing pressure. At all times you must be seen to be handling the fork with great lightness.

Gradually push the head of the fork away from you with your thumb and it will begin to bend. Keep rocking it back and forth and the metal will appear to soften. Soon, you'll feel it break, but don't let go. Instead, shake it horizontally and it will wobble like rubber.

By gently releasing the pressure between your finger and thumb you can make the head seem to melt backward and fall off.

Act astonished and pass around the pieces, saying, "It doesn't even feel hot."

◎ *There are 5,400 items in the Bertha Schaefer Koempel Spoon Collection.* ◎

HOW TO
TEAR A PHONE BOOK IN HALF

This famous strongman trick looks very hard but can actually be done without a great deal of physical strength. Few men could really rip a thousand pages in half in one go, and the method described here works by allowing you to tear a few pages at a time. You can help yourself by starting with a thin directory (700 pages or so) and move up to the thicker ones as your experience grows. A modicum of acting ability and a rugged chin will help sell the effect, but even a skinny introvert should get applause with this fine stunt. As usual, rehearsal of both technique and presentation is vital.

Method

1 Before you start, remove any thick inserts from the directory.

2 To begin, grasp the phone book horizontally, with its front page facing the ceiling and its spine resting on your thigh. Support it underneath at its outside corners with the third and fourth fingers of each hand, your thumbs meeting on top at the front edge, the index and middle fingers resting comfortably underneath.

3 To start the tear, push down with your thumbs on the middle of the book, simultaneously bending up the ends with the third and fourth fingers of each hand, to form a smiling banana shape.

4 Next, squeeze the book tightly and draw the thumbs apart so that the cover and first pages are stretched taut. At the same time, squash the pages nearest the spine into a V shape with your forefingers (fig. a).

5 With your thumbs keeping the cover and front pages taut, bend the banana smile into afrown by turning down the corners of the book. This will stretch the cover and front pages beyond what they can endure, so that they suddenly tear, sometimes with a loud crack (fig. b).

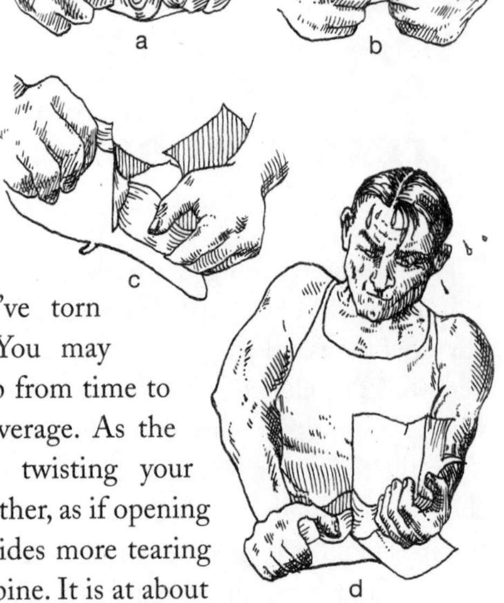

6 Keep bending down the corners until you've torn through every page. You may need to adjust your grip from time to time to increase the leverage. As the tear progresses, begin twisting your hands away from each other, as if opening a fan (fig. c). This provides more tearing power as you near the spine. It is at about

this point that brute force finally comes into its own, and you will need to push half the book with one hand while you pull with the other, completing the tear. A bit of wrestling looks good here, especially if you grunt. After all, this isn't meant to be easy.

7 Finally, fling down the two halves triumphantly and acknowledge your applause.

This is my preferred method, and provides greatly superior control to other procedures that involve fanning the pages before tearing. If you wish to make a speciality of the phone book tear, your community recycling center may be willing to let you have some of their unwanted directories to rehearse with.

◎ *Muscleman Charles Atlas's real name was Angelo Siciliano.* ◎

HOW TO
WEIGH YOUR OWN HEAD

There can't be many problems more vexing than that of weighing your head. For a start, how do you decide where your head ends and your neck begins? And once you've decided this and marked the junction with an indelible pen, what next? It's a riddle that beat even Archimedes. So here is a method that will produce a good estimate of the weight of your head the next time you find yourself at a loose end.

REQUIRED

- *A plastic kiddie pool*
- *A plastic rainwater barrel*
- *A plastic bucket*
- *A plastic measuring jug*
- *A plastic chair*
- *Some bathroom scales*
- *Your head*

Method

1. On a nice day, inflate your kiddie pool in the yard. Divert any bathers from wading into it.
2. Put your barrel into the pool and fill it (the barrel) with warm water, right up to the top. Do not allow it to overflow.
3. Shave all your hair off. You'll get a more accurate measurement this way. Because you are bald no water can be removed by capillary action.
4. Stand on your chair, hold your breath, and lower your head slowly into the water until it is submerged up to your Adam's apple. The displaced water will flow down the sides and collect in the bottom of the pool. Slowly take your head out again.
5. Pour the collected water into your bucket. This is the most annoying part of the experiment because the barrel is full of water and you need to move it without spilling any. You can, if you are ambitious, begin the experiment by digging a deep hole in the lawn, into which you now crawl with your bucket, so as to siphon the water from the pool.
6. Measure, and jot down, the volume of water in your bucket by pouring it into your measuring jug. If the jug's too small, do it in steps.
7. Put the barrel back and fill it to the brim again. Take all your clothes off and weigh yourself.
8. Get on the chair and climb carefully into the barrel, completely submerging yourself. After a moment climb out and pour the displaced water into the bucket and then into the measuring jug, keeping a note of the final amount.
9. Multiply your body weight by the ratio between the two figures. This will give you the weight of your head.
10. Put your clothes back on.

◎ *Hat size is based on head width divided by pi.* ◎

THE TOPOLOGICALLY ANOMALOUS SINGLE-SURFACE IMPOSSIBLE FILING CARD THING

This is one of those tricks you will have to commit to memory because if you try to work it out just by thinking, your brain will catch fire.

1 Take a filing card and fold it to make eight rectangles as shown in the first illustration. Make three cuts with a pair of scissors along the bold lines.

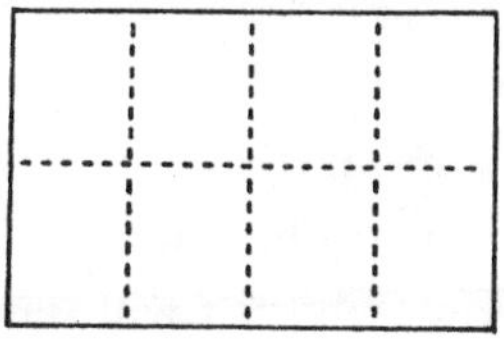

2 Now turn the right-hand bit all the way over, and it's done. It looks weird.

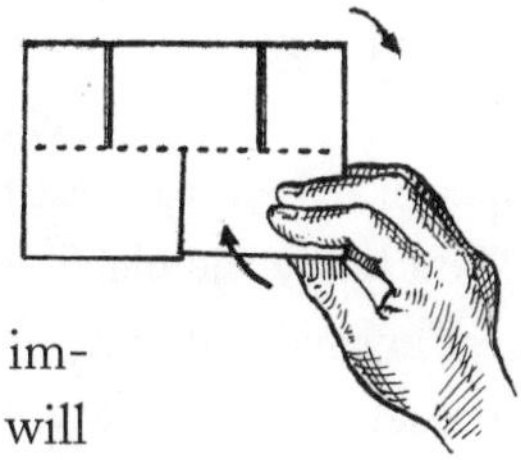

If you hand someone the topologically anomalous single-surface impossible filing card thing he will probably be unable to fold it back flat.

It's even harder if you do the folding and cutting business under the table and then challenge your victim to reproduce the topologically anomalous single-surface impossible filing card thing. His brain will probably melt and his eyes might even fall out.

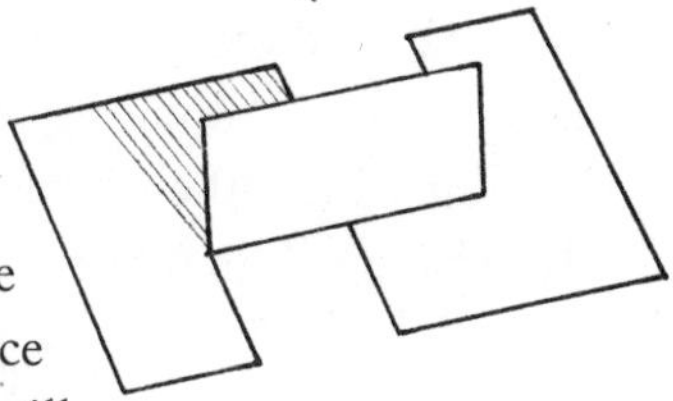

◎ *A sheet of paper folded in half 50 times would be 62 million miles thick.* ◎

HOW TO
MAKE YOUR HAIR STAND ON END

Here's a dodge, invented by myself during a boring German lesson with Mr. Price in 1971. It always has them rolling in the aisles, and is especially good during dreary meetings or while your girlfriend is lecturing you on your various failings as a human being.

Start by taking a large elastic band, of the kind that mail carriers drop along their routes. Secretly pull it down over your head until it is stopped by your ears, just below the widest part of your cranium. Now, tease some of the trapped hair from under the band and arrange it over the rubber to hide it. Push the elastic band up under your hairline at the front, where it will stay quite happily until you are ready to perform, causing you nothing more than an itchy scalp.

When you are ready to go, secretly lift that length of the band that lies over the occipital-parietal region behind your ears so that it is above the equator, where the resistance to its natural urge to contract will be less. Gradually the elastic band will slide up your head, dragging clumps of hair with it and shrinking in circumference as it travels north until it reaches the point where it suddenly closes, snapping your hair up in a ludicrous fountain. You can control the speed to some extent by frowning or raising your eyebrows and if your hair color is similar to the band's, the mechanism will remain invisible throughout.

It is mesmeric in effect.

◎ *Eunuchs do not go bald.* ◎

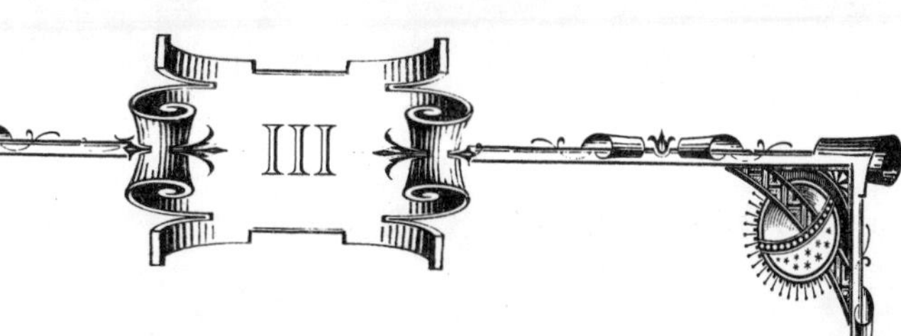

III

THE TREE OF USELESS KNOWLEDGE

EVERYTHING YOU ALWAYS WANTED TO KNOW HOW TO DO BUT WEREN'T SURE WHERE TO START

The passion for play is probably as old, and will be as enduring, as the race of man.

S. W. ERDNASE, The Expert at the Card Table

HOW TO
MILK A COW

A typical cow produces more than 28 pints of milk a day—roughly 10,000 pints a year. This is enough for 30,000 bowls of cereal or 150,000 cups of coffee. Milking a cow isn't as easy as it looks, and is a skill that, once mastered, people will always compliment you on. Practice hard and you'll find you receive many a pat on the back.

Required

- *A spotless stainless steel bucket*
- *A short stool*
- *A cow*
- *A full complement of hands*

Instructions

Make sure the cow's been fed, cleaned, and spoken to in a friendly way. Cows are sensitive creatures and if you're nervous they will pick this up, possibly refusing to deliver the milk. If you have a soothing voice, you might try singing to the cow gently. Psychologists have discovered that slow smoochy music increases milk yield by some 3 percent. Cows' favorites include "Bridge Over Troubled Water" by Simon and Garfunkel, and Beethoven's Pastoral Symphony. You should obviously avoid hip-hop songs about women's behinds, or the animal will be likely to knock over the milk bucket and step on your foot. Don't forget that even well-mannered cows who have been to Swiss finishing schools will kick your head if they feel like it. So stay alert.

1. Wash the udder with a cloth dipped in warm water.
2. Place the milk bucket slightly in front of the udder.
3. If you are right-handed, put the stool on the cow's starboard (right) flank and sit with your right ear resting on the animal's side, looking backward and protecting the bucket with your left leg.

4 If you try to start milking by just grabbing hold and pulling, you will fail. Instead, gently but firmly grasp a teat in the palm of each hand. (Remind you of anything?) Squeeze the top of the teat between thumb and forefinger, effectively making a seal, while your other fingers, in sequence, force the milk downwards in imitation of a calf's sucking action. You'll have to practice, clearly, because there's a knack to it.

5 Let go. (The easy part.)

6 Repeat the process until the udder begins to feel empty and soft to the touch, and only a small amount of milk is released with each squeeze.

What you do with all that milk is your own business.

◎ *Butter's yellow color comes from beta-carotene in the grass the cows eat.* ◎

HOW TO
REPEL AN UNINVITED SOLICITOR OFF THE DOORSTEP

There are few things more annoying than the doorbell going, just as you're about to light a fart or juggle some fruit, and a grinning zealot on the doorstep is often the cause of unhealthy physical symptoms such as foul-mouthed screaming, fist waving, and a snarling Russell Crowe–type face. These foot-in-the-door merchants, a bane of modern existence, are practiced in deflecting polite rebuffs of this kind. So here, for your approval, are a few alternative extreme-prejudice measures to make them go away.

The non-religious caller

The first thing to remember is that you must never answer any of the innocuous-sounding questions that this type lobs at you. Instead, seize the initiative by immediately saying you'll be delighted to speak to them if they will just sign on the dotted line. Hand them your clipboard with an official-looking contract attached. A sample is printed below.

CONTRACT

Name:

Age:

Salary:

Race:

IQ:

Health problems:

Sexual orientation:

I, ______________________________, promise to:

i. Pay the householder for his time an interlocutory fee of $10 per minute, or part thereof;
ii. Pay the householder interrogatory compensation of $20 per question;
iii. Pay the householder a contract arrangement fee of $150;
iv. Make all payments immediately in cash;
v. Provide the householder with details of my home address.

SIGNED ____________________ DATE __________

This is foolproof because it kicks them where it hurts—in the pocket.

Another effective ruse with the commercial caller is to put your hand on his shoulder and say: "I'm so glad you're here because I'm desperately lonely and I need to talk to you about God." As panic flashes across his features, get in your killer question: "Do you read the Bible?"

No matter what he answers, ask him to pay close attention. Now read from Matthew's gospel:

> *Abraham begat Isaac; and Isaac begat Jacob; and Jacob begat Judas and his brethren; And Judas begat Phares and Zara of Thamar; and Phares begat Esrom; and Esrom begat Aram; And Aram begat Aminadab; and Aminadab begat Naasson; and Naasson begat Salmon; Salmon begat Booz of Rachab; and Booz begat Obed of Ruth; and Obed begat Jesse; And Jesse begat David the king; and David the king begat Solomon of her that had been the wife of Urias; And Solomon begat Roboam; and Roboam begat Abia; and Abia begat Asa; And Asa begat Josaphat; and Josaphat begat Joram; and Joram begat Ozias; And Ozias begat Joatham; and Joatham begat Achaz; and Achaz begat Ezekias; And Ezekias begat Manasses; and Manasses begat Amon; and Amon begat Josias; And Josias begat Jechonias and his brethren, about the time they were carried away to Babylon.*

He'll think you've stopped here but it goes on begetting for another 67 words.

The religious caller

For religious prosthelytizers of all stripes, you obviously need a different approach, so once they've flourished their copy of *The Watchtower*, say, "You are certainly the church I've been seeking, for I am troubled and have known evil." As they prick up their ears, reach for your prepared folder containing photographs downloaded from the Internet, and show them a selection. Good examples are full-color autopsy close-ups, gun-shot suicides, and people doing filthy-looking pornographic things to each other—or to horses. Ask, "What do you make of this sort of thing?" and as they recoil hand them a page of squalid obscenities printed in 72-point bold type. You can call these out as they back away, asking them to rank them in order of offensiveness. Tell them to please shut the gate behind them.

THE "DISABLED"
A disagreeable trick is played by a few rogue companies that employ people to sell mops and cloths door to door. This particular variety of fraudulent ruse requires the caller to pretend to some sort of physical disability. Deafness, accompanied by speech problems, is a favorite, though it's interesting to note that, whatever the problem, the ability to collect and add up money never seems to suffer impediment. A polite no is usually effective with these people, but if you are convinced you're being hosed you can have a go at hosing right back with a really good reverse-hose. Try poking your tongue over your lower teeth, adopting a half-closed-eyes look, with maybe a withered arm, and drawl stertorously something along these lines: "Mner nerg mnurb nmerbmernb." This usually works a treat but has the disadvantage that genuinely afflicted callers might feel inclined to fetch your nose a wallop. And who could blame them?

◎ *The door-to-door vacuum cleaner salesman was the idea of William Hoover.* ◎

HOW TO
MAKE A CITIZEN'S ARREST

Under state laws and the Second and Ninth Amendments, any member of the American public has the power to make an arrest (or detain the perpetrator) if he thinks somebody is committing a felony.

You may arrest somebody if you witness a crime being committed or if, without actually witnessing it, you know that somebody is guilty. You may also make an arrest even if you only *suspect* that somebody is committing, or has committed, a crime (you need to have reasonable grounds for this).

If you make an arrest, you must tell the person why you are collaring him, and take him straight to a police station. Try to alert the fuzz as soon as you can, and hand over your charge to them, or your arrest will be disallowed in court. Try also to remember anything the suspect says, and jot down all your recollections as soon as possible, with approximate times. This will help when you are called as a witness.

You are allowed to use only *reasonable* force when you make an arrest; you don't want to end up with a charge of assault. And you cannot arrest somebody just for burping, pushing in line, or calling your sister an ugly cow. Nonetheless, while nabbing a criminal sounds sort of thrilling, most of us are best not quitting our day jobs.

◎ *North Carolina does not permit citizen's arrests.* ◎

HOW TO
WIN MONEY IN A CASINO—WITHOUT CHEATING

The glamor, the girls, the gambling: Las Vegas. If you've ever dreamed of winning big at blackjack, roulette, *or anything* in Vegas, forget it. The odds are that you will almost certainly come out poorer than you went in. Cheating is illegal, the techniques for counting and memorizing cards take years to master, and the big businesses that operate the glitzy establishments will smoke you out pretty fast. But you *can* win money in a casino if you follow these simple rules:

- Learn the odds, which you can easily discover with a computer search. Once you know them inside and out you're ready to go.
- Bet only when the odds are in your favor: so avoid the tables and *target the gamblers*.

Put on your high-roller tux, stride Bond-like into the casino, and sidle up to the guy who is making a lot of noise at, say, the craps table. He'll be kissing the dice and yelling something like, "It's going to be a five, come on you lucky five, I'm in a bettin' mood!" You know that, out of the

36 possible combinations from a throw of two dice (6 × 6), there are four ways to roll a five. The odds are therefore eight to one that he won't roll a five, so you say: "I bet you four to three it *isn't* a five." Chances are he'll forget the odds and bet on his superstition, and you'll win again.

- When you do win, keep very quiet but when you lose, make a big noise about it. This is known as the reverse fruit-machine technique.

To further improve your odds, why not bet on certainties? The following bets should be made in the restaurant or at the casino bar:

- Bet your victim $10 you can tie a cigarette in a knot, without breaking it. To do this, tightly roll it up in the smoothed-out cellophane from the cigarette packet, leaving two long ends, which you twirl into points. Tie your knot. You can even stamp on it and dip it in your beer. Untie the knot and collect your money.
- After a meal, suggest that Lady Luck should decide who picks up the tab. Tell your victim to break any number of matches in half and drop them into an ashtray. Say: "We are going to take a piece in turn till they are all gone and the person left with the last piece pays the bill." The secret is simple: always pick first.

◎ *Citizens of Monaco are forbidden to enter its gaming rooms.* ◎

HOW TO LIGHT A FART

Exactly when it was that the idea bulb went on over the head of the first fart lighter is lost in the mists of time. Perhaps one of our Neanderthal ancestors let rip too close to the fire and shed a surprising light on a new world of cheap entertainment.

Whatever its history, fart lighting is an exciting and educational recreation that need not be confined to student halls of residence and fraternity-house dinners. Lighting a fart rather than a cigar during the interval of Wagner's "Ring" is certainly better for your health, and dress pants are no impediment to its efficacy.

Anyway, if you think this is something you'd like to try, you had better understand a bit of the science first.

Farts consist of five gases in the following percentages: about 59% nitrogen (N_2), 4% oxygen (O_2), 9% carbon dioxide (CO_2), 21% hydrogen (H_2), and 7% methane (CH_4). The gases you are interested in are the last two, hydrogen and methane, both of which are combustible.

Hydrogen is the lightest of the elements and is a potent fuel, burning with a yellow flame. It powers NASA's space shuttle and was the gas responsible for the Hindenburg disaster. Getting worried? Hydrogen's chief advantage is that it burns without producing carbon dioxide, so lighting your farts is not going to contribute greatly to global warming.

Methane (so-called natural gas) is odorless, burning with a blue flame and with more of a flame-thrower effect than its lighter cousin. It is emitted by an exclusive third of the population only. Interestingly, those in this select group are entitled to membership of the esoteric and mysterious Knights of the Blue Flame. Heaven only knows what goes on at their annual meetings.

Instructions

A fart is visible only in low light so, if you are performing for an audience, draw the curtains first. It should be remembered that *fart lighting can be risky*—the ill prepared have been known to injure themselves. Clothing and draperies can catch fire and there have even been reports of flames "backing up." Surveys reveal that some 25 percent of fart lighters injure themselves and it's said that things can sometimes get hot enough to make your eyes water. To avoid Hindenberg-type problems, always follow these rules:

1. Lie on a rug with your knees on your chest, feet facing the ceiling, out of harm's way.

2 Have a friend standing by with a damp tea towel.
3 Use a long kitchen match to avoid scorching your fingers.
4 Keep your clothes on—human hair is highly flammable.

Good luck.

◎ *Joseph Pujol, 1857–1945, could play tunes on a flute with his behind.* ◎

HOW TO
DEVELOP A GIGANTIC MEMORY

Most people find it impossible to remember a shopping list, but few of us ever forget what our car looks like or how to find our way around town. It turns out, in fact, that journeys are singularly memorable and the following technique, which has been used since the time of the ancient Greeks, works by linking the things that you can't remember to a journey that you can. Try it, and you need never write a shopping list again.

First, go through a familiar journey in your head. It might be around your garden, or it could be a trip to the market. Memorize 10 points on this journey. For example, (1) your front door, (2) the pub, (3) the zebra crossing, (4) the vandalized bus stop, (5) the sex shop, (6) the library, (7) the fountain, (8) the pizza place, (9) the concrete church, (10) the war heroes statue with the glasses drawn on.

Now imagine a typical shopping list. For example, (1) eggs, (2) hemorrhoid cream, (3) oranges, (4) 60-watt bulb, (5) bread, (6) milk, (7) bleach, (8) ectoplasm, (9) fear, (10) infinity. You'll have spotted that the last three are not really typical shopping list items. They are there for practice, because they are harder to remember.

The list is most memorable if you attach your objects to the stages of the journey with the rudest or most ludicrous pictures you can think of. You might imagine, say, (1) a broken egg running down your front door, (2) the barmaid at the pub applying hemorrhoid cream

(3) a giant orange on the zebra crossing, (4) a bus full of bright light-bulbs, (5) a sandwich with something very unexpected in it, and so on. Try to convert abstract words into concrete images. So (9) might be a fearful child hiding behind a pew, and (10) could be a never-ending row of veterans. For items such as the 60-watt bulb, remember just the bulb part and the wattage will automatically come along with it.

If you enjoy performing, why not challenge an audience to call out 10 items at the beginning of the evening, and name them at the end. Because they're numbered, you can tell people in a flash what is at any number, or recite them in reverse order.

There was something else I meant to say but I can't remember what it was.

◎ *In Alfred Hitchcock's* The 39 Steps *Mr. Memory is played by Wylie Watson.* ◎

A BEGINNER'S GUIDE TO CALCULATING TIME OF DEATH

Suppose you've stopped by to see your best friend, only to discover that he's lying dead, with a sword in his back—it doesn't look like suicide. It's going to be some time before the pathologist and forensic agents are on the scene, and it will take the doctor half an hour just to wrestle his stethoscope into his bag. All the while, vital evidence is slipping away, so why not get cracking yourself? Here's a basic to-do list; there's no time to waste.

1 Take the rectal temperature

Starting from a normal temperature of 98.4 degrees F, a fresh corpse chills at the rate of about 1½ degrees an hour, until it reaches the temperature of the environment. The skin gets colder about three times faster than the body's core but, if the poor fellow is lying on an electric blanket, or has fallen through the ice, things are going to vary a bit—obviously.

2 Wiggle the limbs around

Owing to chemical changes in the muscles, a body starts to become rigid about three hours after death. This is called rigor mortis. A high ambient temperature speeds the process and a low one slows it. This stiffening begins in the eyelids, working its way down the face and body, with the stiff becoming fully stiff in something like 12 hours. Between 10 and 48 hours later, things start to go floppy again. Frankly, the whole thing is terribly variable, and a bit iffy.

3 Take a look underneath

As soon as a guy's heart stops beating, gravitation causes the blood to drain downward and settle (hypostasis). The parts of the body where this blood is now resting go dark blue and splotchy, taking on the appearance of bruises. After 5–6 hours, the skin will be blue all over but will go white if you push it with your finger. If it stays blue, the body has probably been dead for at least 10 hours. Non-blue patches will now be present where the corpse is touching the ground. If it has been moved after death, revealing discrepancies will be visible, my dear Watson.

4 Check the eyes

Signs of death appear in the eyes in just a few minutes. The whites go a sort of gray color and the cornea acquires a "film." After two hours or so the cornea becomes cloudy, and within a couple of days is generally opaque. These signs are a useful guide to undertakers, who like to check that the person they are about to nail into a coffin is actually dead—which is a relief to know.

5 Examine the stomach contents

How? Use your imagination, or a bit of hose and that old standby: siphoning. It takes between 1½ and 6 hours for a meal to be processed by the stomach. A cheese sandwich is in and out quicker than a five-course meal complete with half a bottle of Merlot, chocolate mousse, and an after-dinner drink.

6 Look for creepy-crawlies

After three days your cadaver will probably be host to the excited larvae of insects. Flies lay their eggs in the body's openings and they hatch quickly, sometimes in less than a day. The process continues over a couple of weeks, with the maggots getting progressively bigger. They are fat-eaters and there's no shortage of food.

7 Be aware of signs of decay

Putrefaction usually begins after two days in areas where bacteria are concentrated, its progress depending on the ambient temperature. Interestingly, fat people rot faster than skinny ones. After two or three days a green taint will appear on the abdomen and the body will start to bloat—until something "yields," to put it politely. In another day or so the green discoloration will have spread and the veins will be going a sort of darkish brown.

After five or six days, the skin begins blistering and slipping off the hands like gloves. Within three weeks or so, tissues begin to soften, things start to go bang inside, and fingernails fall off. It takes about a month for liquefaction to take hold, with the eyes "melting" and the features of the face becoming unrecognizable. Autolysis (cellular self-eating) is now well under way.

Of course, there are easier ways than all this to find out when somebody died. If their final diary entry on September 16 says, "Not feeling very well today," then that would be a good tip. If Thursday's newspaper is open on the table and the rest are on the doormat, that would tell you something too. And you wouldn't need to put a mask on to find it out.

◎ *Alexandros I of Greece died from septicaemia after his monkey bit him.* ◎

HOW TO
PLAY THE BAGPIPES

There are surely ladies who play the bagpipes, just as there are gentlemen who enjoy arranging cushions, but, on the whole, bagpipes are a guy thing—like poker and belching.

I cannot promise to teach you in five minutes how to crank out the *piobaireachd* (pibroch) like Pipe Major Angus MacDonald MBE, but this guide to the basics should enable you to put the right part in your mouth and make a noise of some description. It will take longer before you can master "Amazing Grace."

When you first encounter a set of Highland bagpipes they can appear intimidating and large. But do not allow your anxiety to show, because, like an animal, the pipes can smell fear. Instead, pick them up confidently and look them straight in the eye with a masterful gaze.

You will notice that the arrangement consists of a cloth-covered sort of Hoover bag, out of the long side of which stick three black pipes. The biggest of these is the bass "drone," which is attached to two, smaller, tenor drones with a piece of ribbon (sometimes tartan), or a cord and tassel. The drones are where the threnodic hooting comes out. Dangling from the end of the bag is a fourth pipe with a round "sole." This is the one that makes the tunes. It has finger holes up and down it and is called the "chanter." The fifth pipe, the pointy one in line with the drones, is the "blowpipe" and it is this one that goes in your mouth.

When the great Highland bagpipes are in full steam they produce a persistent wailing and, because this precludes any gaps between notes, tunes must be articulated by stopping the chanter holes with your fingers. Unlike with the didgeridoo, you needn't have mastered the art of circular breathing in order to play the pipes; your reservoir of air is created by constantly inflating the bag.

The best way to get things going is to lift the bagpipes and put the three drones over your left shoulder, with the bass nearest your ear. Stick the blowpipe in your mouth and let the chanter hang down in front of your midriff. Getting the arrangement sorted out shouldn't take longer than six or seven hours. If you can't see any pipes and are holding a hairy pouch with a strap, you have picked up someone's sporran (Scottish man-purse) by mistake. Do not blow into it.

When you are all set up, blow periodically into the mouthpiece as you squeeze the apparatus under your left arm, thus producing a continuous wind across the reeds, which are hidden in the pipes. Coordinating this blow—squeeze business is no more difficult than working the clutch and accelerator in a car, with the bonus that you won't end up in a ditch if you get it wrong. When you are doing things right, a delightful musical sound should fill the air (sort of B-flatish). Once you are making a steady drone (sounds a bit like a bear dreaming he's strangling a monkey), begin moving your fingers up and down the holes in the chanter, and music will come out.

Well, I did say it was going to be a fairly basic lesson. Like the man said when he was asked: "Oi mate, how do I get to Albert Hall?"—"Brother, you gotta practice."

◎ *The current world record for haggis hurling is 180 feet, 10 inches.* ◎

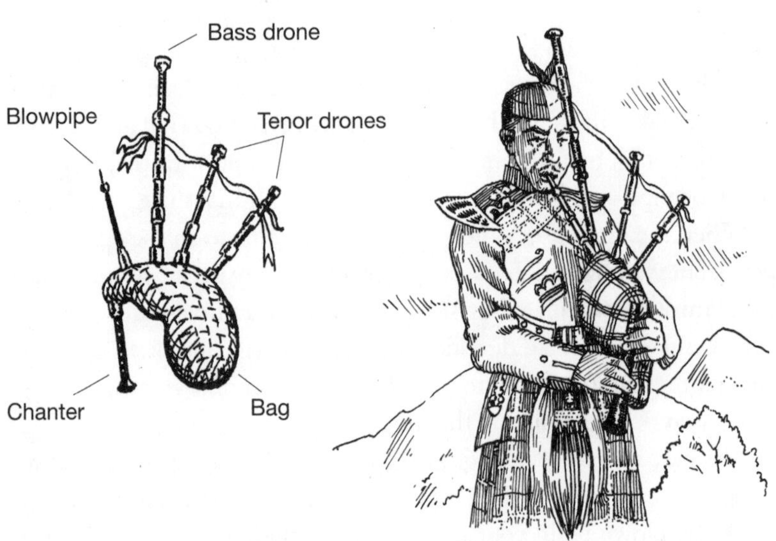

HOW TO
SHEAR A SHEEP

This is not some simplified Johnny-come-lately exercise but the proper old-fashioned Highland-shears method for which I thank crofter-extraordinaire Mr. Angus MacKenzie, the seventh in a knobbly line of Angus MacKenzies. (He's Scottish.)

Shears blunt easily, especially when they encounter the charmingly named "daggings" around the tail, or a heather or grit-filled fleece. So ask your local hardware store to sharpen them for you (it's difficult to get a good edge on a grinding stone). Two pairs should do about 40 sheep.

Choose your hold

- *Very old style*: tie up all four legs and put the sheep on a shearing stool (a kind of "bed" made of turf). In days of yore sheep shearing was a woman's job and this hold reduced backache.
- *Old style*: grip the sheep tightly between your knees, so that it's sitting on its bottom as if watching TV, and hold its front legs with your non-shearing hand. For extra stability you can wrap one of your own legs around its back members. Look out for the horn if you're handling a ram.

Two cutting techniques

1. Start at the belly, where the wool conveniently stops. Lift it up and keep it taut as you clip, working around to the behind, then cutting the fleece from your back leg of choice. Now work along that side of the sheep and then move across to the other side, shearing the legs in turn. With any luck, the fleece will come off in a single piece.
2. Cut the fleece around the neck to the base of the jaw and then, working around the whole body from back to front, "peel" the fleece off, over the animal's head. (If you are doing the very-old-style hold, the belly fleece must come off last.)

THE RELEASE

Your nude sheep may well be feeling a bit miffed so be quick about the release. Take a smart step back, away from the animal, and look all masterful.

◎ *The presence of menthol accounts for mint's minty taste.* ◎

HOW TO PASS YOURSELF OFF AS A PHILOSOPHER WITH THE HELP OF CLASSIC TV SITCOMS

For every Homer Simpson or "Hawkeye" Pierce there are a hundred characters whose aphorisms just evaporate over time. Perhaps the most quotable TV comedy ever is *The Simpsons*, with the most hilariously ornate dialogue coming from lips of the positively Dickensian Mr. Burns. (I therefore make no apology for the preponderance of *Simpsons* quotes that appear below.) But even some of the more garden-variety sitcom fare is funny, and even contains a few unexpected nuggets of wisdom. So get your nose out from those works of classic literature. Commit a few of these TV gems to memory and you will seem a wise and deep thinker indeed.

Love makes you do funny things. It made me get married.
—Buddy Sorrel from *The Dick Van Dyke Show*

This is America. You can't make a horse testify against himself.
—Mr. Ed from *Mr. Ed*

A device is yet to be invented that will measure my indifference to this remark.
—Hawkeye from *M*A*S*H*

This anonymous clan of slack-jawed troglodytes has cost me the election, and yet if I were to have them killed, I would be the one to go to jail. That's democracy for you.
—Mr. Burns from *The Simpsons*

Whenever I'm confused, I just check my underwear. It holds the answer to all the important questions.
—Grandpa from *The Simpsons*

Why can't they invent something for us to marry instead of women?
—Fred from *The Flintstones*

Looking at cleavage is like looking at the sun. You don't stare at it. It's too risky. You get a sense of it and then you look away.
—Jerry from *Seinfeld*

I always wanted to pretend I was an architect.
—George from *Seinfeld*

All right, look if you absolutely have to tell her the truth, at least wait until the timing's right. And that's what deathbeds are for.
—Chandler from *Friends*

Would I rather be feared or loved? Um . . . Easy, both. I want people to be afraid of how much they love me.
—Michael Scott from *The Office*

Right now, this is a job. If I advance any higher, this would be my career. And if this were my career, I'd have to throw myself in front of a train.
—Jim Halpert from *The Office*

◎ The Flintstones *was first aired with a laugh track, which was later removed.* ◎

UNDERSTANDING YOUR DOLLAR BILL

The visual design of the dollar bill is the oldest of any of the US currency now in circulation. The obverse (front) was originally issued in 1963, when the $1 bill first became a Federal Reserve note. (The Fed is a fascinating banking system, well worth reading about.) The reverse is of an older design, first produced in 1935. Handling these promissory notes as frequently as you probably do, you may not pay them great attention. But there is an abundance of interesting detail in the design.

General

- Dotted around on the bill, both front and back, you will find a wealth of small numbers and letters. These excitingly named check letters, quadrant numbers, and face- and backplate numbers indicate the particular printing plate used to manufacture the note, as well as its position on the sheet. A single impression produces 32 separate images of the dollar bill.

Obverse

- The most prominent thing on the front of the dollar bill is the central portrait of a 64-year-old George Washington, as depicted by Gilbert Stuart, a Scottish artist. By the way, that is *not* a funny haircut, it's his wig. They all wore them back in 1796.
- The black seal on the President's left is that of the Federal Reserve. The large letter in its center identifies the issuing bank. The letter *J* (for example) belongs to the Federal Reserve Bank in Kansas City, Missouri, while a *B* means New York.
- The four black numbers in the corners of the rectangular white space indicate the relevant Federal Reserve Bank.
- Under the Fed's seal is the bill's serial number, in green. There is a matching one above the green seal superimposed over the word *ONE*, on the right. This is the seal of the Department of the

Treasury. In its middle is a carpenter's square (a Masonic emblem), below that, the key to the Treasury, and above them, a pair of scales. The letter before the serial number should be the same as that in the seal's center. So a *J* in the seal and a *B* before the number (for example) means a suspect bill. The number's suffix letter shows how often that number has been used. The letter *A* is its first run, a *Z* shows it's the 26th. Simple!

- Below the Treasury seal is the signature of the Treasury Secretary. With some 8,000 million dollar bills in circulation, he must have a really sore signing arm.
- Directly below the serial number is the signature of the Treasurer of the United States. Same goes for his arm. These guys must be heartily sick of signing; I'm amazed they have time to do anything else. I bet the pair of them wish they'd gone into something more glamorous, like garbage disposal.
- On the left of the secretary's signature is the series year date.

Reverse

- The roundels show on the right the recto (front) and on the left the verso (back) of the Great Seal of the United States of America (1782), which is full of interesting details. In the roundel on the right is a heraldic bald eagle with wings "displayed." In his beak he holds a scroll inscribed with the Latin motto: *E pluribus unum*, "From many (comes) one." Over his head, the stars in the "glory" were designed to represent the 13 original colonies "a new constellation in the firmament of nations," and appear in the earliest sketches for the Great Seal, along with the 13 stripes in the escutcheon (shield), the 13 olive leaves (peace), and the 13 arrows (not peace).
- The leftmost roundel shows a pyramid, another Masonic symbol. The eye in the triangle symbolizes the all-seeing Deity. In capitals over the pyramid, the motto *Annuit Cœptis* may be translated as, "He hath smiled on our undertakings," and *Novus Ordo Seclorum* at the foot of the pyramid as, "A new order of centuries."

The pyramid (unfinished) is officially interpreted as symbolizing permanence and strength, future growth and the goal of perfection. Which sounds better than: "We ran out of bricks." The Roman numerals, MDCCLXXVI, at the pyramid's base are a date: 1776.

◎ *A dollar bill costs 4.2 cents to make and typically lasts less than 2 years.* ◎

HOW TO BLUFF YOUR WAY IN SCIENCE

The idea that we should believe just those things that are likely to be true (science) is only about 400 years old. Scientists look at nature, try to guess what might be going on, and then do experiments in an effort to falsify their guesses—and other people's. If a guess doesn't stand up to testing, it's wrong—even if you're Einstein. A theory that is still in one piece after testing is, however, only *provisionally* right.

Useful talking points

- *4000 BC*: Mesopotamians guess that the Earth is the center of the universe—wrong!
- *4th century BC*: the Greeks use arithmetic, logic, and philosophy to explain the world. They suggest that everything is made up of tiny bits (atoms)—a hugely influential and correct guess.
- *13th century*: Europeans begin consolidating scientific theory and practice—much of it false. Progress is patchy and the Church is antagonistic.
- *1543*: Copernicus's (correct) theory that the Earth goes around the sun is published.
- *17th century*: modern science begins. William Harvey's theory reveals that blood goes around the body (1628). In 1666 Newton realizes that gravity affects planets as well as apples.
- *18th century*: the "Age of Enlightenment." Biology and chemistry develop fast.

- *19th century*: long-held assumptions start to fall apart. In 1803, John Dalton reveals the first (useful) atomic theory of matter. Michael Faraday and James Maxwell make giant strides in understanding electromagnetism, gravity and light. In 1859 Charles Darwin's theory of evolution by natural selection annoys people.
- *20th century*: Einstein staggers everybody with his strange theories of relativity (special and general). Quantum mechanics, an even weirder theory, explains what's going on at the teeny-weeny level. Though rejected by Einstein, quantum mechanics has not been falsified by any experiment designed to test it—*so far*. The double helix shape of DNA is determined by James Watson and Francis Crick.
- *21st century*: the human genome project maps our blueprint. "String theory" emerges, and may turn out to be a "theory of everything." Or not . . .

◎ *A jumping flea accelerates 20 times faster than the space shuttle at takeoff.* ◎

HOW TO PLAY EDWARD FORTYHANDS

Have you seen the movie *Edward Scissorhands* (1990)? It stars Johnny Depp as a young man with scissors for hands: enormous great long blades on every finger. Goodness only knows what palaver he must have gone through to avoid inadvertent amputation when pulling off his boxers at night.

In any case, the drinking game known as Edward Fortyhands is named after that classic role. The rules are simple and the entertainment is suitable for home, office, or bachelor party. It might, for all I know, even be apropos during a lull between courses at a state dinner at the White House, although I'm not certain of the protocol. Anyway, here's what's involved.

Required

- *2 40-ounce bottles of cold malt liquor*
- *A roll of duct tape*
- *Two or more players not younger than drinking age*

Method

1 Grasp an unopened bottle of your preferred 40-ounce beverage in each hand.
2 Have the bottles securely taped to your palms.
3 Ask an assistant to unscrew and remove the bottle tops.
4 On the command *Legg mi am Åsch!* (a Bavarian exclamation roughly translatable as "Well, what a surprise!"), drink both bottles.
5 The first player to finish is the winner.

Rules

1 You must not remove the duct tape or either bottle until both 40s are finished.
2 You may do anything while playing so long as you do it with the 40s taped to your hands. If you need to brush your teeth or "sharpen your skates," you'll just have to ask a trusted friend to assist you with your zipper.
3 If you remove tape or bottles before finishing, you lose and must, as a forfeit, chug both your 40s.

Now, those 40s are capacious hummers, holding almost four times the amount of your normal 12-ounce bottle, and it can be wonderfully entertaining to watch players trying to answer the phone or help fellow competitors light cigarettes with their teeth and elbows, hampered as they are by their own bottles. It doesn't help that the temperature of the bottles has an anesthetic effect on the hands and it's not long before they begin to feel like natural appendages. It's somewhat similar to Lee Majors in *The Six Million Dollar Man*, except he had expensive cybernetic bionics surgically implanted into his body, not large containers of highly alcoholic beer taped to his fingers.

Among the delightful variants of Edward Fortyhands are Edward Thirty-two-hands, played where 40-ounce bottles are hard to come by; Edward Winehands (self-explanatory); Edward Ciderhands (2-liter bottles of rough cider—popular in Southwest England); and the French Edouard Champagnemains (for formal occasions).

◎ *"Depp" is a German word meaning "jackass."* ◎

HOW TO
COUNT TO TEN IN CUNEIFORM

The first ever written language was invented by the Sumerians in Mesopotamia some 5,000 years ago, its symbols being pressed into soft clay tablets with a reed stylus. This technique produced singularly characteristic triangular indentations causing modern scholars to dub the writing "cuneiform," from the Latin *cuneus*, or *wedge*.

At first, cuneiform was a pictorial script like classical Japanese but it developed over time into an abstract, syllabic alphabet, the earliest function of which was to record commercial transactions, using a decimal system.

Numbers were initially expressed in a primitive way: if Fred sold Bill half a dozen goats, scribes just made the mark for goat six times. A bit of a nightmare if you were accounting for grains of rice.

Not surprisingly, around 3000 BC, numbers and the articles to which they referred began to be shown separately. So instead of writing say "goat" n times, they began to write the commodity's character next to that representing the pertinent number. This huge conceptual leap allowed numbers now to be recorded and thought about, independent of real things, in a more sophisticated, complex, and useful way. It also freed junior scribes from the torture of such things as writing the number of bricks required for the latest extension to Emperor Tiglath-Pileser's super palace.

THE NUMBERS

Cuneiform numbers are written using a combination of two marks: a thin vertical wedge for 1 and a fatter wedge for 10. The basic scheme (minus some common variations) is shown below.

Practice with a piece of chalk and a big flat rock and you can get quite an authentic looking cuneiform tablet. Sketched on a bar coaster it's worth at least one free pint.

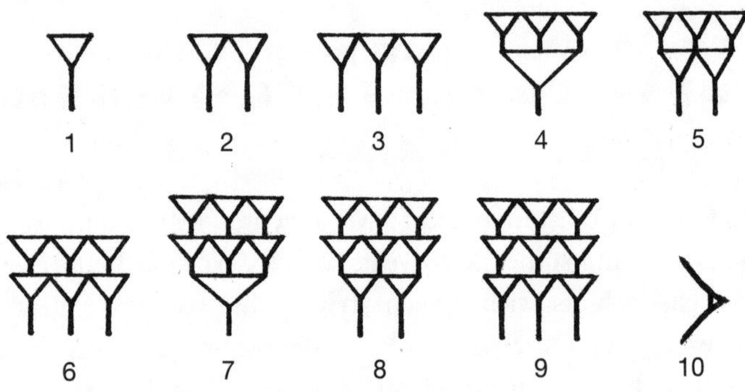

◎ *Arithmomania is an obsessive love of counting.* ◎

HOW TO
PLAY ELEPHANT POLO

Similar to ordinary polo, elephant polo was first played in India at the beginning of the 20th century, with nine-foot-long bamboo mallets. In the beginning, soccer balls were used but the elephants squashed them, so the game is now played with an ordinary polo ball on a pitch ¾ the length of a standard one. The elephants need a shorter pitch because they run more slowly than horses.

The other main difference between horse and elephant polo is that the elephant is ridden not by the player but by the trainer or "mahout." The player tells the mahout where to go and what to do, and the mahout communicates this to the elephant with verbal commands and by squeezing behind the pachyderm's ears with his feet. Trained polo elephants are monolingual, understanding only Nepali, which can, and does, frequently lead to confusion. So, unless your team is composed of some good Nepali speakers it will be a real challenge to play elephant polo.

Some rules

- A team consists of four elephants and four players, a senior umpire presiding, together with an assistant mounted on the referee elephant.
- Play begins when the umpire throws the ball between two opposing elephants inside the center circle.
- The playing time consists of two 10-minute "chukkers" with a 15-minute halftime interval during which, ends and elephants are changed.
- No team may have more than three elephants in the same half of the pitch at any one time.
- It is a foul for an elephant to lie down in front of the goal, as this spoils it for everyone else. The opposing team gets a free hit.
- Men must play with the right hand only, but women may play with both hands.
- No player may hit another player, elephant or umpire with his stick.
- It is a foul for an elephant to pick up the ball with his trunk (what else?). The penalty is a free hit to the opposing team from the place where the ball was picked up.
- No standing on the ball.
- Mahouts and players must wear a polo helmet.
- At the end of play, the elephants are given a sugar-soaked rice ball or two and the mahouts get a cold beer. No swapping of rice balls for beer will be allowed.

◎ *Male elephants have no scrotum.* ◎

HOW TO
BLUFF YOUR WAY IN PHILOSOPHY

Unlike the laws of science and the rules of mathematics, philosophical ideas cannot be proved or disproved. You can't refute statements such as "There is no such thing as 'knowledge'" or "Animals don't have rights" by doing an experiment or looking up the log tables. This means, of course, that you can argue all night without fear of reaching a conclusion, and it's this that makes philosophy—like politics—such a brilliant subject for the artful bluffer.

Types of philosopher

There are two main types of philosopher. With the first type, you often get an inkling of what they are going on about. Take this important philosophical assertion by type-1 thinker Bertrand Russell:

> There may, for aught I know, be admirable reasons for eating peas with a knife, but the hypnotic effect of early persuasion has made me completely incapable of appreciating them.

This is philosophical exposition of crystalline clarity.

In contrast, philosophers of type 2 are, at all times, completely incomprehensible. They say things such as:

> The shift from a homologous concept in which capital is understood to condition societal relationships in quintessentially structuralist modalities as an appreciation of oligarchic or hegemonic constructs—in which capitalistic subjection is contingent on restatement, reconvergence, and rearticulationism—invokes the dilemma of conceptual ephemerality as a notion of a renewed structure, distinguishing a shift from the view of commodities as hypothetical totalities, to one in which the cognition of the contingent potentialities of structure initiates, instead, a revivified

imagining of hegemony as the ineluctable concomitant of the tropes and tactics of the renunciation of might.

This masterly style is the one you should adopt if you wish to bluff your way in philosophy. Learn a few "gorged-snake" sentences of this kind, keeping a variety of vocabularies up your sleeve, and you'll have a ready-made answer for *any* philosophical question lobbed your way.

Wardrobe is important too:

- Stay-press pants, nylon sports jackets, and shirts with collars of a different hue are the costume of the analytical philosopher. You'll also need a few incredibly sharp pencils.
- Black jeans, black T-shirts, and a black leather jacket indicate the continental philosopher, along with a fountain pen for those bleary diagrams: all arrows, and lines, and question marks.
- Corduroy bags and tweed jackets with elbow-patches are the garb of the historian of philosophy. Naturally, a pipe is *de rigueur*. Faced with a tricky question, just start cleaning it. Takes hours.
- By the addition of some expensive glasses a plainly dressed chap can be turned into an instant professor of cultural studies. Easiest of the lot.

◎ *Aristotle thought wind direction decided the gender of a baby.* ◎

HOW TO CHANGE YOUR NAME

Nothing on this earth could be simpler than changing your name. Here is what you do:

- Start using your new name.

That's it. There's no legal process you *have* to follow to change your name in the United States. Once you have changed your name, you can use it officially, so long as you aren't trying to deceive or defraud people.

You can quite legally order up a new passport, change the details of your driver's license, order credit cards, and open new bank accounts all over the place in your new name. As security concerns escalate and the threat of identity theft increases, however, you may find that making these changes requires some kind of legal documentation. The easiest way to get such a document is to petition your state court, achieved by some simple paperwork.

That's all there is to it—so long as you are over 18. If not, it's trickier and involves judges and paperwork.

◎ *Truman Streckfus Persons wrote under the name Truman Capote.* ◎

FINE LIMERICKS FOR THE DISCERNING AESTHETE

A limerick is a five-line humorous poem in strict meter, the first line of which generally introduces a young lady or an old man from a particular place. The limerick's rhyme scheme is AABBA. The first, second, and fifth lines being nine syllables each, in three metrical feet; the third and fourth lines being each two metrical feet. The foot generally used is the amphibrach, a stressed syllable between two unstressed ones (e.g., "a fine way"), or the inferior anapest, two short syllables followed by a long one (e.g., "unabridged"). The best limericks are ingenious, playful, often self-referential—and commonly ribald. Young ladies called Tucker or Hunt may create expectations in the corrupt or indecent listener that are often dashed at the last moment by a surprising final non-rhyme. The rigid metrical code has also led to many waggish anti-limericks that subvert the form by not rhyming or scanning, or by breaking another of the rules. Here are a few of the best limericks around, each one suitable for social situations that require making a good impression.

There was an old man of Calcutta
Who coated his tonsils with butta
This converted his snore
From a thunderous roar
To a soft, oleaginous mutta

There was a young girl of Bermuda
Every man on the island had wooed her
I'm afraid that the rest
Must be sternly suppressed
It gets ruder and ruder and ruder

There was a young lady of Exeter
So pretty the men craned their necks at her
But some, more depraved,
Went much further and waved
The distinguishing marks of their sex at her

There was a young poet named Dan
Whose limericks never would scan
When asked why this was

He replied, "It's because
I always try to squeeze as many syllables
 into the last line as I possibly can"

There was a young man of St Bees
Who was stung on the nose by a wasp
When they asked, "Does it hurt?"
He replied, "Yes, it does
Thank goodness it wasn't a hornet!"

There was a New Yorker named Hannah
Who liked to make love on a piannah
A hell of a fine way
To treat a new Steinway
But such is the star-spangled mannah

There was a young man of Arnoux
Whose limericks stopped at line two

There was a young man of Utrecht
Whose approach was both crude and direct
To a girl he would say
"Are you good for a lay?"
(He did better than one might expect)

There was a young girl of Madras
Who had a magnificent ass
Not what you think
Soft round and pink
It was gray, had long ears and ate grass

◎ Nantucket *is derived from a Native American word for "land far out to sea."* ◎

THE 38 COUNTRIES OF NORTH AMERICA

Yes, you read correctly. At the time of this writing, the number of countries and territories on the continent of North America is an impressive 38. What's more, there are 514 million people living in these 23 sovereign states and 15 dependent territories, except for Navassa Island, which is uninhabited, has no official language, and produces nothing but bird droppings. Rattling off these facts at a party is sure to impress.

Naturally enough, there's some debate about exactly where North America starts and stops. Central America, for example, is generally regarded as the southernmost part of the continent, even though some view it as a region in its own right. In fact people argue about a lot of this stuff. Take Aruba, Netherlands Antilles, Trinidad and Tobago, and Panama, which are all considered to have territory in both North and South America. I've included Panama here as the bottom of North America. I don't mean that in a derogatory sense, but simply geographically; please don't write me with your complaints—write the President or someone.

THE COUNTRIES AND TERRITORIES

Anguilla (UK)
- Language: English
- Main products: sugar, molasses and Sea Island cotton

Antigua and Barbuda
- Language: English
- Main product: tourism

Aruba (Netherlands)
- Languages: Dutch, English, Papiamento
- Main product: tourism

Bahamas
- Language: English
- Main products: tourism, rum, offshore finance

Barbados
- Language: English
- Main products: rum, molasses, tourism

Belize
- Language: English, Spanish
- Main products: sugar, timber

Bermuda (UK)
Language: English
Main products: tourism (this tourism thing is *big*), offshore finance

British Virgin Islands (UK)
Languages: English, Creole
Main products: tourism, offshore finance

Canada
Languages: English, French
Main products: minerals, timber, cereals, manufactured goods

Cayman Islands (UK)
Language: English
Main products: tourism, offshore finance, turtle products (!)

Costa Rica
Language: Spanish
Main product: coffee

Cuba
Language: Spanish
Main products: beans, casava, minerals, coffee, sugar

Dominica
Language: English
Main products: bananas, fruit, tourism

Dominican Republic
Language: Spanish
Main products: sugar, minerals

El Salvador
Language: Spanish
Main products: coffee, cotton

Greenland (Denmark)
Languages: Danish, Inuit
Main products: fish, more fish

Grenada
Language: English
Main products: cocoa, nutmeg, bananas

Guadeloupe (France)
Languages: French, Creole
Main products: eggplants, bananas, pineapples, sugar cane

Guatemala
Language: Spanish
Main products: coffee, minerals

Haiti
Languages: French, Creole
Main products: coffee, sugar

Honduras
Language: Spanish
Main products: bananas, coffee, timber

Jamaica
Language: English, Creole
Main products: bauxite, bananas, sugar, tourism

Martinique (France)
Languages: French, Creole
Main products: bananas, flowers, pineapples, sugar cane

Mexico
Language: Spanish
Main products: oil, minerals, textiles, steel
Montserrat (UK)
Languages: English, Creole
Main products: electronic components, vegetables, plastic bags (severe volcanic activity has decimated this economy)
Navassa Island (USA/claimed also by Haiti)
Language: None
Main product: guano (bird leavings)
Netherlands Antilles (Netherlands)
Languages: Dutch, English, Creole
Main products: tourism, oil refinement, offshore finance
Nicaragua
Languages: Spanish, English
Main products: coffee, cotton, meat
Panama
Language: Spanish
Main products: canal traffic, banking, bananas
Puerto Rico (USA)
Language: Spanish
Main products: minerals, cotton, fish, fruit, hydroelectricity
Saint Kitts and Nevis (UK)
Language: English
Main product: sugar
Saint Lucia
Language: English
Main products: bananas, cocoa, textiles
Saint Pierre and Miquelon (France)
Languages: French, English
Main product: fish
Saint Vincent and the Grenadines
Language: English
Main products: bananas, arrowroot, tourism
Trinidad and Tobago
Language: English
Main products: oil, sugar, cocoa, coffee
Turks and Caicos Islands (UK)
Language: English
Main products: seafood
United States
Language: English
Main products: foods, minerals, manufactured goods
US Virgin Islands (USA)
Languages: English, Creole, Dutch
Main product: tourism

◎ *The geographical center of North America is in Rugby, North Dakota.* ◎

HOW TO
IDENTIFY AMERICAN WILD ANIMALS

We are surrounded by a plenitude of native wildlife, from the New World porcupine to the tree-dwelling wood duck, but I guess many of us would be at a loss if called upon to identify them by name, beyond the obvious ones like the robin. In case you'd like to brush up on your wildlife identification skills, here's a quick guide to a few of the more interesting specimens.

- *The American alligator*: gets its name from the Spanish *el lagarto* ("the lizard"), and lives along the bottom portion of the United States, where it is warm and wet. Alligators are difficult to miss really. They will eat almost anything, including fish, birds, turtles, frogs, snakes, raccoons, pet cats and dogs, and possibly even KFC—they're not fussy. A big alligator will take on cattle, Florida panther, bears, other alligators, and slow-moving grandmas. So watch out, especially for its tail, in case it attempts to knock you over and drag you screaming into the water, where it will then drown you. Climb a tree; alligators have poor climbing skills, as you've no doubt spotted.
- *The rattlesnake*: the broad, triangular head, skinny neck, and heavy body are all characteristic identifiers of the rattler, while the rattle on the tail is a dead giveaway. Rattlesnakes generally bite only when threatened or provoked and will usually retreat. But for advice on snakebites see Chapter 4.

  Most rattlesnakes live in the deserts, plains, forests, river bottoms, and coastal prairies of the southwestern United States, growing up to 6 feet in length and ranging in color from brown or gray through pink. Other distinctive attributes include a series of light and dark bands near the tail, rather menacing hooded eyes, and a penchant for gaudy silk neckties.

- *The pygmy sperm whale*: a small, toothed cetacean, rare in Nebraska but known to swim all around the US coastline, though sightings are uncommon. Growing up to 13 feet in length and weighing more than 600 pounds when adult, this whale is dark on the top with a pale belly and a small dorsal fin. It has a short spear-shaped blowhole along with a blunt rather rude face. Its teeth are slender and widely spaced, and it has long blond curly hair (no, I made that up about the hair).
- *The skunk*: Even if you've never seen one, you'll have no problem identifying a skunk, if you possess a nose. The exquisite perfume of burning tires, horsehair, and sweaty shirts is often the sign that there's a skunk about. Two scent glands flanking the exit of the skunk's wind tunnel offer a persuasive defense. When threatened, the skunk will first display his black and white tail. If you see him bending into a *U* and pointing his head and fundament in your direction, don't ask questions: run for it. He can squirt two jets of foul-smelling yuck more than 15 feet, quicker than you can say, "Pepé le Pew," befouling the air for a mile around. Think about that for a minute: just one skunk sitting outside the venerable stage at Carnegie Hall could bring the whole of Midtown Manhattan to a shuddering halt. I wish I could do that.
- *Attwater's prairie chicken*: these grouse-like birds are endangered and only to be found in Texas. But they're hard to miss if you can catch up with them, with vertical brown-and-white zebra-like markings. The males sport a bright orange inflatable "air ball" on either side of the neck, with which they make a strange mating call. (Perhaps Attwater himself, whoever he was, had a similar signature call.)
- *The American black bear*: You'll find this cuddly killer in 40 of the 50 states. They're called black but confusingly vary in color from white through brown and blond. Beady eyes, round ears, a long

nose and a short tail are also black bear identifiers, along with the characteristic shuffling gait, the result of his hind legs being slightly longer than his forelegs. They are not usually aggressive and will often run away before you see them.

- *The hairy-legged vampire*: A large, dark-brown bat with a narrow, hairy interfemoral membrane, short round ears, and a pug-nosed snout. (This sounds like a woman I used to work for.) It lives in the southern United States and is more solitary than the common vampire. Its favorite dinner is the blood of domestic birds, including chickens.
- *The raccoon*: Frequently seen drinking beer out of paper sacks in shopping malls, the raccoon often suffers from black "raccoon eyes." Aggressive if cornered, he will readily fight a larger predator who has been hitting on his girl. Typically smokes malodorous stogies and belches rudely. Best keep away.
- *The coyote*: Coyotes, also called prairie wolves, have adapted well to urban living, looking after themselves in the human environment with little trouble. Indeed, a coyote named Hal was captured by wildlife officials in Central Park during March 2006; but only after they had chased him for two days.
- *The roadrunner*: A large, skinny, streaked ground bird with a distinctive head crest and long legs. The state bird of New Mexico, the roadrunner can sprint at a very respectable 15 miles an hour. Beep beep!
- *Daffy Duck*: Sorry, my mind's playing word-association games with me after the roadrunner and coyote stuff above.
- *Eastern brown pelican*: The brown pelican weighs about 9 pounds and has a 6-foot wingspan. Very fond of spicy tortilla chips and semiotics.
- *The moose*: A lanky ruminant with a long fleshy muzzle, and, in the case of the male, a sort of jowly neck-sporran. His range includes the Dakotas, much of New England, and the upper Rockies. I am reminded of the man in charge of the elks at the Alaska Zoo who wanted to boost moose numbers but was unsure whether

he should ask his supplier for two moose, two mooses, or two meese. Finally he wrote his contact: "Please send me a moose. Please send me another one with it."

◎ *Mel Blanc disliked the taste of raw carrots.* ◎

HOW TO MAKE A WILL WITHOUT SPENDING A PENNY

About 66 percent of American grown-ups don't have a will. Dying without a will is known as dying intestate and it is as painful as it sounds.

If you snuff it without a will in America and you are married with children, your wife and kids automatically get all your personal stuff like your motorbike, favorite armchair, old pants, MP3 player and Spiderman Timex, and the income from whatever money is left over.

If you are married without children, your wife gets your belongings and any money left over. The rest goes to your parents or to your brothers and sisters if they are dead (your parents, that is). If you have no living parent or siblings, the state can quite legally lay it's cold, gnarled paws on your assets.

So you should definitely make a will, then you can leave your 18th-century farmhouse and the Manhattan penthouse (yeah right) to whoever you like, say your mistress, and nominate trusted friends as executors to sort the thing out.

Types of will

- Most wills are "attested," that is, prepared in writing and signed by witnesses who confirm that the document reflects the wishes of the person who made it, and that he wasn't bonkers at the time.
- A will of a less common type is the "nuncupative" will. This is a will croaked out to witnesses on the deathbed, who jot down

what they think you said and then show it to lawyers. Wills of this kind are fraught with problems, as you might imagine.

- Lawyers go on about how they should always do your will, but, since they commonly charge a not insignificant sum for the privilege, this advice should be taken with a pinch of salt. Why not do it yourself?
- You can buy will software, or, if you live in a state that considers them valid, you can do it absolutely free by making a "holographic" will. This is nothing to do with those 3-D laser pictures, it's just the name for a document written entirely in your own hand. Holographic wills are especially good if things are simple (like you aren't the part-owner of 17 companies in various tax havens and a serial husband with scores of dependent children around the world).

Holography

- Provided a will is written out in your own hand (you could even sign it) you don't need a witness. Storm-tossed sailors and soldiers under fire often find themselves knocking up a quick holographic will and the absence of a fatuous lawyer must invest their impending immolation with a wonderful serenity.
- The shortest will ever, according to the *Guinness Book of World Records*, is "All to wife," written on the bedroom wall by a chap who realized his end was extremely nigh. It was perfectly legal too, being plainly his own work and nobody else's.
- Another enterprising fellow, a farmer, finding himself mortally squashed under his own tractor, distributed his chattels by inscription on the muddy bumper. It went through probate (the legal bit) without a murmur—surely an inspiration to us all.

◎ *The first coins were made from electrum, an alloy of gold and silver.* ◎

HOW TO
ESCAPE FROM A STRAITJACKET

Do you remember Jack Nicholson in *One Flew Over the Cuckoo's Nest* (1975)? Even in a straitjacket he looks like the kind of person capable of causing considerable mayhem at an auction of fine china.

Escaping from a straitjacket is, let's face it, possibly the single most useless article of knowledge in the long, extensive, and tortured annals of useless knowledge. That's just an opinion—please don't write me with long lists of knowledge even more useless than this one; my precarious constitution couldn't stand the onslaught. Anyway, if you'd like to know how it's done, here's an exploration of the details.

The straitjacket is a robust vest of canvas and leather. Attached to the ends of its closed sleeves are long leather straps used to bind the arms around the trunk. It was designed to prevent mentally disturbed patients from running amok and hurting people. Harry Houdini first introduced the straightjacket escape into his act after touring an insane asylum in Canada. It's not a trick, as such, but a combination of opportunism and brute force, performed in plain sight often by a daredevil suspended upside down high above the ground by a burning rope. This actually makes the escape dramatic, convincing, and also *easier*, allowing a greater degree of wriggle so as to allow the arms over the head (the key to success), as well as lending a gravitational helping hand. This is a précis of Houdini's own explanation as it appeared in his *Handcuff Escapes* (1910).

> *First place the elbow, which has its hand under the opposite elbow, on some solid foundation and exert force sufficient to gradually move it up towards the head. By persistent straining you can squeeze your head under the lower arm, so bringing both of the arms in front of the body. You now undo the buckles of the cuff straps with your teeth, after which*

you open the buckles at the back with your hands, through the canvas sleeves, and then remove the straitjacket.

TIPS

- Always use your own straitjacket, which you know well.
- Be sure to have it strapped on by someone who has never done it before (preferably a little old lady). Every inch counts, so gain slack by expanding your chest and bracing your elbows against your sides as it is strapped on. Extra space can be had by surreptitiously gripping handfuls of fabric under the arms.
- Once it's tight, relax the muscles, hunch the shoulders forward, and push your arms deeper into the sleeves. This maximizes the slack in back, allowing you to proceed as above.

◎ *Harry Houdini's real name was Eric Weiss.* ◎

HOW TO
BLUFF YOUR WAY IN ART

Unlike science, it's easy to bluff your way in art. I've met expert art bluffers who can talk for hours, utterly uninfected by the slightest knowledge of the subject. One famous bluffer, named Richard, once showed me a sketch of Picasso he'd done. It was abysmal, yet he often wrote on the subject for newspapers. So don't feel abashed—no one will spot your fakery.

SOME PERIODS AND "STYLES" USEFUL FOR BLUFFING PURPOSES

- *Greek and Roman*: great vases and sculptures of ladies with no arms. Lots of temples and such. Good mosaics too.
- *Medieval (1200–1400 ish)*: this is when painting took off. Many biblical, especially Christian, pictures being done, but perspective and 3-D all a bit funny-looking.

- *Renaissance*: started in 15th-century Italy. Endless portraits but perspective now sorted out.
- *High Renaissance (16th century)*: oil on canvas supplanting paintings on wood.
- *Mannerism*: an offshoot of Renaissance often featuring men with bare chests and show-offy realism.
- *Baroque*: huge, busy, crowded, dramatic paintings with classical references cropping up a lot (loads of writhing women, mainly, and people playing lutes).
- *Rococo*: early 18th century, all curly and Louis XV-looking. Lots of drapes and cushion covers, like Graceland. Brushwork more modern in appearance.
- *Neo-classicism*: landscapes take off. Many sporting and outdoors pictures churned out, along with stuffy portraits of fat men and their ugly wives.
- *19th century*: paint in tubes now available. A busy century, with the self-consciously arty Pre-Raphaelites in England and, toward the end, the Impressionists in France loosening up subject matter and treatment. Lots of ladies with bare bosoms and out-of-focus haystacks. A rapid relay from Manet to Monet to Degas to Seurat to Van Gogh to Cézanne to Gaugin to Matisse to the modern age.
- *20th century*: Totally crazy—Expressionism, Fauvism, Cubism, Vorticism, Futurism, Dadaism, Neo-plasticism, Surrealism, Abstract-Expressionism, Op Art, Pop Art, Conceptual Art, and so on. Artists now commonly become global "brands," like your Picassos, Dalís, Hockneys, Warhols, and Bacons.
- *21st century*: a desiccated time of sponsored art prizes, competitions, and self-conscious "controversy." Bring back the ladies with the bare bosoms.

◎ *The Guggenheim was first called the Museum of Non-Objective Painting.* ◎

A GUIDE TO
DIY FUNERALS

Now that churchyards are simply bursting with dead bodies, people are increasingly looking for alternative places, and different ways, to inter their loved ones. Many people's first choice is burial in the yard, but this can reduce the value of your home by 25 percent. So here are some better ideas for your do-it-yourself disposals.

Burial at sea

We buried my seafaring father-in-law this way—or part of him, anyway—in the form of some of his ashes shaken from a plastic bag over the side of the Boston ferry on a windy day off Cape Cod. I am able to confirm, as a result of this experiment, that eating a sandwich dusted with somebody's mortal remains does you no harm.

If you want to bury a person off the American coast without cremating him, you'll need to adhere to the Environmental Protection Agency's fairly basic regulations on ocean dumping (sounds romantic). The EPA requires that the remains be prepared according to the Naval or civil authority that has jurisdiction, and stipulates that the burial take place at least three nautical miles from the shore in water that is at least 600 feet deep. Once the burial has taken place, you have thirty days to submit the Burial at Sea form to the EPA regional office.

You can arrange the burial through a funeral director, or you can do it all yourself. It's common sense mainly: weight the coffin properly—not forgetting to drill a few holes—make sure the top won't come off and get hold of a willing boatman with a vessel from which he can launch your loved one into the sea without a lot of undignified straining and swearing. You also need to weight the corpse with chains and secure a metal tag around it in case the worst happens and the body has to be returned to you.

Other DIY options

Talk to the experts early on—before anyone's actually snuffed it. There's no requirement to have a funeral director run the operation and much can be learned from ordinary people who have organized the whole thing themselves.

As well as sorting out the practicalities, you might want to consider taking along a priest, shaman, or actor to pronounce a bit. Dignified formality and ritual are important to people on momentous occasions, though there's no obligation for supernatural talk. If you're an atheist, The American Humanist Association can supply a funeral "officiant" to come and say nonreligious things. Check their website to find a chapter near you. Alternatively, members of the family can speak: it's up to you.

The Natural Death Centre has plenty of information about "natural" burial grounds, private burials, the law, and biodegradable coffins of cardboard, bamboo, willow, and jute; though the more stylish corpse might prefer the sleek, German Uono Cocoon, a sort of giant headache capsule.

If you really want to go out with a bang, rather than a municipal whimper on the crematorium conveyor belt, why not copy Hunter S. Thompson who had his ashes fired from a 150ft cannon? "He loved explosions," explained his widow.

Good luck.

◎ *The 10th Duke of Hamilton's legs were cut short to fit him into his coffin.* ◎

HOW TO
IDENTIFY AIRCRAFT TAIL INSIGNIA

The identification of aircraft by their tail insignia used to be a doddle once but now they come and go like nobody's business. Here's a selection of the more graphically interesting ones so that next time you're by the runway-side window in Customs you can issue fellow jet-setters a tail-spotting challenge. See illustration on page 103.

1 *Aer Lingus*. The name is an anglicized form of the Irish Aer Loingeas meaning air fleet. They are Irish so their tails are green with a shamrock—what else do you need?

2 *Aeroflot*. Aeroflot once had a reputation for gruff air hostesses with beards. They may have changed but the tail insignia still features the red, blue, and white of the Russian flag.

3 *Air Canada*. Their red maple leaf has appeared over the years in different guises on their tail fins. But if it's a maple leaf, it's Air Canada.

4 *Air France*. No, not a frog but a conservative design of diagonal blue and white stripes, with just a cheeky little red one near the bottom. Very French.

5 *Air New Zealand*. The koru is the Maori symbol of the uncurling fern. It's still there in white.

6 *Alitalia*. Once again it's a nationalistic theme: the red, white, and green of the Italian flag. A highly visible one, not too rich in subtlety.

7 *British Airways*. Flags again. A cleverly stylized portion of Union Jack on the tail, with added flutter.

8 *Cathay Pacific Airways*. I've no idea what that is on the tail either—a headless bird? A bit inscrutable if you ask me.

9 *Easyjet*. Orange all over with a white word: easyJet. Small *E* big *J*, very, very annoying, but easy to spot. Stelios Haji-Iouannou is your man. Looks quite orange himself, I think.

10 *Japan Airlines*. All it is is part of a red circle from the flag of the land of the rising sun. Doubtless the design cost millions.

11 *Qantas*. Yes, it's a kangaroo I'm afraid, so no awards for originality. The only surprise is that they didn't put it on upside down.

12 *Ryanair*. Probably the worst-drawn symbol in the history of aircraft tail insignia. After much tooth-sucking, I've decided it's meant to be a flying harp-woman. Hopeless!

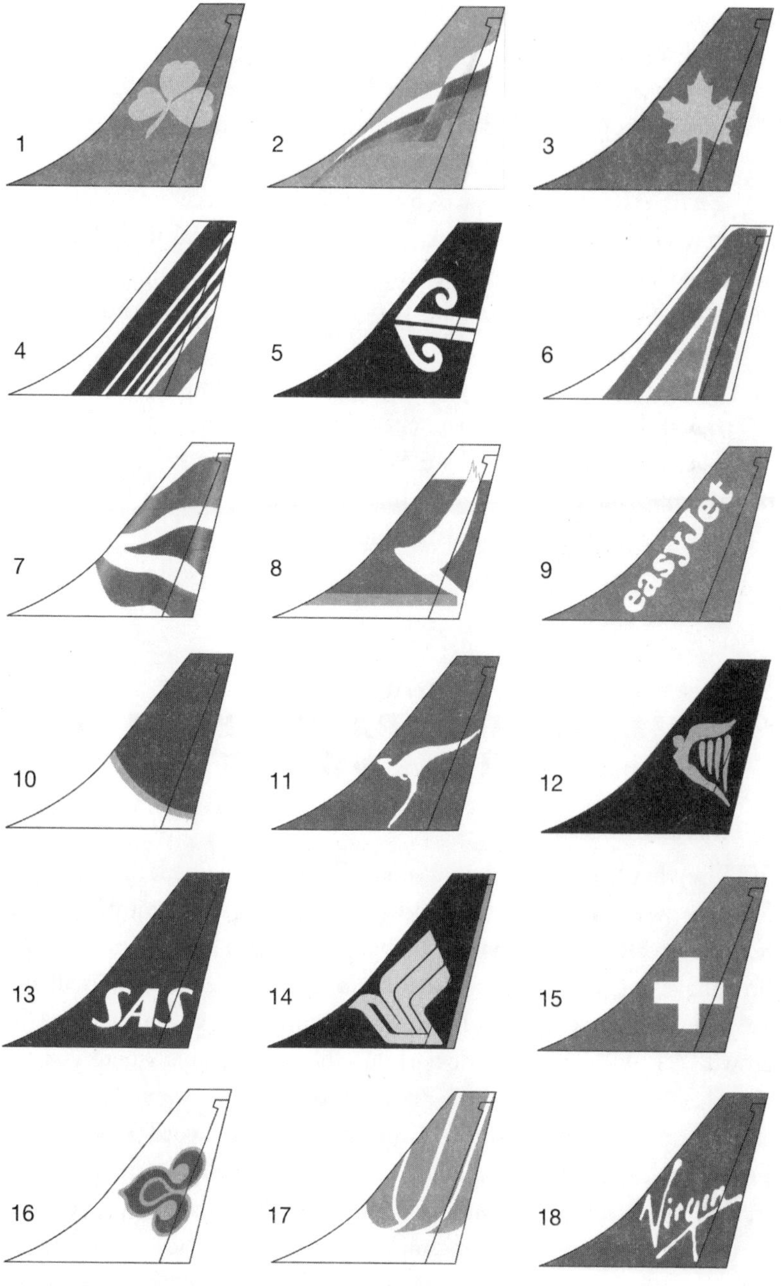
1
2
3
4
5
6
7
8
9
easyJet
10
11
12
13
SAS
14
15
16
17
18
Virgin

13 *Scandinavian Airlines.* White SAS on a dark blue field. Straightforward as can be.

14 *Singapore Airlines.* It's a stylized pale bird on a blue background and is about as well designed as the stylized birds on the tail fins of other airlines. That is to say, not very.

15 *Swiss.* After the collapse of Swissair in 2001, successor Swiss made few changes to the tail insignia. It's the national flag again and one of the simplest and best tails around.

16 *Thai Airways International.* Very curly and stylized. And tremendously purple.

17 *United Airlines.* After years of money problems (like other airlines), United recently launched a new tail insignia based on the old one. A bit more stylish? Possibly.

18 *Virgin Atlantic.* Brash, teetering on vulgarity, but subtly executed, the Virgin brand is unmistakable.

◎ *The Wright Brothers' first flight was shorter than the wingspan of a 747.* ◎

HOW TO
OPEN A CHAMPAGNE BOTTLE WITH A SWORD

Elsewhere in this volume you will find explained the textbook method for uncorking a bottle of Champagne. The trouble with textbook techniques, however, is that they lack panache and pizzazz. So I have included here this exhibitionistic procedure that will not only get the cork out in double-quick time but will also wow the crowd. You will find it particularly useful in situations where you are already carrying a hussar's saber on your belt.

The opening of a bottle by means of your sword is what the French call *le sabrage.* Napoleon's *Hussards* (cavalry) were always at it, yelling, "*Sabrer la bouteille!*" ("Saber" the bottle!), when they should have been practicing chopping the enemy's heads off. Maybe that's why the British were able to give them such a thrashing at Waterloo.

In essence, *le sabrage* involves using the back (blunt) edge of your saber to break the neck off the bottle. Beheading a bottle in this showy fashion is not difficult but does require diligent practice, and the sacrifice of half a case or more of low-grade bubbly. You need to be prepared to invest, say, $100 (up to a dozen bottles of sparkling "bum's wine").

Method

1. Using a linen napkin, dry an unshaken bottle of chilled Champagne, and remove the foil and wire.
2. Locate the hemispherical seam that marks the vertical join created during the bottle's manufacture. This is known as the crease. The bottle is weakest at the point where the crease meets the lip (the round bump your finger encounters if you run it down the neck from the fat end), and it is here that you will strike.
3. Hold the bottle firmly and point it upward (away from living creatures, e.g., your grandma) at an angle of about 45 degrees.
4. Lay your sword against the bottle with the blunt edge facing the cork. In a swift, firm, masculine movement, slide the sword impressively down the seam, toward the lip (a bit like a slow backhand tennis stroke). Hit at just the right speed, and with the proper amount of force, the lip will be knocked clean off the bottle, taking the cork with it, and will fly off in a pleasing and most satisfactory fashion.

Safety

1. Unless you know what you are doing with sharp swords, use a metal ruler instead.
2. The edge of the neck will be sharp; so wear leather gauntlets and a welder's face mask, and, if possible, a full suit of armor.
3. Don't rehearse in your living room. The backyard is the best place, but be careful not to mow the lawn before you've picked up all those corks and shards.

4 Discard incorrectly decapitated bottles and do not drink from any that do not display a clean break.
5 Or you could just open a can of beer.

◎ *Half the world's cork is produced in Portugal.* ◎

HOW TO
FIGHT A BULL

Bullfighting is a lot more fun than stamp collecting and it only takes about half an hour. It's performed after lunch in three acts, starting with the matador in his golden figure-hugging "suit of lights" processing into the ring with his assistants to the sound of the paso doble played usually on a bugle. For the novice matador here's a guide to the rudiments.

First act

- First the bull is released into the ring and your number two waves his yellow-and-magenta *capote* (cape) at him. You can just watch this part.
- Your turn comes next, as you do a series of "passes," each with its own fancy name, the most notable being the *veronica*. These are all a bit tricky to describe and probably the best thing for you to do, as a beginner, is just wave the cape around at arm's length, keeping your trouser-region as far from those horns as you can. Forget the artistry for the moment.
- Soon you'll see the mounted picadors coming in. Their job is to get the bull to charge their padded horses and stick a lance into his neck to keep his head down during the third act.
- The end of the first act is signaled by the sounding of a bugle and the picadors are escorted from the ring.

Second act

- This is the easy bit and most matadors just let their teams get on with tiring the bull out, girding their loins for the finale. I recommend you do the same. Stand back and text your girlfriend or something. The act ends with another of your assistants, the *banderillero*, thrusting short fancy harpoons into the bull's shoulders.

Third act

- The third and final act is the *faena*. To the sound of more bugle calls you remove your funny-looking black hat (the *montero*) and dedicate the death of the bull to somebody in the crowd by handing her the hat, or to the lot of them by putting it on the ground.
- This is the most artistic section of the fight, in which you demonstrate your valor and finesse with a piece of red cloth on a stick (the *muleta*). You also carry the killing sword (the *espada*) and this is the time for a few applause-getters such as kneeling before the bull. You must encourage him to charge you, swishing the *muleta* away from your vitals at the last moment. With any luck he might not stick his horns in you. (Those big fences at the side of the ring are good for running behind if things start looking a bit dodgy.)
- When you are ready for the kill, make sure the bull is looking at the *muleta* and not at your crotch. Then, leaning over his horns, plunge the *montero* between his shoulder blades—oh no, that's your hat, I mean the *espada*. This is the most hazardous moment of the whole fight, so best to cross your fingers, and maybe your legs too.
- If the sword goes in up to the handle (an *estocada*) the bull normally collapses and expires. But if it strikes bone you may have to use the *descabello* to finish him off. This is a sword with a distinctive cruciform handle, with which you cut the spinal cord.

The man in the pub who explained all this to me seemed to be a great fan, but upon reflection the whole thing strikes me as a bit unfair to the bull.

◎ *The New Birmingham Bull Ring was opened in 2003 by Sir Albert Bore.* ◎

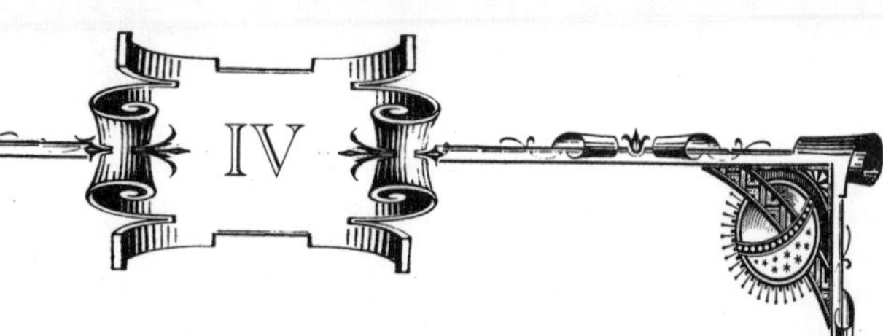

THE COMPLEAT OUTDOORSMAN

BRACING SPORTS, HOBBIES, AND GAMES, IN THE FRESH AIR

It is to be observed that "angling" is the name given to fishing by people who can't fish.

STEPHEN LEACOCK

HOW TO
PADDLE A CANOE

Do not be misled by the swanlike poise of the Indian chief gliding over the balmy rill. His serenity conceals years of flailing and foul language as he struggled to grasp the higher mysteries of his art. These instructions are not for the likes of experts such as he, but for the initiate canoe-paddler. Though they will not enable you to tackle the rapids after 10 minutes, they should at least protect you from the grim humiliation of shuddering around in circles, whimpering for help.

Method

1. Put on your life jacket. This can take a while, even with two of you.
2. Get into the canoe. This is an art in itself and involves quite a lot of getting wet. You had better practice a bit before you go on to the next step. (Now is the time to make sure you are in a canoe and not a kayak. Your paddle should have a flat blade on just one end of the shaft. If it has a curved blade on each end, you're in a kayak, so get out.)
3. Kneel or sit in the middle of the canoe, facing the front end (the bow). Kneeling pads make your life easier—but only if you're kneeling.
4. Grasp the paddle with your right hand, knuckles out, 2–3 feet down the shaft, and your left hand toward the top, knuckles out.
5. Reach as far forward as you can, without lurching, and submerge the blade. Keep the handle perpendicular, like a garden spade, not angled like an oar. And remember: no lurching.
6. Keeping the top of the paddle's shaft below eye level, pull your right hand back, drawing the blade through the water about as far as your bottom, and no farther. Push your left hand forward to counteract the water's resistance. Do not make the mistake of following the curve of the hull—keep the line straight. And do not "dig up" the water; that just wastes energy, forcing the canoe down.

7 Pick the blade out, turning it parallel to the water as it travels forward, back to the starting position, to begin the cycle again. To avoid unilateral muscle development, you can use the paddle on the other side of the canoe some of the time. The actions are much the same, though your hands change position.

On a nice calm day, these instructions should keep you pointing forward, with your head above water. But if the wind is blowing, do something else.

◎ *There are no rivers in Saudi Arabia.* ◎

HOW TO
FIND FOSSILS

Should I be asked to choose between being the kind of guy who wanders the beach detecting bottle caps with a circular carpet sweeper, or one of those fellows who discovers a new species of dinosaur with a single blow of his hammer, the choice would not be a difficult one. So here are some tips on becoming an instant palaeontologist.

The complete history of the Earth in 115 words

Our planet is about 4,600 million years old (older, if you're reading a handed-down copy of this book), and its layers of rock reveal its chronology. Fossils are new, originating only around 570 million years ago. Their history is sorted into three "eras": the Palaeozoic, from the Greek for "ancient animals," the Mesozoic (middle animals), and Cainozoic (new animals). These eras are subdivided into eleven "periods," the names of which make fascinating research in themselves—grab a dictionary. They begin with the Cambrian and move forward in time through the Silurian, Carboniferous (forests), Jurassic (famously), Cretaceous (ending in the extinction of the dinosaurs), Tertiary, and Quaternary, after which the Ice Age begins and humans appear.

What fossils are

Fossils are the remains of ancient animals (and plants), the soft body parts of which have rotted away. Over time, bones, teeth, and the tougher plant structures slowly absorb minerals from the surrounding sediment, turning eventually to stone. Fossilization can happen only underwater and it's funny to think that every fossilized dinosaur ended his life in the drink.

Equipment and collecting

- *Notebook and pen*
- *A magnifying lens*
- *Sturdy waterproof boots*
- *Whacking tools (see below)*
- *Flask of hot chocolate*
- *Goggles and a hard hat for serious walloping under falling cliffs*
- *A strong bag for the big ones*

Fossils can be found in exposed sedimentary rocks such as shale, limestone, and sandstone in several parts of the United States, including the high desert and mountainous regions of the Western states. Beware though of climbing high crumbly cliffs, and don't go fossil hunting on your own in the dark under hazardous escarpments with unpredictable tides.

Younger deposits are softer and their fossils can be picked up loose or levered out with a knife. Small bones and teeth may sometimes be sieved out of sand if you are by the sea, and a bit of sloshing of your sieve in the water can reveal smaller specimens. Talk to other collectors for a few tips; it's a good way to meet people. Once removed, fragile finds should be wrapped and put in a box for travel.

Older fossils require smashing with a hefty hammer and chisel. A geological hammer of hardened steel is ideal, its head being flat at one end and chisel-shaped at the other. A 2- or 3-pound hammer is fine for most purposes but for really serious rocks, one of between 7–14 pounds is better.

Practice is required to get an unwilling fossil out of a hard matrix without damaging it but before you start digging out a whole *allosaurus* make sure it's a manageable task and that you are not going to destroy it in the process. If you find yourself preparing a plaster of Paris jacket for your find, you are showing signs of moving beyond the realm of the dilettante.

Always keep a proper record in your book and label each fossil with details of where it was found. The scientific value is lessened if you haven't made a note of the place where you unearthed the thing. By the way, indiscriminate walloping in areas of outstanding natural beauty is generally not a good idea.

When you get them home, give your finds a good wash. Don't try to remove too much stone—they often look best embedded in the rock in which you discovered them.

◎ *The largest complete dinosaur fossil is* Brachiosaurus. *It's 75 feet long.* ◎

HOW TO
MAKE AND FLY A KITE ON A SHOESTRING

Most kite flying I've observed consists of a lot of filthy swearing, running, pulling, rending, and crashing. Nonetheless, here, for those with a strong constitution, is a cheap and reliable method for making a kite, together with important tips on flying it.

THE INGREDIENTS FOR A GOOD HOMEMADE KITE

- *A roll of garden twine*
- *A sharp knife*
- *A long ruler or tape measure*
- *Some strong glue*
- *A 40-inch square of brown parcel paper*
- *Brown gummed parcel tape*
- *2 boxes of cornflakes (or similar)*
- 2¼-inch dowel rods: *one 35 inches, and one 40 inches in length*
- *A bicycle pedal*
- *Some ribbon*

1 Cut a diametrical notch at the ends of each of your dowels to accommodate the twine. For goodness' sake, be careful with that knife.

2 Cross the short dowel horizontally over the long, a quarter of the way from the end of the long one. With the notches parallel to the table, tie the two together in their centers. Put a little glue on the join before you start and use your cereal boxes to keep the right angles true as you work.

3 Cut a length of twine long enough to go around the kite, with some to spare. Tie a small loop an inch or so from one end and fasten this at the top of the kite by wrapping the end of the twine around the dowel. With the loop at the top, take the twine through the notch

and then through the notch on the right-hand end of the horizontal spar. At the foot, tie another loop like the first and take the twine through that notch, running it then through the notch on the horizontal spar's left end. Tie it off at the top by wrapping it around the dowel and cutting off the loose end. The whole arrangement should be taut, without the dowels being bent.

4 Lay the paper flat on the table and put the frame on top. Cut around it making the characteristic diamond shape, allowing a border of about 1½ inches.

5 Fold the edges over the twine, and glue them down with some glue. Wet a few pieces of your gummed parcel tape and stick them here and there to strengthen the join. The less you put on, the lighter your finished kite will be. The paper should be fairly taut when you've finished.

6 You are now going to make what's called the bridle. This is the piece of twine that holds the line on to the kite. Cut a four-foot length and tie one end to the head loop, the other to the tail loop. Next, tie a small loop in the bridle itself just above the point at which the dowels cross. This is where your line will be attached.

7 Now for the tail. Tie a length of twine to the tail loop and attach some brightly colored ribbons every four inches or so. Optimum tail length is a matter of experimentation. Start with one about five times the length of the kite and trim it to size after a bit of trial and error in the field. Extra ribbons add stability (but also weight).

8 Finally, check the balance of your kite. Dangle it by the twine and, if it hangs funny, stick on some gummed paper as a counterbalance. Continual adjustment will be necessary once you're out there, as every kite is different.

The Line

Polyester or nylon fiber line is best for your kite or you can use the leftover garden twine like in the olden days, but this adds drag. You'll find that a bicycle pedal, or just a piece of stiff cardboard, makes a fine reel.

Flying it

Without wind a kite won't take off, let alone stay up. Moderate, steady winds with speeds of 5–15 miles an hour are best. Stronger winds will shred your kite, and light breezes won't lift it. If you find you are running to keep your kite up, the wind is probably not strong or steady enough.

Without its line your kite would blow all over the place like a plastic grocery bag, and in a way, it is the line that really makes your kite fly. Since the wind cannot push the kite farther than the length of the line, it (the wind) is deflected downward, producing an upward force in perfect accordance with Newtonian laws.

Treeless fields are the best places to fly. Not those containing power stations and overhead electrical lines, of course. Unless you want to appear on the evening news, don't fly in thunderstorms or near airports.

1. Stand with *a steady wind behind you* and get a friend to launch the kite gently.
2. Once it's in the air, release enough line for it to reach a decent height. You'll lose lift with a longer line because of the drag. Too short a line and the thing will be unstable. About four stories is a nice height but you can go higher if you like.
3. If the wind drops, reel in the string slightly to increase the lifting force.

On a windy day you can tie the line around a post and have a picnic while your kite flies itself. To lower it, just reel it in and once it's within grabbing distance, catch it—ideally before it smashes into the ground.

Tears can be repaired with gummed parcel paper or spray glue (smells fantastic).

◉ *Men are six times more likely than women to be struck by lightning.* ◉

HOW TO
AVOID SNAKEBITES

You have probably seen nature programs in which a man in bush gear picks up huge snakes by the tail and, with the aid of a stick, describes the horrible effects of their deadly toxins. This is entertaining from the perspective of your armchair but it is probably not something you would want to try for yourself with a rhinoceros viper. In fact, most encounters with deadly snakes are accidental—people often step on them—so here are a few rules of thumb to avoid being bitten when you're in snake country.

THE IDIOT'S BITE

Snakes love dark places, such as hollow branches, clefts in the rocks, and heavy undergrowth. If you drop your sunglasses into a cranny you can't see into properly, and then put your hand in to rummage around for it, you are likely to get bitten. Don't be so stupid.

THE WALKER'S BITE

Snakes like long grass so don't walk through heavy underbrush or tall grass without paying close attention to the area around your feet. Obvious really.

THE NIGHT BITE

If you know there are dangerous snakes around, have a bit of common sense—don't sleep next to long grass, undergrowth, boulders, or trees. These are some of their favorite hiding places. Instead, put your sleeping bag in a clear area and tuck a bit of net curtain or mosquito netting around yourself. This will discourage inquisitive snakes from getting into your pajamas.

But look out for the lions.

The log-lurker

OK, so there's a fallen tree in your way. What are you going to do? Step over it? Wrong! Snakes just love to lurk behind a fallen branch or mossy log. Instead, step on to the log and take a look at the other side. If there's a snake there, ask him to leave, or choose another route. Better still, go and read a book in the car.

Picking up a snake

Don't be so stupid.

Picking up a dead snake

Some guys have a desire to flourish a freshly killed snake for their photo albums. Don't fall for this one. Many a pith-helmeted hero brandishing his kill has been bitten unceremoniously. A freshly executed snake may still have a nervous system in good working order, and excellent reflex actions. If you must wave a dead snake around, cut its head off first with a blow from a sharp knife.

What to do if you are bitten

First and most importantly, don't be on your own or you'll be in trouble. Bite victims should keep *completely* still and be taken to the hospital very quickly. Most venoms are spread by the lymphatic system, and any movement speeds this up. The process can be slowed by firmly bandaging and splinting the bitten limb.

Don't cut the bite or suck it, and don't put an arterial tourniquet on—you'll just make things worse. Instead, keep still, quiet, and calm, and get a friend to:

- Move you away from the snake.
- Quickly identify the snake (if possible).
- Remove your watch and jewelery.
- Quickly apply a broad pressure bandage (clothing or towels will work).
- Get you to the hospital fast, keeping you still and quiet.

◎ *ACE inhibitors (blood pressure drugs) were developed from snake venom.* ◎

HOW TO
MAKE AN UNCOMPLICATED RAIN GAUGE

Wet outside? Don't worry there are plenty of things you can do. For a start, you could go and sit in the shed and listen to the patter of raindrops on the corrugated roof. There's nothing better than this for reducing stress and lowering your blood pressure. But if you're looking for something a little more active, and requiring an element of skill, here's an idea. It's easy to do, and you don't need much in the way of equipment.

Required

- *A big, clear, plastic bottle*
- *A marker pen*
- *A sharpish knife or scissors*
- *Masking tape*
- *A ruler*

Method

1. Cut the top off the bottle at its shoulder and take the label off.
2. Upturn the top and rest it in the lower section, taping the junction closed. This will let in rain and reduce evaporation.
3. Pour about an inch of water into the bottle and mark its level as zero. Continue by gradating the outside of the bottle in ¼ and ½-inch increments.
4. Put your rain gauge outside. You can make a holder from a bent coat hanger and attach it to a fence so people don't knock it over, drink it, or throw it away.
5. Try recording what happens over a month. Ten years ago this would have produced loads of sensible rain results but with global warming you may now get absolutely nothing, or seven years' worth in five minutes. Not my fault.

◎ *Rainfall record: 6 feet in 24 hours on Reunion Island in the Indian Ocean.* ◎

HOW TO
YODEL

Yodeling is a kind of ancient mountain "throat-singing" common in Austria, Bavaria, and Switzerland that evolved from the hollering of Tyrolean goatherds across the echoing crags and snowy gorges. It is characterized by sudden changes of pitch between the normal and falsetto registers of the male voice.

Most guys have tried a little yodeling at one time or another. Sitting down suddenly on a seatless bicycle, spilling iced water into the lap, and receiving a fastball in the privates are some common causes of the involuntary form of this art. For the serious student, however, the difficulty of finding somewhere to practice can hinder progress. The car offers a suitably solitary environment, but is cramped, while the bathroom, although especially rewarding acoustically, is antiseptic in a particularly un-Alpine way.

On the plus side, studying the technique of accomplished yodelers is not as hard as once it was. There are many fine records on the market, and live performers are occasionally to be found, decked out in authentic Bavarian lederhosen, belting out medleys in pubs of a certain kind.

Starting out

The key to yodeling is getting the hang of the falsetto or "head-voice." Although this upper register lies outside the normal male *tessitura* it is easily reached. Indeed, it's the voice that fathers use unconsciously when speaking to their babies. Some people imagine the falsetto to be an index of effeminacy or eunuchoid sterility, but nothing could be further from the truth. Many a hairy yodeler is to be found at the bar after (or sometimes during) his performance, ordering beers in a lusty baritone before returning home to his wife and ten children.

So, to start, practice singing in your falsetto as you go about your daily activities. Once you've got the hang of this you'll need to try switching suddenly between your normal "chest-voice" and the high yodely one. This is tricky but comes with a little application.

If you read music try your hand at the brief phrase below, which must be one of the best known tunes in the whole world. I've put it in C major to make everyone's life easier but you can change the key to suit your vocal range. The last two notes should be yodeled in your falsetto; the leap across the octaves is highly characteristic of the yodeler's art.

Got it? Now try the next phrase. Again, just the last two notes should be in the falsetto.

See where we're going? When you've mastered the technique, take a flying leap at "High on a Hill sat a Lonely Goatherd" from *The Sound of Music*. (Not "goat turd," as I once heard someone sing.) No yodeling is required until you reach the characteristic "Yea, oh de lay, old lady who?" just like Julie Andrews. The only syllables sung in the falsetto are "-dy" of "old lady," and "who?"

You'll have noticed by now that you can't help tapping your foot to yodeling tunes. This is because the emphasis falls on the weak beat of the bar—the famous oompah—lending the music a syncopation, just as in reggae.

Right then, now for the big one: the world's most famous folk-tune (outside China, of course).

Now you're really in business and your performance should be conjuring up pictures of sylvan mountain pastures, the colourful von Trapp family, and the lonely goatherd with the horn. Even if you're only yodeling in Cleveland.

◎ *The thyroid cartilage is better known as the Adam's apple.* ◎

HOW TO
DO A FIVE-MINUTE SHOW WITH JUST A BLADE OF GRASS

A summer's day in the country just as the picnic basket is being packed away—this is the time to perform a few tricks with a blade of grass. Not only will people find it entertaining, but you will have evaded some of the tedious cleanup.

The shrieking monkey

Put your hands into the praying position with a long blade of grass pinched lengthways between your thumb knuckles. Now form an "O" with your mouth and press your thumb knuckles firmly against your lips. Blow hard through the almond shaped aperture and the grass will vibrate like a clarinet reed, producing an ear-splitting shriek. It's not very musical but is excellent for attracting the attention of your buddies across a millpond—and for annoying your sister.

Magic climbing grass

On the blade of grass you have just picked are thousands of almost invisible filaments, all pointing the same way. If you pinch the grass very lightly between your thumb and first finger, and move your thumb rapidly up and down, the grass will climb mysteriously upward. (If it goes down, you have it positioned the wrong way.) For those not in the know, this is a puzzling demonstration, which they will want to imitate. For extra points, show them how it works.

Catchum

Attach a firm blob of mud to the bottom of a blade of grass not longer than your finger. Hold it by the tip with the mud ball hanging between your victim's extended thumb and forefinger, which are slightly apart. Bet him he cannot catch the grass by closing his thumb and finger if you let it go without warning. Nine times out of ten he will fail because his eyes, brain, and nerves take a little longer to register the drop and tell his fingers to close, than it takes you to let go and the grass to fall out of reach.

The nose cannon

While nobody's looking, pick a long blade of grass and roll it into a tight ball just large enough to stuff into your right nostril. Tamp it in firmly with your thumb. When you're ready, get everybody's attention by shouting: "Look out—flying booger!" Close the empty nostril by pressing on it with the extended forefinger of your left hand, and shoot the grass ball into their midst with a sharp puff through the nose. Ejected with sufficient force it will travel a surprising distance, but make sure your sinuses are clear before trying this; people dislike being struck by particles of extraneous nose matter.

◎ *Hayfever affects 15–20 percent of the US population.* ◎

THE PROPER WAY TO BUILD AND LIGHT A CAMPFIRE

Before the days of TV and central heating, men sat around the fire and told stories. Today they carry on a version of this ritualistic activity by incinerating sausages on the barbecue, dressed in a primitive costume of silly apron and hat. Forest folktales have given way to stories about football, cars, beer, women, and burping.

One of the most important skills every young man should acquire is proper fire-making technique. Here's a good way.

Building the fire

Build your fire methodically, in stages. There's no need for a monster fire—keep the thing small. Huge bonfires easily get out of hand, setting alight neighbors' fences and cars, and, in the wilderness, threatening entire forests. So find a safe place, using a circle of rocks to mark the fire's perimeter. Before you start, read through the instructions below to see what sizes of wood you will need to collect.

1. Lay two arm-size logs in the center of your ring, parallel to each other and with two logs' width between them.
2. Collect a handful of tinder. You are looking for twigs about as long as your foot that break with a dry snap. A good place to find these is at the base of trees, where they have been protected from the weather. Avoid the temptation to use dry bark. This tends to spit when alight, shooting sparks into the forest or torching the neighbor's shed.
3. Place the tight tinder bundle between the logs, at right angles. Lean the bunch up against one of them, making the crossbar of a capital H.
4. Collect two more bunches of tinder and rest them up against, and at right angles to, the first bundle, like a little roof. Leave enough space for you to lean in later and light the bottom bundle from above (fig. 1).
5. At the ends of, and at right angles to, the first two logs, lay two more of the same size on top. In the gap between them, and parallel to them, lay some kindling: pieces of branch, about the diameter of a circle made with your thumb and finger (fig. 2).
6. Cover this with more of the same, at right angles. You will see that you are alternating, north–south, east–west to allow plenty of room for the air to flow between the sticks.
7. Top the pile with some small thick logs. Once the fire's under way, these will burn steadily (fig. 3).
8. Surround this rough cube with an upright wall of kindling: thin branches, about as long as your arm.

9 Lean a tripod of logs around your cube, wigwam style. These should be about as long and thick as your leg (fig. 4).

10 Lean a further dozen of these long logs around the wigwam, leaving a triangular hole so you can get in and light the fire.

11 When you have everybody's attention, reach in and light the tinder with a match, closing the aperture afterward. Don't use bits of cardboard or pints of lighter fuel to get it going. Not only is this cheating, it can cause your fire to burn inefficiently.

12 Now watch, as volumes of smoke pour impressively from the

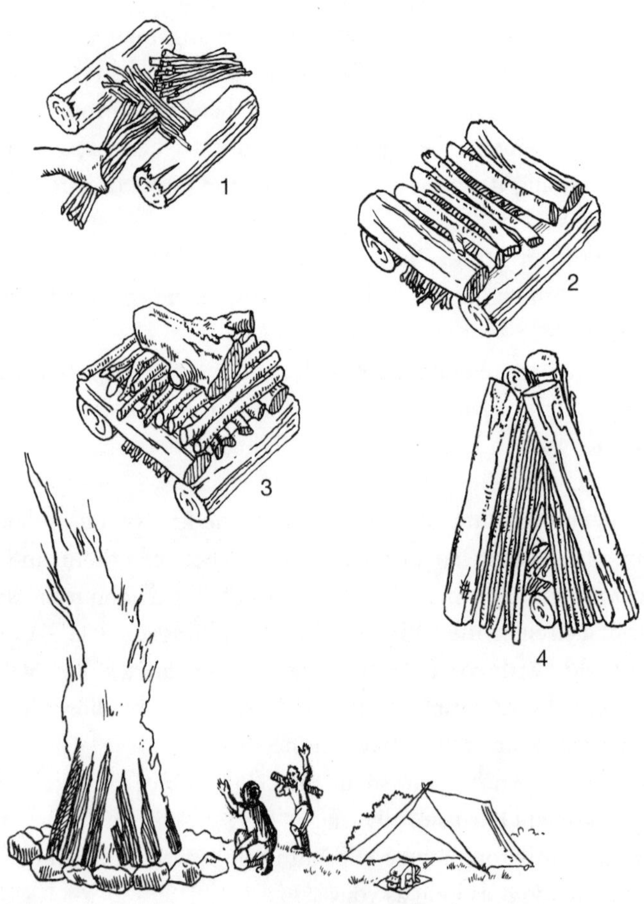

chimney. After only a few minutes you will have a magnificent blaze.

To put your fire out at the end of the evening, pour on a lot of water and stir the embers with a long stick. Be careful of the fire ring, which may still be hot. In the wild, turn everything over thoroughly and water well.

◎ *The first marshmallows were made from the root of the marshmallow plant.* ◎

HOW TO SKATE BACKWARDS

There are few things more humiliating than standing on a public ice rink for the first time. While all around practiced skaters glide and swish, you wobble gingerly round the circumference, holding on to the sides for dear life. "If only I could skate backwards," you think, wanting to run before you can walk, "I could hold my head high on frosty ponds." Here's how.

Go forward first

I'm afraid there's no way around it: you'll have to learn to skate forwards before you can go backwards. So put on the skates and walk about on something that isn't ice for five minutes to get used to the crazy sensations. When you're ready, get on the rink. Don't try normal walking—you'll either shuffle forward like Nanki Poo approaching the Mikado or you'll be down in seconds. Instead, stand with your feet together and turn your right toe outward until the skates are nearly at 90 degrees, with the right slightly behind the left. Press against the right blade and you will slide forward on the left foot. Immediately lift the right skate and, at the end of the glide, put it back on the ice, pointing forward.

Now turn your left foot outward and push against it as you did before with your right. It's thrust and glide, thrust and glide. Learning this cycle should minimize the step, scramble, shriek, and tumble that many beginners go in for. If you do fall over, fall forward, relaxing as you go. Your arms and knees will break your fall. Ice is hard, and falling backwards is a good way to smash your head open.

Some novice skaters, especially children, find themselves skating confidently around the arena after only an hour's practice so don't be disheartened by the roars of derisive laughter as you go down inelegantly on your wet knees for the umpteenth time. In the olden days, beginners supported themselves on the backs of kitchen chairs as they learned the moves, but your local rink might take exception to hundreds of these on the ice. Anyway, after a bit of application, your thrusting leg will begin to stick out in the air as you glide, more or less gracefully, your head will be up, and your skating knee will be well bent.

Skating backwards

Right. Let's assume you can skate forward without clinging on to somebody's arm, and are now ready, finally, to try going backwards. You'll be relieved to hear that there's not much more to it than going forward. To begin with, keep both feet on the ice, knees sharply bent, and sweep your feet out, leading by the heel, until you begin to travel in the intended direction. Before long, you will find you are able to go

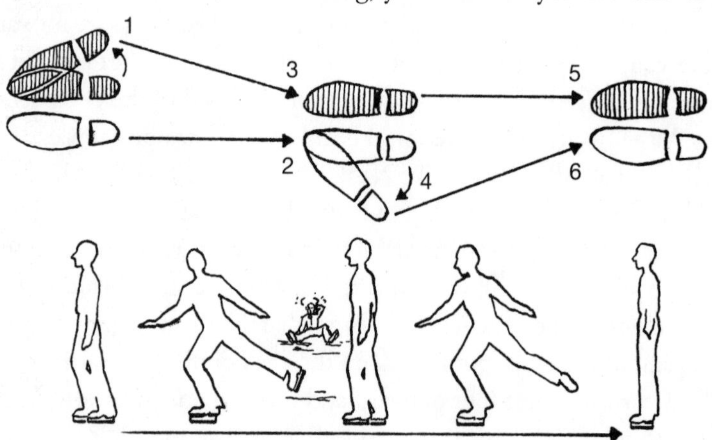

backwards fairly fast, with first one foot, then the other. You can now start concentrating on your glides, as you did going forward. Thrust against each foot in turn, turning the toe inward and gliding on the other blade in the normal way. Look over your shoulder to avoid bumping into people. What could be simpler?

◎ *The first ever ice hockey puck was a piece of frozen cow dung.* ◎

HOW TO
SPIN A ROPE, COWBOY STYLE

First described some 2,000 years ago by Herodotus, rope tricks have fallen out of fashion in recent times. But a rope-spinning act performed by an accomplished artist is a beautiful thing to see, and ropery is a fine hobby for a young man. As an introduction to the craft, here's a description of the most basic of spins, the flat loop, which, once mastered, will open the door to a new and exciting world of ropiness. You needn't wear a cowboy hat to spin a rope, but it helps. And remember, this is outdoors work; don't practice in a house full of china, unless, of course, it's someone else's house. Yee ha!

REQUIRED

A lariat. For current purposes, this is a 14-foot, medium-weight, braided rope, roughly 3/8 inch in diameter, whipped at one end, and with an eyelet or *honda* at the other. The rope must be pliable and unlikely to kink. Sash cord is worth experimenting with. The *honda* is made by lashing a small piece of rope back on itself to make a loop, the whipped end being threaded through the eye.

The flat loop spin

The flat loop is so called because you spin the rope in a horizontal plane, like a revolving pancake parallel to the ground. Take a look at the illustration. This is how you should stand. The left hand holds the loop loosely, so it can be dropped smartly once it begins to whirl. You'll see that the free end or "spoke" is about the same length as the loop's radius. The right holds both spoke and loop.

Action!

Throw the right hand in a counterclockwise direction, at the same time releasing the rope with both hands, in such a way that it is whirling before it has a chance to touch the ground. Keep the loop small and the speed low, holding the spoke in your right hand far enough away that the rope does not strike your legs. Make a counterclockwise circle with this hand and you'll notice that the loop, supported by the spoke you are holding, will be kept open by centrifugal force (*see* picture). One of the things you'll also notice is the tendency of the rope to twist and kink. You can largely prevent this by letting the free end continually untwist in your hand.

There's a lot to remember, so practice slowly until you begin to get the hang of things.

◎ *Cowboy wisdom: don't squat with your spurs on.* ◎

THE PROPER WAY TO CATCH A BUTTERFLY

Catching butterflies isn't just for little girls. To catch a butterfly you will need:

- *A warm day*
- *A net*
- *A jam jar with a lid*

The net is a specialist item but, for a few bucks, you can pick up a rather flimsy one from a toy shop. Cheap ones—often advertised as fishing nets—will certainly catch butterflies but their main disadvantage is that the net part is often made from a cheap and relatively unfloppy plastic material, and can be rather too small.

Whatever net you have—and you could always make one yourself—there is a knack to catching butterflies. It's trickier than you'd think, so here are a couple of tips.

When you've identified your prey, sweep the net through the air sideways and, once the butterfly is inside, quickly turn your hand so that the open ring of the net is facing the ground, forming a closed "bag" and preventing the butterfly from getting out again—a common problem with too-small nets and beginners.

You can now examine the thing at leisure, but don't handle it unless necessary. Butterflies are delicate creatures and life is hard enough for them without you rubbing all the colored dust off their beautiful wings or accidentally breaking legs off.

Let your butterfly go when you've finished looking at it—it's rather a nice feeling.

◎ *The 1973 film* Papillon *starred Steve McQueen in the lead role.* ◎

HOW TO
SEND SEMAPHORE MESSAGES

Now that it is possible to transmit an instantaneous video message on your cell phone from the pool table of your local bar to the top of a Nepalese mountain, the ability to signal by flag from hill to hill seems quaintly obsolete. But next time you find yourself camping in the woods across the valley from the convenience store, who's going to be the one who knows how to semaphore for a pint of milk or a half dozen eggs?

Flag handling

You are going to spell out your message in groups of letters (usually words), moving the arms smartly from one letter to the next and bringing the flags back to the ready position after each group. If one arm is already in the correct position for the next letter of the group, you must keep it steady while you move the other flag decisively into place. Suppose you are transmitting the word "milkman." If you look at the illustrations showing the letters of the alphabet (see opposite) you will notice that the right arm stays in the same position throughout the word, with the left doing all the work. Each letter of the word "ass," however, requires a new attitude for both arms.

At the end of your message, send the letters "AR" as a group. If your message has been read successfully you will receive the reply "R."

Hints and tips

Use flags of the same color and stand against a flat-looking contrasting background.

- When sending, stand up straight and push the flagpoles into the sleeve of each arm, resting your first finger along the shaft.
- When making a new letter put your arms in precisely the right position. Doing otherwise causes unnecessary confusion. "I am

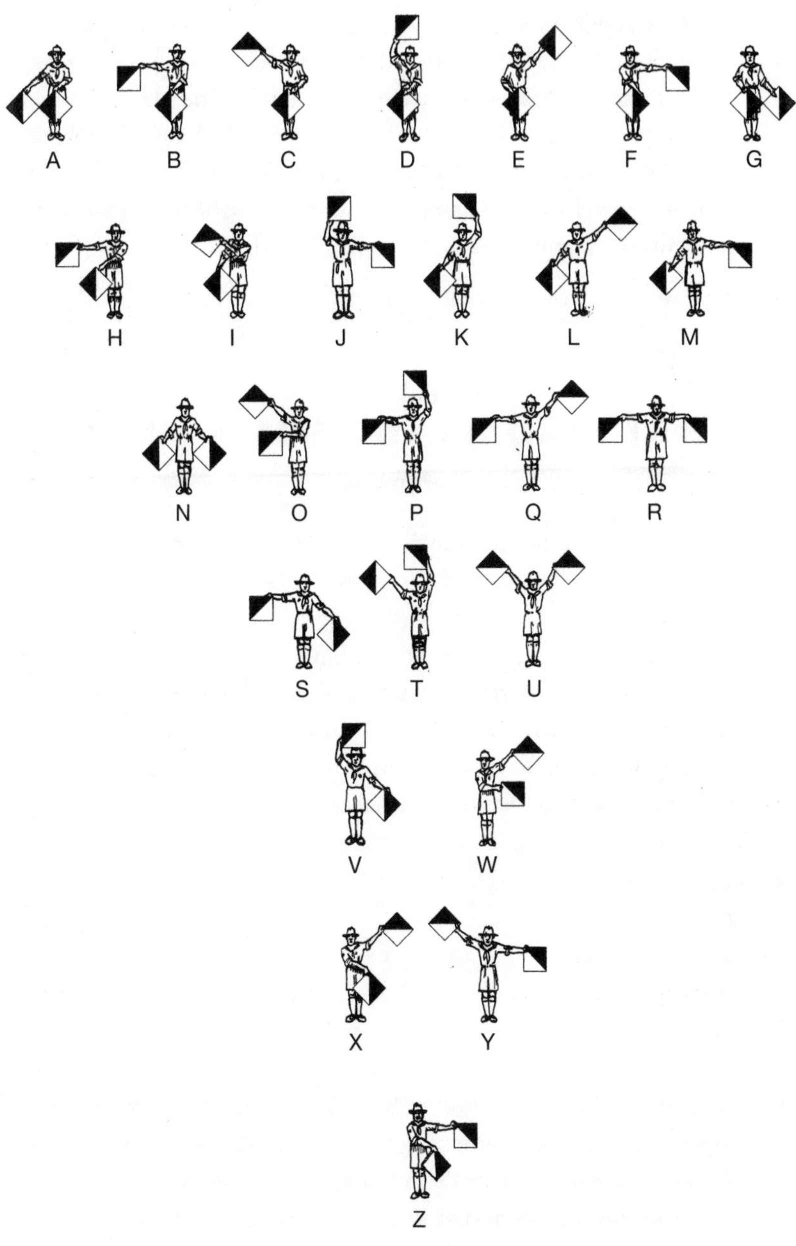
A
B
C
D
E
F
G
H
I
J
K
L
M
N
O
P
Q
R
S
T
U
V
W
X
Y
Z

much stronger than yesterday" can very easily become "I am much stranger than yesterday."

- In between double letters, bring the hands well into the body, poles pressed into the legs. Send double letters at the same speed as single.
- In letters requiring one arm only, don't wave the other flag about. Bring it in front of the body and hold it still.
- When practicing, don't stand in front of a mirror or you will learn everything half-backward and go mad.

◎ *"Semaphore" comes from the Greek words meaning "sign-bearer."* ◎

HOW TO
TRAP AND SNARE WILD GAME

You can catch more for lunch with a few traps or a well-placed snare than you ever will sitting in the brambles with a rifle and a cold behind.

When you're trapping, know what it is you are trying to catch and set your traps to suit. For example, it's no good fishing for squirrels in a creek. Just like humans, animals have bedrooms, pubs, and cafés, with trails leading from one to another. Put your snares and traps near these places. Good areas include those with signs of:

- *Tracks*
- *Droppings*
- *Chewed or abraded vegetation*
- *Nesting*
- *Feeding and watering*

You smell—and don't you forget it. Smoking a trap over a fire will disguise your scent without frightening away your prey. Animal urine and odoriferous mud are also good scent-maskers. Cover your hands with the stuff—but not before dinner with a promising date.

Camouflage your trap naturally, and arrange things so as to channel your prey into it. Peanut butter and salt are big favorites with mammals so drop some around as tasty bait. Animals aren't stupid, though. They will steer clear of newly stirred-up vegetation and freshly turned earth. If you have to dig, remove freshly dug soil from the area.

Here's how to make some simple snares and traps.

A basic noose

Flexible wire is best for the purpose. Start by making an eyelet. Do this by doubling an end back on itself and neatly tying it off. Thread the long end through the hole and test it by inserting two fingers into the loop and moving them away from the long piece. The noose should tighten smoothly.

A snare

The snare is a noose positioned on a trail, or over the entrance to a burrow, with its long end held down by a stake. The noose must be large enough to go over the prey's head, where it will tighten as the creature moves forward. Small twigs or blades of grass are ideal for holding it up. Strands of spider gossamer will hold the noose open without breaking.

The twitcher

Strip a small sapling and bend it down, holding it taut with a piece of cord attached to a stake, which you push into the ground at an acute angle. Lay the noose flat on the ground around the stake, on which you have securely tied some bait. Small animals will tug at the bait until they dislodge the stake, whipping the sapling upright with great force, and drawing the noose tight quicker than you can say "strangulated bunny."

Squirrel poles

A squirrel pole is a long stick leaned against a tree where squirrels cavort. Position a few 2-inch diameter nooses along the pole so that squirrels climbing up and down will have to pass through them. After an initial cautious period, the squirrels will become bolder and it won't be long before one will get caught in a noose. It will struggle briefly but will soon lose its grip and fall off the pole, where it will be hanged by the neck until it is dead. Being a bit unobservant, further squirrels will suffer the same fate, providing enough squirrel meat for a good stew. Don't allow sentimental friends to tut about this—it's dinner!

Apothecary's bottle trap

Although you don't need an apothecary's bottle to make an apothecary's bottle trap, it does help. Start by digging a hole and put a narrow-necked bottle into it. Fill in with earth around the bottle so that its top is just below the surface. Position a few stones around the small hole and cover it with a roof made from a large piece of bark or something, supported above the ground by the stones. It won't be long before mice seek shelter under the cover, where they will absent-mindedly fall into the hole. When you come to check the trap, pop a cork into the neck before you dig it up, just in case there's a deadly snake lurking in there.

◎ *Rabbits re-ingest their droppings so that food passes through them twice.* ◎

A BEGINNER'S GUIDE TO SUPER BEERSBY

Europeans are odd. Take the following outdoor games: Portuguese sardine racing, rhubarb thrashing, pétanque, conger cuddling, marrow dangling, dwile flonking, and passing the splod. Those aren't games, surely, they're anagrams! At least with an American game like Beersby you know what you're getting, namely beer and a Frisbee. Here are the rules.

Required

- *2 8-foot poles (you must improvise)*
- *A Frisbee (or straw hat in an emergency)*
- *4 grown-up persons*
- *Several cans of beer (say 48; it's unlucky to go short)*

Preparation

1 Empty two of the cans by drinking the beer.
2 Stick the poles in the ground about 25 feet apart. This can be a game in itself.
3 Balance an empty beer can on top of each pole.

Rules

Form two teams, with each team stationed at its pole. Each player now opens a can of beer, which he must hold at all times during play. If he finishes the beer in his hand, he must open a new can.

Taking turns, each team throws the Frisbee at the opposition's pole-perched can, trying to knock it off. Players may, if they wish, aim at the pole rather than the can. The receiving team tries to catch the Frisbee *after* it strikes their pole or can, and attempts to catch the can if it is knocked off the pole. They then take their turn to attempt a de-poling of their rivals' can. The first team to score 10 points wins and the losers pay for the beer.

Points and penalties

- If you fail to catch the Frisbee after it knocks your can off the pole you must drink a can of beer, and it's a point to the opposition.
- If your can is knocked off its pole and strikes the ground, you and your teammate must say: *Cinnamon aluminum linoleum* and share a can of beer. And it's one point to your rivals. If both or either of you misspeak the tongue twister you must share another can of beer.

- If you catch the Frisbee *before* it reaches your pole, the other team scores one point and your team must share a can of beer.
- If you drop, or are forced to set down, your drink you must at the next available opportunity swallow the remaining beer in your can without stopping for breath.
- If you or your teammate can catch the Frisbee after it hits the can or pole but before it strikes the ground, the opposition doesn't score and you don't perform the tongue twister above. (Is this making *any* sense?)
- If you catch the Frisbee *and* the can after a strike, it's a "Super Beersby," you win a point and the opposition drinks two cans of beer each.

For seasoned or expert players, the game can be combined with the name game, sometimes called "drinking while thinking." Following the rules set out above, the starting player must, as he throws the Frisbee, say the name of a famous person—usually the President or a foreign potentate. The opposing players must then say the name of another celebrity, whose *first* name begins with the first letter of the previous famous person's *last* name. For example, George W. Bush could be followed by Béla Lugosi, which might itself be followed by Leonard Nimoy. Names may not be repeated; repetition being penalized by the sharing of a can of beer between the teammates of the offending team.

The game (whether in its simple or combined-drinking-while-thinking form) usually proceeds without event until everybody has consumed about four cans of beer. Then it goes rapidly downhill. I've seen people trying to drink the Frisbee, totally unable to remember the score—or, sometimes, which team they're on. By the time each player has drunk 11 or 12 cans the situation is more like a scene from one of those zombie movies where various vacant-looking undead people are wandering around a graveyard with their arms waving in front of them.

Good luck!

Remember, the playing of Super Beersby impairs your ability to drive a car or operate machinery, and may cause health problems. Don't say I didn't warn you.

◎ *Béla Lugosi was buried in one of his* Dracula *capes.* ◎

A SURVIVAL KIT IN A TIN

Marooned in the wilderness? Here's the answer to your problems: a portable survival kit that provides all the essentials for preparing shelter, food gathering, fire making, water cleaning and storage, signaling, and first aid. The entire kit has everything you need to keep you going for at least three days.

Contents

- A tobacco tin or breath mints tin. As well as holding everything, the inside of the lid is highly reflective and can be used to signal to rescuers.
- A folded square of tinfoil. This can be fashioned into a small pan for collecting and boiling water, for cooking, washing, and drinking out of.
- A loud whistle of your favorite kind. For instructions on whistling with grass, see page 123.
- A short piece of sealed drinking straw, containing household bleach for water purification. This provides about eight drops of bleach. One drop should be enough to sterilize a pint of water.
- A condom for water storage (or other purposes if you are lucky).
- A dozen matches dipped in paraffin wax. Dipping them in wax keeps them completely dry—what's more, you can eat the wax scrapings.
- A candle stub. A combination of uses: a waterproof light, lubrication, and foodstuff.
- Three 1-inch squares of inner-tube rubber: amazing waterproof fire lighters.

- Three Vaseline-covered cotton balls. Another multi-use tool: an effective waterproof tinder, first-aid swab, and lubricant.
- A soft pencil. This is a good message writer, obviously, but its lead will also provide an excellent lubricant, and its shavings can be used as dry tinder.
- Three over-the-counter antihistamine and three diarrhea tablets. These stop you being disabled by allergic reactions and dehydration.
- A small roll of waterproof surgical tape. In addition to its obvious first aid uses, you can make essential repairs with this or even put some on a branch to catch insects—a protein-rich food or bait.
- A sugar cube. Use in combination with your surgical tape to catch bees and insects for dinner. Bee soup is very nourishing.
- Six safety pins. You can use these for emergency clothing repairs, and as an aid to shelter construction. They make good fishing hooks too. Just attach a caterpillar, and a piece of foil as a lure, and you're all set.
- A stock cube. This simple item will improve the taste of some of the ghastly stuff you might have to eat.
- A small Swiss Army knife. For skinning, gutting, sawing, and so forth (its tweezers are good for plucking your eyebrows if you are at a loose end).
- 10-foot multi-strand parachute cord, wrapped around the tin. In addition to its uses as shelter suspension, strung between trees, it can be used for hanging food out of the reach of animals and its inner filaments are perfect for sewing, snare-manufacture, tying off your water container and, especially, fishing. The filaments also make ideal dental floss.

How to start a fire with your survival kit

Gather together a heavy flat stone, your foil, a wax covered match, and something to strike it on such as a rough stone. Fold the foil into a bandshell shape to make a windscreen and hold this down with your big flat stone. Have a Vaseline-coated cotton ball ready and shave some pencil sharpenings on to it. Prepare a kindling bundle of whatever *dry* grasses and bark you can find, and you are ready to go.

1 Scrape off wax from the match head and eat it (the wax).
2 Strike the match on the rough stone and throw it inside the windscreen (the match).
3 Hold a rubber square over the match until it catches fire (the rubber).
4 Place the burning rubber into your waterproof tinder.
5 Blow on the tinder and, once it's going, transfer it to your kindling bundle.

A good signal flare can be produced by making a fire under a dry pine tree. The whole tree will catch light. Don't burn down the forest if you can avoid it.

NOTES

1 Remember, alcohol is the enemy of survival. It dehydrates the body, lowers body temperature (by opening peripheral blood vessels), and impairs performance.
2 If you find yourself lost in the wilderness, *stay where you are.* However, if you must move—say to find water—*see* page 3 for instructions on using your watch as a compass.

◎ *Alexander Selkirk spent more than 4 years alone on* Más a Tierra *island.* ◎

SUMO WRESTLING FOR BEGINNERS

Sumo is the genteel art of Japanese wrestling, the aim of which is to force the opponent out of the ring or cause him to touch the ground with any part of his body other than his feet. No punching, kicking, hair-pulling, or grabbing of the nether regions is allowed.

That's the rules. The higher mysteries of this sport take many years to master but beginners can get to grips with things without too much trouble and become quickly proficient—especially if bulky.

The basic goings-on

The *dohyo* (ring) is a 15-foot circle marked by a hoop of straw, *the shobu-dawara.* Before entering the ring you must first do a fair bit of clapping and stomping with bent legs to scare away the evil spirits. Throw a few handfuls of purifying salt into the arena for good measure.

After the ring-entering ceremony, you should stare commandingly across the space at the other *rikishi* (wrestler). This can be tricky with your hair in a bun and dressed, as you are, in just your *mawashi*, the thong thing that goes around your waist and between the legs to cover your embarrassment.

The match begins, politely, only once you and your adversary have motioned to the *gyoji* (referee) that you are set. This politeness is encouraged by a fine of 100,000 yen (roughly $800) for any wrestler who starts before the other chap is ready.

When you've signaled your preparedness, the ref will display the *gunbai* or so-called war fan and give the command "*Gunbai wo kaesu!*" (flip the *gunbai*). Don't wander away now or you'll be out.

After touching the ring with your fists, you're off, charging into your opponent with a sound like a cricket ball hitting a frying pan when your heads collide. Pretend you don't care. As you struggle with the other chap's huge carcass (lots of hugging and *mawashi*-gripping) the *gyoji* will keep shouting "*Nokotta!,*" which is a sort of carry-on signal. Should you at any time find yourselves in a deadlock the referee will invite you to get on with things using the command "*Yoi, hakkeyoi!*"

Bouts can be short and in a tournament wins are simply accumulated, the fellow with the highest score becoming the overall victor.

Preparing your body

There is no truth to the terrifying rumor that sumo wrestlers squeeze their testicles into the inguinal canal to avoid injury. Have you tried it? You'll have a loincloth under that belt and it's quite good enough protection. Anyway it's illegal for your opponent to grab your *mae-tatemitsu*—that part of the belt that lies over the hills and far away.

It will help you as a novice, though, if you can get extremely fat as soon as possible. Skinny sumo wrestlers look a bit sad and are knocked over all the time by their huge opponents, who have low centers of gravity.

SUMO WEIGHT CATEGORIES, ADJUSTED TO THE WESTERN SYSTEM

- *Lightweight:* lighter than 187 pounds
- *Middleweight:* lighter than 250 pounds
- *Heavyweight:* heavier than 250 pounds

The way to plump up is to do just as authentic *sumotori* do: eat a great deal of sticky rice. For a while you will gain weight only slowly until one day your body gives up the fight and you suddenly start to swell like a balloon with a gas pipe stuck in its bottom. But beware: sumo wrestlers are nearly all type-2 diabetics as a result of their gigantic size; chess might be a safer bet.

◎ *British wrestler Big Daddy's real name was Shirley Crabtree.* ◎

HOW TO MAKE A BOOMERANG ACTUALLY COME BACK

The boomerang is the Australian Aborigine's greatest contribution to the science of hunting animals with a bent stick. Designed as a tool for whacking food on the head from a distance, the first boomerangs came back only when unsuccessful. Indeed, the homing properties of a boomerang are incidental to its superb efficiency as a projectile, the curved shape and wing-like profile of which lend it accuracy, stability, and lift, as it spins toward some unhappy kangaroo.

Making a boomerang

You can make a boomerang in a variety of shapes, from a cross or triangle to the V-shape Aborigine type. A boomerang cut from the trunk of a tree at the junction with a main root will give you an angle of curve somewhere between 95 and 110 degrees.

Here's how to make a basic cross-boomerang. It is simple to construct and easy to trim with snips of the scissors. Be prepared for plenty of trial and error.

Required

- *A cereal box*
- *Some scissors*
- *A stapler*

Method

1. Draw on to a piece of cereal box two identical strips 8½ inches × 1 inch.
2. Cut these out, curving their corners attractively, like your doctor's tongue depressor.
3. Lay one on top of the other in a cross, and staple them in the middle.
4. Fold both tips of each blade ¾ inch from the end, and you're set.

Making your boomerang come back

There are three keys to success in getting a boomerang to come back: (1) practice, (2) practice, and (3) practice. Like anything else you throw, boomerangs are governed by Newton's laws of motion. Inertia, the Bernoulli effect, gyroscopic precession, and centripetal force are all involved, too, in case you care.

A boomerang should always be thrown vertically. As it spins, the

ends of the blades rotate faster than the center, creating a difference in lift that gives the boomerang its characteristic wobbly-circle flight pattern.

1 Go outside, away from people with bare heads.
2 With your arm raised against your ear, grip the 'rang tightly by a blade tip so that it points upward—with the folded parts bent toward you.
3 Aim just above the trees about 200 yards away and whip the boomerang out of your hand vertically, with a snap of the wrist, finishing the throw with your arm against your leg.

You can throw a boomerang in the wind but it's hard enough for beginners when it's fairly still. On windy days, try the indoor miniature boomerang on the next page.

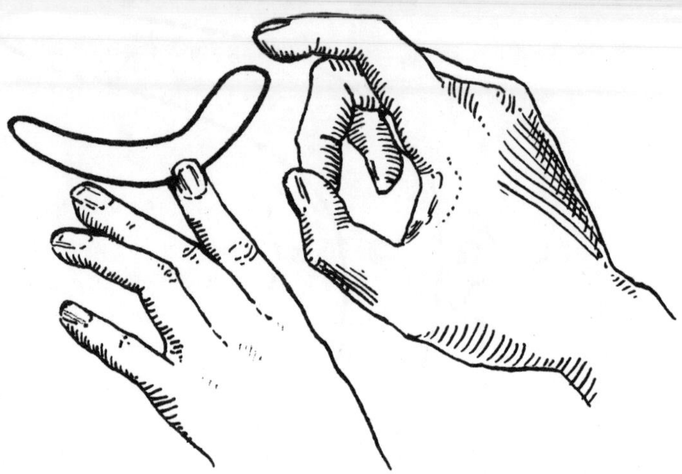

THE MINI-RANG

Cut an old-fashioned curved boomerang shape from your cereal box about 3 inches long (see illustration), making one end slightly fatter, therefore heavier, than the other.

To launch, hold it vertically between your left finger and thumb, tilted very slightly to the left and flick it hard at the top of the blade with your right middle finger. Alternatively, you can tuck it under the nail of your left forefinger and try launching it horizontally. Give it an upward tilt of about 45 degrees before flicking it away with your right forefinger.

If things aren't working, never throw a boomerang away in disgust—it may well come back and hit you.

◎ *Kangaroos smear themselves with saliva to cool down.* ◎

HOW TO
MAKE A SLED THAT REALLY GOES

John Gale's marvelous book, *Clean Young Englishman*, includes a description of the toboggans of his youth, which were hammered from a sheet of corrugated iron. Hard to beat on snow and ice, they also gave a good account of themselves in slush and mud, unlike those mass-produced wooden numbers.

Making one

Get yourself a sheet of corrugated iron about 8 feet × 2 feet, and remove with a pair of pliers any bent nails or screws. Using a wire brush and plenty of elbow grease, clean the metal of rust. This can be exhausting but will warm you up beautifully in an east wind. Next a good going over with coarse, medium, and then fine sandpaper will bring up a robust shine, though even a cursory scrape to get the worst off will do. An oily rag works wonders as a final buffer. Now your sled is ready to be bent and you must hammer it into shape.

The best hammers are hefty wide-headed things. If you have a heated metal pipe-bender you are well away. Otherwise it's a job for you, your friend, and the gatepost or handy tree. Telephone poles are ideal too but can be few and far between.

Whack and pull the end of the metal around the pole to create the rounded prow of your sled. You are trying to create a curve like that of a Turkish slipper—fairly steep at the front but at the same time elegant. Smooth, pleasing lines mean faster, safer travel so try to be artistic. Trial and error are your best teachers and you may find yourself making last-minute adjustments between goes down the snowy hill. Once you get it right a crew of two or three will smash a fat channel through the cool kids in their fancy hats: unstoppable and almost uncontrollable.

Stout gloves are a must because you'll need to grip the front or edges of the sled as you hurtle along, and the metal isn't very forgiving, especially when cold. A piece of rugged garden twine attached through two holes at the bow makes a serviceable handle for dragging the monster back uphill. But don't try to hold on to it as you whistle down the slope; you'll risk taking fingers off.

With a well-watered surface, a high-speed run can be achieved. For a more expert move, you can toboggan in the dark, with your front passenger holding a flashlight. Never try to stop the thing by sticking limbs out—they'll be snapped off like bread sticks. A slight shifting of your center of gravity by leaning left or right can have a marginal effect on steering but frankly your sled has a life of its own. A bit of practice will help you control it a little but, once launched, prayer is really your best bet.

◎ *Residents of Maine made the tallest snowman ever. He was 113 feet high.* ◎

HOW TO
SKIP STONES

Among the top films every boy should see is *The Dam Busters* (1954), in which Vanessa Redgrave's dad plays Barnes Wallis, inventor of the "bouncing bomb," which spun backward when dropped on water, making it stable, accurate, and *bouncy*. The British navy used a similar idea, firing their cannonballs short of their targets so that they bounced off the sea and punched holes in the enemy's ships from an impressive upward angle.

As with cannonballs so with stones. Along with the angle of trajectory, the secrets of stone skipping are velocity and rotation. According to one expert, the optimum skip speed is 25 miles an hour at a spin rate of 14 rotations a second, though how one is supposed to measure this is a mystery to me. Forty skips is the current world record, but most of us are lucky, even after a lot of trying, to score six or seven.

The best stones to skip

To stand any chance you need a good projectile. The best skipping stones are smooth, palm-size, flatish, and triangular not round, with a slightly curved underside. And they should be just heavy enough—let trial and error be your guides. Sea-worn slate and flint are both excellent materials and one world record has been achieved with a piece of limestone. Beaches near cliffs are the ideal place to find suitable stones but unless the sea is unusually calm, lakes or large ponds are the preferred skipping places. Waves are your enemy.

The science

As a stone hits the water it is "pushed away" from the surface by the density of the liquid, just like a water-skier. The force of this "push" is proportional to the stone's (or skier's) squared speed. Unlike a skier, though, each bounce of the stone is shorter and steeper than the one before because its energy is running out, and, just like it says in Newton's third law of motion, the stone's momentum is conserved, being transferred to the water. The visible result is ripples.

However, the overriding factor for skipping success is the angle at which the pebble hits the pond. Twenty degrees has been proved best by some laboratory Frenchmen. Coming in acute like this the stone will skip even if thrown by your mom—all slow and with rotten spin.

Stones striking the surface at less than 20 degrees (more horizontal) do bounce, but lose much of their energy to the water. Those that hit the pond at more than 45 degrees (more perpendicular) don't bounce, they just break the surface and sink—if you'll pardon the not very illuminating simile—like a stone. So *this angle business is critical*, and not only with stone skipping. It's one of the things that must be taken into careful account when a space shuttle is being guided back to Earth. Too sharp an angle and it will skip off the atmosphere straight back into space.

The throw

Stand up straight, feet apart, at an angle to the water. Pinch your stone horizontally between thumb and middle finger, your elbow four or five inches from your hip. Your forefinger, the motivating digit, should be lying around the stone's circumference. Now, preceded by a little backswing, throw the stone fast at the aforementioned 20-degree angle, uncurling your hand with a flick of the wrist at the last moment. As the stone is released, the forefinger imparts the critical spin.

◎ *Some flying sequences in* Star Wars *were based on those in* The Dam Busters. ◎

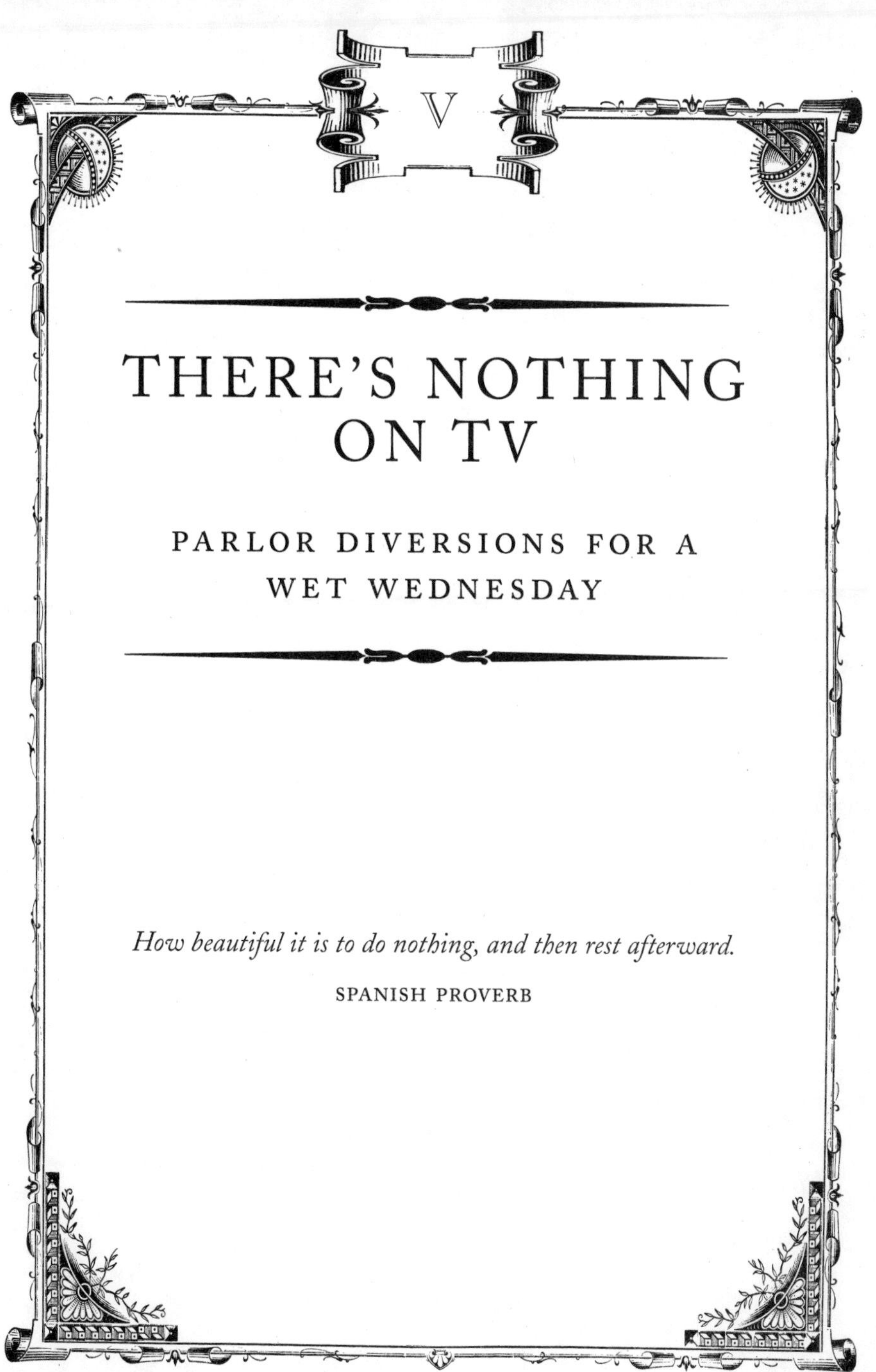

V

THERE'S NOTHING ON TV

PARLOR DIVERSIONS FOR A WET WEDNESDAY

How beautiful it is to do nothing, and then rest afterward.

SPANISH PROVERB

THE ACROBATIC FORKS

This incredible stunt is hundreds of years old but is surprisingly little known. In the years before we all toiled like slaves in the salt mines from dawn till dusk, and decompressed couch-potato style in front of the evening's sitcoms, this beautiful after-dinner amusement was a favorite with families.

What you are going to do is push a large coin between the prongs of two forks and balance this by its very edge on the rim of a glass. The effect defies belief and its preparation is almost as much fun as the dénouement.

REQUIRED

- *A coin*
- *2 forks*
- *A glass (a tall one is good)*

"The acrobatic forks" works best with a large coin like a quarter or half-dollar. With smaller forks, a nickel will work. The size of the coin you use will depend on the weight of the forks and the gaps between their prongs, so some experimentation is required beforehand. As with anything spontaneous, good preparation is a must.

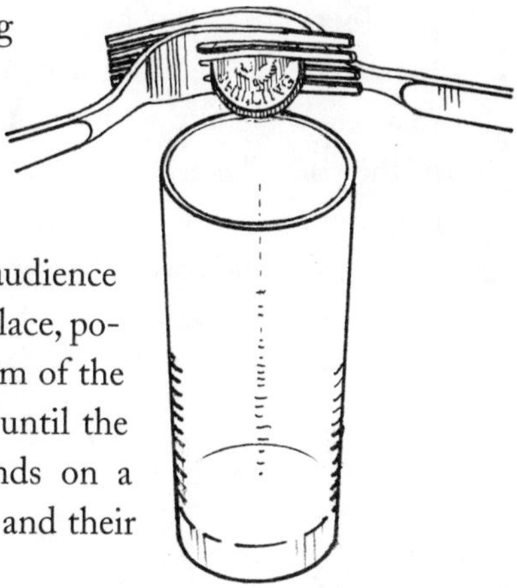

First, insert your coin between the tines of the two forks, as in the illustration. This bit can be tricky but your audience will be intrigued. Once everything's in place, position the flat edge of the coin on the rim of the glass, as shown. Keep adjusting things until the equilibrium is established. This depends on a combination of the weight of the forks and their distance from the center of gravity. A little judicious bending can help reluctant cutlery.

The arrangement is more stable than it appears and, to add a bit of drama, you can fill the glass with beer and then pour this into another glass without the coin and forks falling off. Do this from a point diametrically opposite the coin. With practice and care you'll even be able to pour the liquid into your mouth.

For the ambitious, there are two interesting variations:

1 THE BURNING MATCH

When you have mastered the trick using a coin, why not try it with a matchstick, as shown? Once you have the thing balanced, light the match head. It will burn all the way through, while your spectators hold their breath, until the flame reaches the rim, where it will go out, leaving the whole contraption balanced on the very tip of the burnt match. It is an amazing sight and looks comprehensively unlikely. Try blowing gently on a fork handle and the whole thing will sway in the breeze, without falling off.

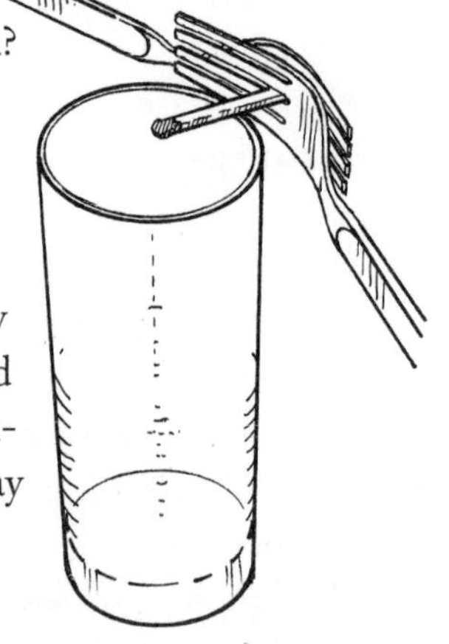

2 THE EGG AND CORK

Instead of a coin, take a wine cork and hollow out one end just enough to accommodate the blunt end of an egg. Stick a fork into either side of the cork like arms hanging down at shopping-bag angle. Place the contraption on the egg and, after some adjustment, you should be able to let go of the cork. The sharp end of the egg may now be balanced perfectly safely on the rim of a wine bottle with the cork and forks on top of the lot.

◎ *The earliest forks had just two tines.* ◎

MAKE YOUR OWN "TADPOLES"

Tadpole manufacture is the acme of wet Wednesday afternoon diversions. The tadpoles can be made in a jiffy and there is something seductive in the way they glide and turn. You will spend many a happy hour devising games for them to play.

Required

- *A few marbles*
- *A few friends*
- *A roll of tinfoil*
- *A smooth tabletop or floor*
- *A few cans of beer (optional)*

Instructions

1. Steal a roll of tinfoil from the kitchen.
2. Find some marbles. Everybody has a few marbles somewhere. Often you'll find them at the bottom of the drawer that contains a bulldog clip, somebody's glasses, an ancient cell phone, and a bunch of keys. Two marbles each is plenty.
3. Put the marbles into a bowl and sit down at the table. (This is a good time to open the beer.)
4. Each person must now tear off a roughly rectangular piece of foil about as long as his middle finger and about two-thirds this width. Don't worry if it's a bit misshapen and the edges are all ragged, this isn't origami.
5. To make a tadpole, take a marble and put it on the table in front of you. Loosely squash your foil over it, a bit off-center, so that the marble forms a "head," with the rest of the foil flaring out behind, like the tail of a comet.
6. Tighten the foil around the marble and squeeze the flared end into a tail shape. It's quite normal for a flattened "skirt" to form

where the head meets the table. This skirt will add stability to your tadpole.

7 Now give him a little push. With any luck you will have left just enough space around the marble for it to roll about smoothly under its foil shell. But if the foil is too tight you'll have to fiddle with it to loosen things up. Your tadpole is working correctly when you are able to nudge its tail or body so that it sails smoothly across a surface.

Ovarian petanque (A tadpole game for 4–10 players)

If you have access to a shiny wood or laminate floor you can play a wonderful game called ovarian petanque. This is based on the resemblance of your tadpoles to spermatozoa. The rules are simple.

1 First, clear the floor of children, rugs, tables, and newspapers to provide a large space.
2 Position your players around the edge of the room and place a cushion in the middle of the floor. The cushion is your "ovum," the target of your sperm-tadpoles.
3 On command, each player attempts to hit the cushion with a single launch of his tadpole. Any player who is unable to do so is declared "sterile" and is out; the remaining players go again.
4 The last man out is the winner, and buys the drinks.

◎ *Marbles were once made from white marble.* ◎

HOW TO
MAKE A PAIR OF PANTS FROM POSH RESTAURANT NAPKINS

Making a pair of pants out of a few posh napkins will increase your chances of survival in a whole variety of hotel and restaurant scrapes, perhaps the most unfortunate of which is the well-known "Gentleman's Trouser Emergency." This is usually the result of a serious quickstep-style "follow-through" after a rash "cheese-cutting" in the ornate restaurant of some very fancy hotel.

1 The first thing you'll require is a good supply of napkins: probably between 12 and 15, depending on the napkin size and the thickness of your legs. Don't be shy: whisk them off the tables without shame. If there's a choice, remember that dark colors are more flattering, especially to the fuller figure. Paper napkins *will not do*; the seams will bulge and tear and, frankly, you'll end up looking like trailer trash.
2 Ask at reception for one of those nifty sewing kits containing needles, thread, and scissors. If they demur, cause a fuss.
3 Now make your way to the restroom, where you can get on with your needlework in peace. Once you have discarded your pants, and availed yourself of the ablutions, sit down in a cubicle and pass a yard of doubled-up thread through the needle.
4 Starting at the ankle, wrap the first napkin around your leg. (Be discreet with branded table linens, keeping the restaurant's logo, if there is one, on the *inside*.) If you are well built you might not have collected enough napkins for long pants and may have to make do with shorts. Start higher up (think lederhosen). For everybody's sake, guys, make these loose fitting.
5 Begin by sewing the bottom corners of the napkin together, behind your leg, and tie this off with a knot. Keep going up the leg with an ascending helical (spiral) stitch. Don't concern yourself with

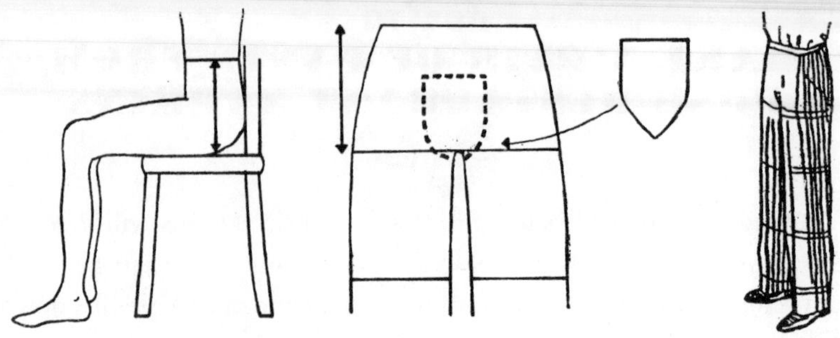

the look of the seam, this is the *least* of your worries. Use the same stitch around the circumference of your leg, to connect the next layer of napkins, and continue upward until you have a tube of material on each leg as far as the crotch line.

6 The most crucial measurement for a comfortable pair of pants is the crotch depth. A good way to work this out is to stitch a long strip of napkins together and sew these around your waist like a wide belt. Depending on the drop (the width of the napkins), you should be able to stitch the bottom of this piece to the top of the leg pieces, with plenty of wiggle room. Do this sitting down and you'll automatically allow enough material.

7 Finally, cut a crotch hole (see illustration) and adjust its width for comfort. Cut out a trowel-shape piece of napkin wide enough to accommodate your requirements and sew it into place at the crotch hole, like a codpiece, closing any gap between the legs.

8 Things should now feel fairly comfortable, if somewhat unusual. Put your shoes and socks back on, and you're ready to go. The pants should hang nicely and feel perfectly comfortable, but a word of warning: linen napkins are highly absorbent. Don't go out in an electrical rainstorm or you'll be a human sponge.

◎ *Richard Feynman solved his physics problems on the napkins of a topless bar.* ◎

HOW TO
MAKE A SPARTAN CODE STICK

The 5th-century Spartan army didn't have access to elaborate message encryption software. In any case, what they needed in Greece for writing secret messages during military campaigns was something quick and easy that could be deciphered by the recipient without a lot of fuss.

Their brilliant solution was called the *scytale* (pronounced *skee ta lee*)—essentially a wooden cylinder with a parchment strip wrapped around it, on which the message was written. It was fast, easy, and reliable—ideal qualities when people are firing things at you.

To encode the message, the sender would coil the paper around his stick in a helix and write the text along the cylinder's length. He would then unwind it and send the resulting strip of jumbled characters by messenger. The recipient would decipher the code by winding the paper around a scytale of the same diameter. If captured by the enemy, the message took ages to decode without a rod of the right size.

Required

- *2 cylinders of the same diameter*
- *Paper, scissors, and sticky tape*
- *A felt pen*

Broom handles and paper-towel tubes make good Spartan code sticks. You will need two, of course, together with a long strip of paper about 1 inch wide. You can cut this from a sheet of paper and tape several pieces together.

Writing the message

1. Tape one end of the paper strip to the tube. Wrap it around in a tight coil, so that the edges meet without overlapping. Tear off any spare paper at the other end and tape it down.

2 Write your message in a straight line along the length of your code stick. The spiral junction, where the edges of the paper meet, acts as a separator between each letter. When you come to the end, rotate your code stick away from yourself and start a new row underneath. Indicate word spaces with a space, or, if you wish to be devious, a Z.

3 When you have finished, remove the paper. You'll see that your text reads as gobbledygook.

4 To decode your message, your recipient must wind the strip around his broom handle—or whatever—until the rows of letters line up.

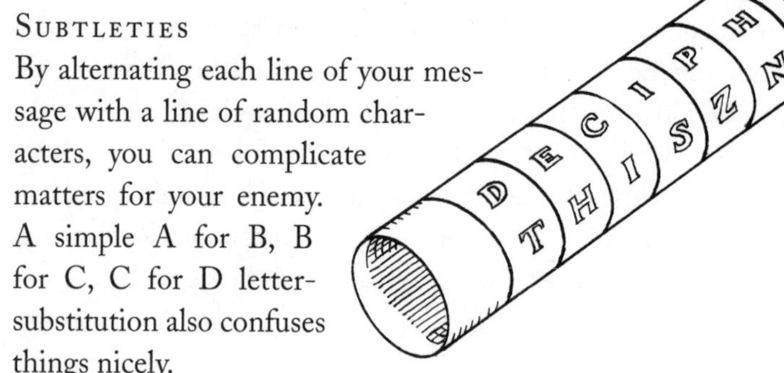

Subtleties

By alternating each line of your message with a line of random characters, you can complicate matters for your enemy. A simple A for B, B for C, C for D letter-substitution also confuses things nicely.

⊚ *At the Spartan Festival of the Cleaver, sausages were nailed to the wall.* ⊚

HOW TO
MAKE A PERISCOPE

Those Greeks had a word for everything. "Periscope" comes from the Greek words *peri* meaning "around" and *scopus* "to look at." A periscope is essentially a tube with tilted parallel mirrors at its ends. These peek out of holes in opposite sides of the tube and any image striking one mirror is bounced off the other into the viewer's eye.

Periscopes are famously used by submarines, but before 1902, when the first naval periscope was invented, subs had to surface so that the crew could look out of the windows to see what was going on upstairs. This was not very secret.

To make your own periscope you will need the following.

- *2 large orange juice cartons (empty)*
- *A piece of scrap paper*
- *2 small square mirrors*
- *A sharp knife*
- *Masking tape*
- *A ruler*
- *Fun-Tak*
- *A pencil*

CONSTRUCTION

1 Cut the tops off the cartons and throw them away (not the cartons, obviously), then tape them together at the open ends to make a long tube. *Note:* the longer the tube, the smaller the final image.

2 When they go in, the mirrors must be positioned at a 45-degree angle, opposite the holes you are going to cut. To get an accurate angle for the mirrors, stand the carton on your piece of scrap paper and draw its footprint. It should be square. Cut this out and fold it in half diagonally.

3 To calculate the right dimensions for your holes, draw a horizontal line a quarter of an inch from the end of the carton. Place one of the short sides of your paper triangle along the horizontal, and draw a diagonal line on the carton, down the triangle's long edge.

4 Now, place the long side of your triangle against the horizontal line, with one of its short edges along the diagonal you have drawn. Mark the carton with a dot at the corner of the triangle and draw a horizontal line across the carton at this point.

5 Slit along this line, stopping a quarter of an inch from each edge. Cut a similar slit along the original horizontal line, finishing a

quarter of an inch short of the edges. With two vertical cuts finish the rectangular hole.

6 Tape a mirror inside the carton, shiny side out, with its bottom edge in line with the bottom of the hole. You can measure this precisely with your ruler. Tape this edge down neatly and put a large blob of Fun-Tak on the corners opposite the tape. Now flop the mirror toward the hole, resting it on the Fun-Tak and adjusting it so that the angle is correct. When you are satisfied, tape the mirror in place.

7 Repeat the moves on the opposite side and at the other end of the carton, and presto!

8 Now you can look over the fence at the girl next door without her brother threatening to push your face in.

◎ *Peeping Tom was the fictional tailor blinded by spying on Lady Godiva.* ◎

HOW TO
FOLD AN ORIGAMI GIFT BOX

A plain origami box is a thing of austere beauty but is arguably trickier to fold than the fancy container described on this page, whose flounces craftily disguise any minor shortcomings of the folder. At its simplest, paper folding is pretty basic mechanics, so, even if you're a fingers and thumbs kind of person, you ought to be able to manage this little number.

Required

- *A square sheet of plain paper (fancy paper works too)*
- *Some chocolate-covered raisins*

Method

1 Make two corner-to-corner folds and crease them down to make an X across the square (fig. 1).

2 Open up the paper and neatly fold the four corners into the middle, to make a smaller square. Turn this over and repeat the actions, to get an even smaller square (fig. 2).

3 Turn the paper over again and carefully fold each center point back to its respective corner, creasing the fold. These new creases describe a still smaller square.

4 You'll notice that the paper is not flat on the table but is "bouncing" a bit. Turn it over and fold one of the center points back on itself so that its tip projects beyond the edge by about a thumbnail's length. Repeat this move with the other three points, aligning the folds as best you can (fig. 3).

5 Eat a few chocolate raisins.

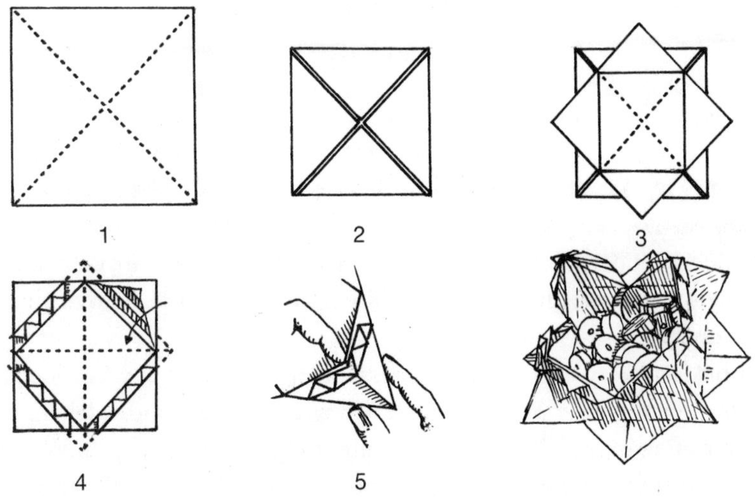

6 Turn the paper over, lift one of the little triangles—just the top sheet—and make four concertina folds, toward the center, then back toward the corner, and so on, so that you end up with a narrow strip, with a zigzag pattern running along it (fig. 4). Repeat with the other three triangles.

7 Now comes the dénouement: poke your left forefinger into one of the corner pockets and pinch the paper around it from the

outside, slipping your finger out at the last minute, as you pinch the paper into a flat, triangular point (fig. 5). Repeat with the other pockets.

8 Finally, flatten the feet and tidy things up.

Girls are always impressed if you make one of these in front of them and then put a small present inside, such as a few chocolate-covered raisins or an engagement ring. It's dirt cheap too.

◎ *The Japanese words for paper and God are the same:* kami. ◎

INSTANT MASKS WITH YOUR FINGERS

Suppose for a minute that you're in one of those films where you are trapped in an elevator or towering inferno with a group of archetypes from central casting. Usually this bunch will contain a plain-speaking, booze-sodden widow in a frightful wig and fur coat; a hysterical flibbertigibbet prone to weepy shrieking fits; an unctuous creepy fellow (usually suspiciously foreign); and a virile hero with a serious chin.

This is all very well for our fearless and active hero but what about those quiet nights when everyone is sitting around the candle debating the meaning of life? Virile-man is going to be out of his depth. What you need are a few things to cheer everyone up, and what could be better than making some masks with your fingers? It's immediate, amusing, and it doesn't require expensive—or any—apparatus.

Batman

Unquestionably the best finger mask is Batman. Start by making circles of your thumbs and forefingers, while extending and spreading your other fingers. Invert the circles so that your thumbnails point at the floor, and touch your chin with your middle fingers. Now rotate the circles up to sit over your eyes. Your third and fourth fingertips will automatically fall into place against your jaw. Have a look in the mirror; it's just like Batman.

Star Trek Klingon

The permanent frown of the Klingon race is hard to perform yourself but is great done on a willing boy of seven or eight. Simply put your hand on his head, palm down, with your fingers extended over his forehead. Now lower your fingers until they touch the top of his brow and push downward. This will have the effect of wrinkling his forehead in a malevolent frown. Very Klingon.

Picasso

Here's a quickie, especially suitable for glasses wearers. Ask your spectators: "Do you want to see my impression of Picasso?" When they all shout "Yes!" move your glasses to the right slightly, such that the frame of the left lens rests on the bridge of your nose. The idea is that you resemble one of Picasso's Cubist portraits.

I don't know why, but people fall over with hilarity when I do this bit of business. It must have gotten me more laughs over the years than any of the more complicated stuff.

◉ *Surgical masks cannot reduce the spread of viruses.* ◉

SHADOW PORTRAITS IN A JIFFY

During centuries gone by, many a parasol-twirling young lady had her svelte outline immortalized by the skillful scissor-craft of the seaside silhouette cutter. These days, the charm has gone out of the thing: the modern equivalent being a bleary passport photo of a creepy guy brandishing a bag of chips. All the more reason, you might think, for a renaissance of the shadow portrait. It's not difficult or expensive, and the apparatus is elementary. So what are you waiting for?

Required

- *A few large sheets of black construction paper*
- *A few large sheets of white paper*
- *A soft but sharp pencil*
- *Some scissors*
- *Glue*
- *Fun-Tak*
- *Your grandma*
- *A lamp*

Method

1 Wait until dark and then attach a piece of black paper to the wall, portrait-style.

2 Position a chair sideways in front of the paper, between the wall and a table.

3 Put a lamp on the table—one of those with a bendable arm is good.

4 Get your grandma or pipe-smoking uncle—or somebody else who can keep still for more than a few seconds—to sit on the chair. They must face sideways, obviously, or you will end up with a silhouette that looks like a huge lightbulb instead of one that has a nose and things. If all you see is a gray smear, your light is too far away, or your subject isn't close enough to the wall. Fiddle around until you are happy. There should be plenty of sharp detail.

5 When you have settled the subject to your satisfaction, and asked her not to leap up every time her cell phone rings, carefully draw around her shadow with your pencil.

6 When you've finished, take down the paper. Although it is dark, your pencil outline should be clear, so cut around it, taking special care wherever you have detail such as spectacles, wisps of hair, and so on. Don't be tempted to leave these out—they bring the portrait to life.

7 Now glue your black silhouette on to a white sheet of paper and you've finished. If your pencil line is noticeable you can turn the paper over before you glue it. It's interesting how different, yet still recognizable, a silhouette looks in reverse.

If you make yourself a pantograph (see below) and trace your portraits with it, you can reduce their size, and make miniatures on finer paper.

◎ *Etienne de Silhouette (1709–67) was finance minister under Louis XV.* ◎

HOW TO
MAKE AND USE A PANTOGRAPH

The pantograph is a simple draftsman's tool that has been used for centuries to copy, enlarge, and reduce flat artwork. The geometric principles involved are Euclidean, and Leonardo da Vinci is believed to have used one to reproduce his own work and transfer drawings to canvas.

The pantograph is a flexible parallelogram, with extended "arms" projecting from the diagonally opposite ends of its long sides, one being fixed at its terminal, the other having a pencil near its tip. The joints are loose and move easily, so that if a point close to one of the corners of the instrument is traced over a line or diagram, the pencil will duplicate its movements and make a copy. Here are the instructions for a homemade pantograph.

REQUIRED

- *A cardboard box*
- *A sharp pencil*
- *Sharp scissors or knife*
- *4 long push pins*
- *A short screw*
- *A tack*
- *A hammer*
- *Masking tape*
- *A thin piece of plywood about the size of a playing card*

Method

1 Following the corrugations, cut four cardboard strips about ¾ inch wide and 13 inches long.

2 Arrange these as shown and mark the positions of the holes. In the illustration below, these are indicated by the figures, which represent the distances in inches *between the holes*.

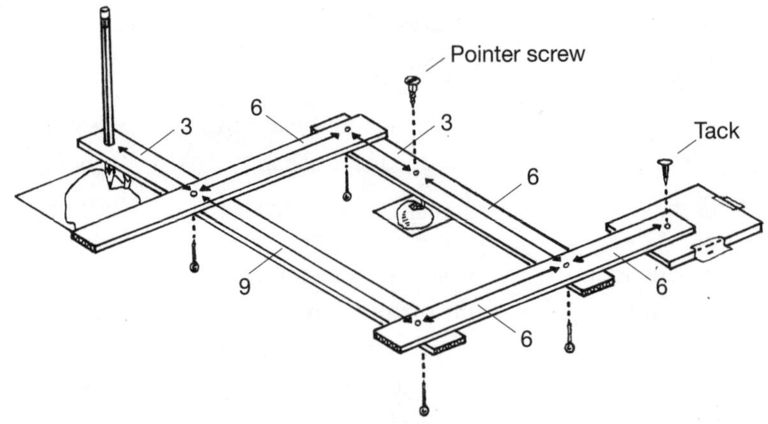

3 Make the holes with your pencil. This is one of those times when a bit of wiggle room is permissible.

4 Insert the four push pins from underneath.

5 Twist the screw into place through the cardboard.

6 Tape the plywood to the table on your left, first making sure that the owner doesn't mind. Explain that she is very kind, and that you will be clearing up afterward. (This is called psychology.)

7 Hammer the tack through the cardboard into the plywood. No need to go crazy, just tap it—you don't want to knock it into the table.

Using your pantograph

1 Put the pencil into its hole. It might help to use tape to hold it in place.

2 Adjust the screw so it just touches the table. This is your pointer.

3. Take a small line drawing that you want to enlarge and position it under the screw.
4. Put a blank sheet of paper under the pencil and move it about, making sure that the pointer covers the whole area of the drawing and that the pencil covers the whole of the blank sheet. When you are satisfied, tape the drawing and blank sheet to the table.
5. To enlarge the picture, hold the pencil very gently, and, without twisting the apparatus, follow the path of the pointer over the original as you hold the pencil against the paper.

There's a knack to it that depends partly on the idiosyncrasies of your pantograph. But it *does* work. If you want to reduce an original, simply switch the positions of your pencil and screw. Experimentation will reveal how to make bigger enlargements and smaller reductions.

◎ *Leonardo da Vinci left only about 30 paintings.* ◎

HOW TO PLAY ANCHORMAN

British drinking games are as old as the hills and include the satanic "Schmidt the shape-slitter," in which a circle of friends, playing against each other, recite the rhyme:

Sitting still in the slitting pits
Schmidt slit the shapes and shaped the slits;
Slitting shapes and shaping slits
Schmidt shaped and slit in the slitting pits.

Each time a player makes a mistake, he has to drink half a pint of beer and try again. At the end of each successful round everyone is rewarded with half a pint of beer. The game is rather easy at first but by about 11 p.m. it is quite usual for the entire group to be comprehensively bladdered, with nobody able to get much further than "Sitting" without going off script.

Anchorman is an American game of this kind but reflects the more competitive character of the red, white, and blue. It is played by two teams of at least four players, though bigger teams have a distinct advantage, as will be seen.

Anchorman

1. The teams sit opposite each other at a table and, after a coin toss to decide who goes first, players from that team take turns trying to get a penny to land in a pitcher of beer in the center of the table. They must use the heads-tails thumb flip and mustn't take their fists off the table. Players may shoot only once, whether or not they get their penny into the pitcher.
2. Once the players have each had a flip, the second team takes over. The first team to get all four pennies into the pitcher wins and the losers must then drink the contents. But in a special way.
3. The winning team picks a member of the losing team to be "Anchorman." The losers then take it in turns to drink from the pitcher in a single quaff, without taking their lips from the vessel. Anyone who fails must pass the pitcher to the team member on his left.
4. The anchorman drinks last, and it is his job to finish any and all beer left in the pitcher, whether it be just a mouthful of brown saliva or almost the entire pitcherful. He is accorded the privilege of removing his lips at any time he pleases, but he must drink its contents within two minutes, while being heckled by the other team.
5. The anchorman's team have to make both strategic and tactical decisions, as the game progresses, about how much beer they will leave for him to finish off, based on his size and known booze-absorbing capacities. Bigger teams are clearly at an advantage at this point.
6. Once empty, the pitcher is refilled and the game begins again.

Anchorman is not recommended before operating a guillotine, or having a job interview with Air Traffic Control.

◎ *Hippocrates recommended beer for strengthening the heart and gums.* ◎

A PAPER HAT IN SECONDS

There's one thing you don't want when you come to make a hat out of a sheet of newspaper, and that's a long exercise in origami. Once you've learned the folds for this, the simplest of methods, you'll be able to turn out a paper hat in 20 seconds.

Required

- *A sheet of newspaper (bigger is better)*
- *Sticky tape*

Method

1. Place the open sheet on the table, with centerfold horizontal. Fold it in half toward you, firmly creasing the fold.
2. Now, fold the left edge over to the right, as if closing a book. Crease the vertical centerfold, and open it again.
3. Next, fold the top-left corner over and down, making a diagonal crease, so that what was the top edge now abuts the centerfold. Repeat with the opposite corner and you should be looking at a shape resembling a chalet with a steep roof (fig. 2).
4. Grasp the long, horizontal bottom edge of the paper and fold up the top leaf. Crease it against the bottom of the two triangular pieces.
5. Turn the paper over and repeat with the other leaf (fig. 3).
6. Grasp the protruding right-angle corner on the left—both leaves—and crease it down diagonally, taping or twisting it closed. This will prevent the fold from opening and undoing the hat (fig. 4).
7. Turn over the paper and repeat.

You can wear a small hat pointing forward like a military side cap, or sideways if it's bigger.

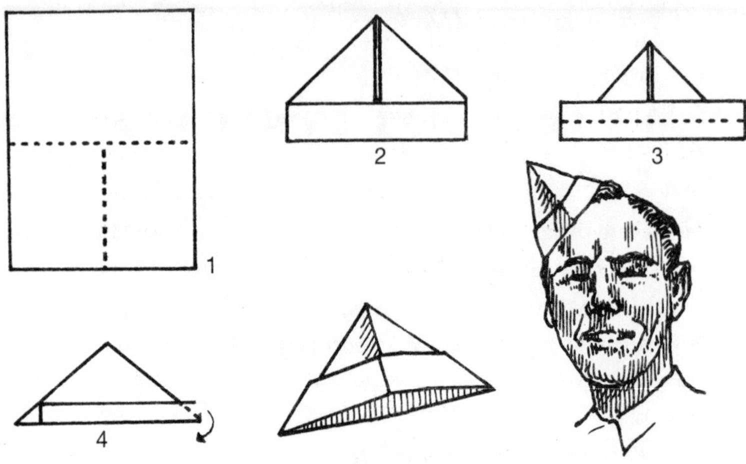

◎ *Joseph Merrick, the "Elephant Man," wore a hat 3 feet in circumference.* ◎

HOW TO
GROW AN ORANGE TREE FROM A SEED

The orange is a hardy evergreen, with a penchant for hot days and cool nights. If properly looked after, it will live happily out of doors during summer. Even a bad gardener can grow an orange indoors; with a little care and attention, and some re-potting, in just a few years your orange tree can reach a height of 6 feet. Don't expect edible fruit, though, unless you are prepared to do some professional husbandry.

Required

- *An orange seed or two*
- *A jam jar*
- *A couple of handfuls of ordinary seed compost*

Planting

- You can plant an orange seed at any time of year and get results, but it is best to do it during the early spring, so that the young tree can take advantage of the lengthening days, with their extra hours of light and warmth.
- To prepare, put some pieces of broken shell or small pebbles into the bottom of a jam jar for drainage, and sprinkle a couple of inches of compost on top. Although it won't spend long in the jar, your plant will live happily in this sort of compost for its first couple of years. After that, take advice from the nice person at the garden center.
- Push a couple of seeds from a ripe orange into the compost—not too deep. Give the seeds a sprinkle of water. In its natural home, the rain is warm, so don't shock it with icy tap water, and make sure you don't waterlog the thing; it won't like it.
- Seal a polythene bag over the top of the jar with a rubber band, put it by a radiator near a sunny window, and wait. The ideal temperature is between 60–70 degrees F. Germination should be under way in two weeks but can take up to two months. Once the leaves are open, take out the best seedling with an ordinary table fork and transfer it to a small pot. Put this into a polythene bag, which you can close with a bit of wire or something, and water it with warm water every three or four days. Check it regularly so that it doesn't dry out. After a season's growth it should be a few inches high and can come out of the bag.
- Your young orange likes full sun and enough water. It dislikes a draught in the early months. Feed it every two weeks in summer and spray its leaves occasionally with warm water.
- After a season's growth it should be a few inches high and can come out of the bag.

◎ *Orange peel is used to repel garden slugs.* ◎

THE THUNDER-FARTER

You can now buy remote-control electronic gadgets that produce some terrifyingly realistic farting noises. But they are expensive. A much cheaper and prodigiously loud substitute is that old schoolboy favorite, the washer and wire coat hanger thunder-farter. Why not give it a whirl?

REQUIRED

- *A wire coat hanger*
- *A pair of pliers (that will also cut wire)*
- *2 long thick rubber bands*
- *A large washer*

METHOD

1. Snip the hook off the coat hanger and discard it, leaving a piece of wire about 1 foot long.
2. Bend this into a squared-off *U* shape as best you can.
3. Fashion with your pliers a sort of unclosed eyelet at each end. These should curve away from the *U* and allow just enough room to slip a doubled-up rubber band under the wire and into the hole (fig. 1).
4. Thread an rubber band through the washer and double it back on itself. Grasp the two hanging loops of the rubber band and let go of the washer so that you could, if you liked, swing it like a pendulum. Now squeeze the two pieces of rubber that you are holding and slip them under the wire into one of the eyelets.
5. Thread the other rubber band through the washer and attach it in the same way on the opposite side of the *U* (fig. 2). You should now have something that looks like the illustration.
6. Next comes the exciting bit. Wind the washer with both hands until the apparatus becomes very taut (fig. 3).
7. Keeping hold of the washer in the left hand, slip the bottom of

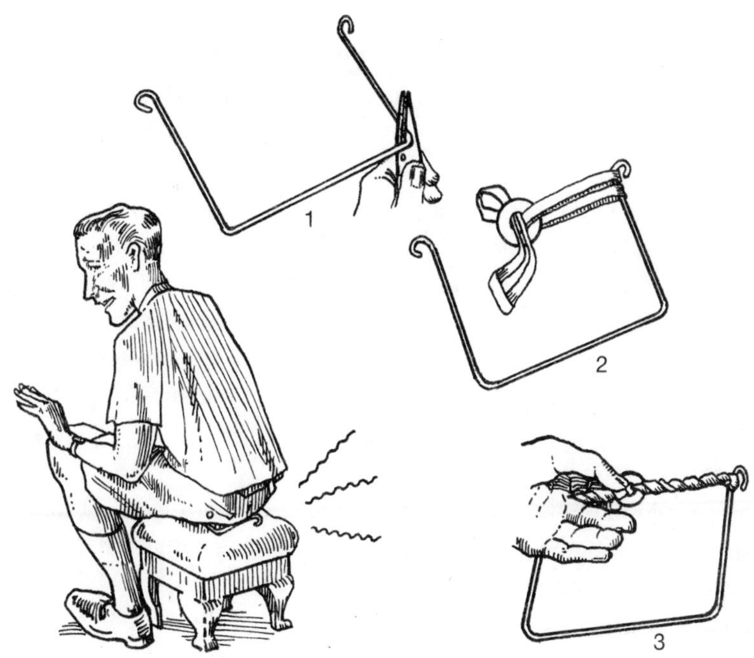

the *U* under your right buttock. You are going to hold the thing still with this cheek.

8 Lower your left buttock on to the washer but do not let go with your fingers until it is held fast between the seat and your left cheek.

9 The position now is this: you have the whole contraption held tightly against the seat. By releasing the pressure of your left buttock you will allow the washer to unwind with tremendous force, causing a long and realistically gruff farting noise. Do not feel self-conscious about tilting over when you let fly, as this only adds to the realism of the effect—especially if you wince while doing so.

10 The best seats for this are vinyl banquettes such as you find in some bars or diners. A leather armchair, director's chair, or hard church pew also produce distinctive results, and always monstrously loud.

⊚ *Rubber bands last a lot longer when kept in the fridge.* ⊚

HOW TO
TAKE YOUR UNDERPANTS OFF WITHOUT REMOVING YOUR PANTS

This very funny gag may not be as dazzling an escape as one from a straitjacket, suspended by a flaming rope over a pit of alligators but it's a lot safer and, with practice, can be built into quite a party trick.

The key to success is elasticity, so stretchy underpants are best. The cotton shorts type are pretty hopeless and my own laboratory experiments reveal that those with a Y at the front are the ones to go for.

Rules

You are allowed to bend your body and to stretch or twist your underpants, but tearing holes in any of your garments is forbidden. You can increase your chances of success by wearing loose pants, and underpants of a size larger than normal, though there must come a point, I suppose, when this constitutes cheating.

Method

1. Begin by standing upright with legs slightly apart in the military Stand Easy position.
2. Placing the index and second fingers of the right hand inside the seam of the left inside-leg, drag the pants leg up with the help of the left hand, as far as it will go, exposing your bare thigh.
3. Reach up inside the pants leg until you can pinch the material of your underpants between your index and second fingers. If you're struggling here, be of good cheer, for by pushing your left arm down the waistband of your pants you can help things along.
4. Grasping the underpants with the first two fingers of your right hand, pull firmly on the material until the waistband slips over your left hip (under your trousers) and the left leg hole of your underpants appears outside the trouser leg.

5 Pull the leg hole and waistband down over the bent left knee and secure your underpants there for a moment while you take a breather.
6 Keeping the left leg bent, pull the underpants over your foot and slip it out of the leg hole and waistband. Release the material so that the underpants spring back up inside your trousers. Be careful that the tense elastic does not cause your underpants to fly up so fast that your pride is injured.
7 It should be smooth sailing from here. By reaching up inside the right pants leg, you should now be able to grasp the material of your underpants and simply slide them down your leg and off your foot with a flourish.

It is possible to put your underpants back on by reversing these moves. Or you could just do it the normal way.

◎ *In 2000 a man tried to smuggle a boa constrictor into France in his boxers.* ◎

LEARN MORSE CODE

Every boy must have wondered, while crawling through a concrete pipe, how he would communicate with rescuers on the outside should he be sealed up inside the thing. Tapping in Morse code seems the obvious answer but beyond *dot dot dot, dash dash dash, dot dot dot,* most of us are pretty helpless. Here, therefore, are the basics, so the next time you're trapped in a pipe, you can try things like, ".. – ... – .. –. –.– ... ..–. .... . .–. ." ("It stinks in here.")

The alphabet

Morse code gives the shortest signs to the most commonly used letters and the easiest way to learn the alphabet is to group the characters as follows.

Simple

E .
I ..
S ...
H ....
T –
M– –
O – – –

Mirror image

A .–	–. N
B –...	...–V
D –..	..–U
F ..–.	.–..L
G – –.	.– –W
Q– –. –	–.– –Y

Sandwiches

K –.–	R .–.
P .– –.	X –..–

No mirror image

C –.–.
J .– – –
Z – –..

A good way to begin learning Morse code is to call the dots "iddy" and the dashes "umpty," with the emphasis on umpty, in imitation of the sounds of a tapper. So the letter F would be, "iddy iddy umpty iddy." When you've learned the easy letters, try sending and reading words made up of them, such as "it, is, hot, shoes," and so forth. Then go on to the mirror image letters and make words with those, in combination with the ones you have already learned.

Once you have command of the alphabet and can readily form and recognize whole words, you can begin a few simple sentences. Don't try to run before you can walk. Better to be able to send "Get help" than "Extraction equipment required most quickly."

Important rules

- Make a dash-length pause at the end of each letter.
- A dash is *always* three times the length of a dot.
- Do not pause between the component dots and dashes of a letter. The word "she" is ... . but will be rendered incomprehensible except by Germans if broken inappropriately, like this: . ... ("esse").

- Before long, you will be able to send messages such as: "This is a pestilential nuisance and the other passengers are complaining about the incessant tapping. Send your cell number at once."
- At the end of a session send the letter group "GB." This stands for "goodbye" and means you are signing off. –.–. ....–. ...

◎ *The first Morse code message: "What hath God wrought?"* ◎

HOW TO
MAKE A 12-FOOT PAPER TREE

Carelessly producing a newspaper tree as high as the ceiling has a definite tendency to attract people's attention and is a real winner at children's parties. What's more, if you use those free newspapers, the equipment won't cost you a penny.

Required

- *A newspaper*
- *A kitchen floor*
- *A glue stick*
- *A rubber band*
- *A pair of sharp scissors*

Preparation

1. From the audience's viewpoint, it looks as if all you do is roll up a sheet of newspaper and produce an instant tree. But, like almost everything in life, it's not as straightforward as it seems, and you'll have to make some secret preparations.
2. First, get down on the kitchen floor with a newspaper. Open it flat and spread 6–10 sheets into a long vertical strip. Sheet sizes vary more than they once did so some experimentation may be needed to produce a tree of the size you want.

3 Carefully stick the bottom of the first sheet to the top of the next, overlapping them just enough to make a firm join, and keep going until you have made a strip running the length of the kitchen—and out the door if you want a longer tree.

4 Once the glue has dried, roll the paper into a fairly tight cylinder, allowing enough room to poke your forefinger comfortably into the middle. Then glue down the edge.

5 With a pair of *sharp* scissors, make two cuts down the opposite sides of the roll, to a point just over halfway. It may all flatten out a bit, but the next step will conceal this.

6 Roll a separate sheet partly around your tube, attaching it with enough glue to secure it and make everything look neat and tidy.

PERFORMANCE

1 Make your entrance, rolling up your cylinder as if it's an unprepared sheet.

2 Secure it with the rubber band, which you have around your wrist or under your watch.

3 Tear the outer sheet with your forefinger, along the line of the cuts, and allow the strips of paper to flop down on either side.

4 Holding the tree trunk in your left hand, put your right forefinger into the middle, and pull it up and out, twisting and tightening as you go.

5 You can increase the apparent height of a shorter tree by slipping it on to a kitchen roll holder on the table.

◎ *The first printed newspaper was published in 1605.* ◎

SPECIAL EFFECTS MAKEUP WITH HOUSEHOLD INGREDIENTS

Some of the classic Hollywood special makeup effects, from slit throats and the ravages of old age, to demonic rotating heads, began their lives in the garages and back bedrooms of the young enthusiasts who invented them. The dean of special effects makeup is without a doubt Dick Smith, whose experiments with dental impression alginate, fake hair, and ordinary kitchen products led to groundbreaking effects in such films as *The Godfather* and *The Exorcist.* Hours of fun can be had researching your own special effects makeup. Here are a few ideas.

The cellophane-tape scar

You can make a horribly convincing scar by sticking a length of old-school cellophane tape to your hand or face—or wherever you need it. Apply the tape and then sponge it gently with water. After a while the cellophane backing will detach itself, leaving just the sticky adhesive in place. Carefully fold the skin along this sticky strip so that its edges are brought together. They will cling tenaciously, producing a horrible-looking wound, which is especially effective on the cheek. To make it appear fresh just add "blood" (see recipe that follows).

Rubber cement

This malodorous product, which usually comes in a pot with its own brush, acts like the latex that Hollywood professionals use to make such things as prosthetic noses. Stipple it on to the back of your hand and dry with a hair dryer to produce aging, or diseased skin effects. Sprinkle on some hair cuttings for that werewolf look.

If you press a finger or nose into a lump of soft clay and then coat your mold with rubber cement, you can make a horrible, lumpy, withered finger, or old man's nose. Make warts by poking a blunt pencil tip into the clay and apply Vaseline to the impression before painting it with glue. When dry, dust it with talcum powder (important) and peel it off. You can then attach it to yourself with more glue. A little of your girlfriend's foundation makeup will blend it in with your skin. Horrible boils may be made in the same way.

Rubber cement comes off easily with soap and water.

Dick Smith's blood recipe

In the early 1960s, movie blood was made of red pigment and glycerine. It looked like paint, tasted foul, and was unsafe. So Smith began experimenting with corn syrup and food coloring to make a better tasting and more translucent product. His superior recipe was first used in the film *Midnight Cowboy* and was quickly adopted by the industry.

Blood is usually shiny and bright red. On the skin it appears translucent and warm but is much darker, bluer, and more opaque in a pool or test tube. Experiment by mixing red and yellow food coloring and corn syrup in varying amounts to get the appearance you are after. You can achieve increased opacity by adding more dye. There's nothing like pricking your finger and comparing real blood with your formula to improve results.

Food coloring can stain surfaces so take care, and don't drink large quantities—it's not good for you.

Corn syrup has a tendency to bead unnaturally when it flows over skin or textiles so Smith adds a photographic wetting agent to his recipe. If you decide to do this, don't put it in your mouth.

◎ *Balkan lore: melons kept 10 days after Christmas turn to vampire fruit.* ◎

GENERAL BROOM HANDLING

Self-explanatory really. All you need is a broom.

1 The Australian broom game

I don't know how this game got its name, but it certainly passes the time. A group of players—each numbered—surround a nominated Broom Master who holds a broom upright on the floor by just his forefinger, hairy end up (hairy end of the broom, that is). He calls out a number, removing his finger at the same time. The player called tries to catch the broom before the hairy end hits the floor. If successful he returns to his place. If not he becomes Broom Master.

2 Broom stepping

This is good when there are three or four of you at loose ends. Hold the broom horizontally in front of you with both hands, level with your knees. Step over it, first with one foot, then with the other. Immediately reverse the moves so you are back in the starting position. Keep going and after a while you will begin to wish you had never been born. It is at this point that one of your feet will accidentally touch the broom and you will be out. The next person now takes over. If there are ladies playing, you can require the removal of an item of clothing each time a foot touches the broom. Dress in many layers and practice beforehand.

3 How to break a stick balanced on two wineglasses with a blow from a broom handle

First, push a pin into each end of a five-foot-long dowel rod. Rest the pins on two wineglasses positioned on the seats of two hard chairs. Lift the broom handle over your head as in the illustration and bring it down with an almighty wallop in the middle of the stick, which will break in two, leaving the wineglasses undamaged. This happens because the force of the blow smashes the stick before its energy has time to be transmitted to the glasses.

4 The ugly-finder

Hold a broom at the tip of its handle and move its bushy end slowly around the faces of your seated guests, stopping in front of some fellow who won't mind a bit of joshing. Say: "Guess what this is." When he shrugs, say: "It's an ugly finder, and guess what, it's working." Always gets a laugh. This piece of funny by-play works well before the next game.

5 The busy beadle's beastly broom

This ancient and annoying game is one of those that require players to catch on to some secret which all the others seem to know.

Seat people in a circle and have someone pass you the broom. Thump

it on the floor five times, saying: "Behold the busy beadle's beastly broom." Pass it to the left with instructions to that fellow to do and say exactly what you did and said. The secret is to receive the broom in the left hand and pass it to the right hand for the thumping business. Naturally enough most people take it in the right hand, and when anyone gets it wrong, those in the know yell: "Bogey bogey bogey! Bogey bogey bogey!" The game continues until everyone has caught on or stormed off in disgust.

6 LAMB TO THE SLAUGHTER

Fill a plastic bowl or cookie tin with water and hand a broom to a volunteer. Stand on a chair and explain that the air pressure is lower at ceiling level than at floor level. While people are sagely nodding in agreement, position the bowl against the ceiling and ask your victim to hold it in place with the broom. Once he's holding it independently, get down and leave him to it. It won't be long before his arms start aching and he begins to whimper. Never do this in your own place.

◎ *Only the feet of the Wicked Witch of the East are seen in* The Wizard of Oz. ◎

INVISIBLE INK WITHOUT FUSS

Round about 500 BC, during the Ionian Revolt, Histiaeus branded a secret message on the shaven head of a slave, dispatching him across enemy lines once his hair had re-grown. Presumably the note wasn't very urgent. In more recent times, finding it hard, no doubt, to write anything very meaningful on their own heads, prisoners of war settled on invisible ink as the best instrument for the clandestine message, using at various times both sweat and saliva. There are numerous recipes for invisible ink but I have tried to avoid those complicated formulas that demand such chemicals as phenolphthalein extract from crushed laxative pills, and potassium ferricyanide, and have stuck instead to things you might have lying around.

There are two main methods here for writing and revealing secret messages. The first depends on heat, the second on an acid-alkali reaction.

Required for heat-sensitive ink

- *A piece of white paper*
- *Lemon or onion juice*
- *A toothpick or matchstick*
- *An iron*

Method

1. Juice a lemon or cut an onion in half. Dip your matchstick in the juice and carefully write your message on the paper. If you like, you can use your finger but this will require a huge piece of paper, presenting problems if your fellow spy has to swallow the message after reading it.
2. Once the ink is dry (be patient), the paper will appear blank and can be overwritten, though some practice is required.
3. When you heat the paper on a radiator, over a 100-watt lightbulb or with an iron, the juices "cook" causing the words to appear faintly in brown.

Required for chemical reaction ink

- *A piece of white paper*
- *White vinegar*
- *Bicarbonate of soda*
- *Half a red cabbage*
- *A toothpick or matchstick*
- *A small brush*

Method

1. Dip your match into a pickle jar containing white vinegar and write your message as before, allowing the paper to dry properly.
2. While it is drying, prepare an "indicator fluid" by boiling half a

red cabbage in $1\frac{1}{2}$ pints of water. This indicator works by changing color depending on the acidity or alkalinity of your ink.

3 Discard the cabbage, and paint the juice over your secret message. Because it is acid, the writing will turn pink.

For an alkali ink, use a 50/50 solution of water and bicarbonate of soda. The indicator will reveal your message by turning it blueish.

◎ *Early inks were made of soot and linseed oil.* ◎

HOW TO
MAKE A SIMPLE GLOVE PUPPET

Making a glove puppet is one of those things that demands patience. But it is a rewarding exercise and worth all the bother.

REQUIRED

- *A lump of modeling clay*
- *An old newspaper*
- *A kitchen roll or toilet roll*
- *Fine sandpaper*
- *Wallpaper paste*
- *Vaseline*
- *A very sharp knife*
- *Water-based paints*
- *A piece of thin fabric*
- *Water-based glue*

METHOD

1 The first thing to do is to make a head from clay. Take a lump about the size of a large orange and begin to mold it. You don't need to be artistic; even a dolt can fashion a roundish lump with blobs for a nose and chin, and a mouth of some kind. Spoon out

two eye sockets and roll yourself a couple of eyeballs. Insert these into the holes and overlay some eyelids. Try to imbue the face with character. Round cheeks and a smiling mouth look happy. A downward pointing mouth on a thin face looks sad or sinister. You can add ears, if you like. Either leave the head bald, or model the hair in clay. And don't forget the neck—you will need it for attaching your puppet's head to the body.

2 Leave the features bold and exaggerated, and don't try to make the proportions realistic. This will add to the expressive quality of your puppet. When you have the features roughly finished, smooth them down with the end of a spoon.

3 After finishing modeling the head, mix up a packet of wallpaper paste and tear a few sheets of kitchen roll into strips. Coat your head in Vaseline (the clay head, I mean), dip the strips in the paste, and lay them all over it. With a small stiff brush, push the paper around contours, up nostrils, and so on. Cover the head in five layers of the tissue paper, making sure there's plenty of paste. Finish with two layers of newspaper, in pieces about the size of postage stamps. While still wet, go over the features with a sharp tool to emphasize the detail, some of which will have been lost.

4 Put the head on a plate, take the cat out of the airing cupboard, and leave your head in there for a few days until it is thoroughly dry.

5 Remove the paper from the clay in two halves by cutting around the head from ear to ear with a razor-sharp knife. Scrape out all the clay and reassemble the shell, sealing the join with two or three layers of paper strips. Allow these to dry thoroughly.

6 When the head is dry, give it a bit of a sand with some fine sandpaper, to smooth out any creases and folds. Then it is time to paint the face, which is fun. Make the features bold, not subtle, using water-based paints mixed with a little glue. This helps to stop the paint coming off when dry. You can also use dilute glue as a protective varnish when you have finished.

7 If your character is bald, you can now add hair. String, wool, fur, and theatrical crepe hair are all successful, but plenty of glue is required to get the stuff to stick. An alternative is to make a hat for your puppet.

8 To construct the simplest of bodies, cut two T-shaped pieces of material and glue them together around the edges with a neck hole in the middle, and an opening for your hand. Glue in the head and put cardboard hands at the ends of the arms. A ghost or Roman senator is the work of a minute with a piece of old sheet. Or you can make something much more elaborate. It's up to you.

◎ *Comedian Jon Stewart once worked as a puppeteer.* ◎

THE COMPLEAT SECRET AGENT

One of the most important things for a spy to do is not get caught spying. In his book *My Silent War*, British agent Kim Philby describes a number of professional countersurveillance techniques that his Soviet spymasters had trained him to use whenever he had to go to a secret meeting with one of his handlers. These techniques might best be described as painfully obvious. They include the following:

- Making sure you are the *last person* to get on the train.
- Frequent use of the "having a good look around to see if you are being followed" technique.
- Plausible "reason for being where you are" activities, e.g., buying a hat.
- Wandering around a lot, getting on and off buses, accompanied by supplementary use of the "having a good look around to see if you are being followed" technique.
- The "movie theater trick," that is, taking a seat in the back row and slipping out in the middle of the show.

- Meeting your contact in a noisy restaurant with piped music in the booths.

It turns out, almost incredibly, that Philby's techniques are still the basis of spy tradecraft. In addition to the points above, the good secret agent should remember the following.

Letters

Of course, a suspected agent is going to have his letters opened. The simplest countermeasure is to ask your correspondents to tape down the edges of the envelopes in which they send their secret messages, and sign across the tape with an indelible pen. It's crude, but effective.

If you wish to get into a sealed envelope yourself, do not steam it open. Instead, insert a long pencil into the gap at the top of the flap and poke it out the other side. If you now put the envelope facedown on the table, flap toward you, and roll the pencil away from yourself, the gummed part will be detached without tearing. You can then read the letter, put it back, and seal it up again and nobody will be any the wiser.

When preparing covert messages wear gloves, and don't lick the envelope or stamps. DNA is a dead giveaway. Post your secret letters from distant locations.

Using code

The most versatile and secure code is the onetime pad. (For details, see page 192; for invisible ink, see page 185.)

Be unpredictable

- Vary your behavior and integrate your clandestine activities into your life, so that routine surveillance becomes more difficult.
- Use public transportation and buy "rover" tickets or get one for a destination several stops beyond your own. Go out suddenly for long drives and visit strange towns on a whim. Talk to strangers all the time.

- Security cameras monitor almost everything we do these days so avoid secret meetings in streets and parks or on public transportation. Busy pubs, cafés, and restaurants are a better bet.

Alerting your contact

If you need to communicate with a contact in a hurry, why not do what Woodward and Bernstein did during their Watergate investigation? Put a red flag in a flowerpot on your windowsill so that Deep Throat knows you need to talk to him.

Using money

Always use cash; never pay by credit card, and don't withdraw money from a machine if you are somewhere you are not supposed to be.

Using phones

Use pay phones whenever possible and keep your cell phone turned off when you travel, or ask someone else to carry it around and use it occasionally to create an alibi trail. Use pay-as-you-go, and change the handset and phone number often.

Using the Internet

Use cyber cafés or public libraries and keep up a variety of disposable names and addresses. Messages for your contacts can be left on obscure message boards.

Intruder detection

There are a number of steps you can take to reveal whether someone has been in your room. The simplest is the match trick. To do this, close the door as normal, but just before it shuts insert the end of a matchstick between door and jamb low down on the hinge side. Once the door is closed the match is held securely and you can snap it off so that its end is held invisibly. When you return, the stump will be on the floor if the door has been opened.

◎ Get Smart *was created by Mel Brooks and Buck Henry.* ◎

MAKING AND USING A ONETIME PAD (OTP)

The onetime pad is a simple, versatile, and theoretically unbreakable encryption tool ideal for short messages between two people. It was the favored device of Soviet spies based in Britain after the Second World War, and, being flexible and quick, was also used for the encryption of messages sent over the hotline between the White House and the Kremlin during the Cold War. It is tremendous fun and works with nothing more than a pencil and paper, and some basic arithmetic.

Making an OTP

The quickest way to make a onetime pad is to put 26 letter tiles from a Scrabble set—one for each letter—into a big jar and give them a good shake. Now remove a tile and jot down the letter, return it to the jar and repeat the process until you have a sequence of letters, enough for a short message—let's say 50 words. If you get the same letter more than once jot it down anyway. This process is reliably random.

Write the letters in key-string groups of five (for convenience) arranged in columns on two sheets of paper (you can use carbonless copy paper if you like). Now mark the pair of sheets with the same serial number. One sheet is for the sender, the other for the receiver. The number of pages you create for your pad will depend on the number of messages you expect to send and receive. For professional use, very small, thick, sometimes edible booklets were made up.

Encryption

To encode your message, you must systematically combine each character with the randomly generated letters from the top page of your onetime pad. The page must be used once only and both key sheets (sender's and receiver's) must be destroyed immediately after use.

EXERCISE

Constructing the code is simple. First give every letter a numerical value. A = 0, B = 1, all the way up to Z = 25 (not 26, you started with 0 not 1). Jot these down.

Suppose you wish to send your handler the message "HI BUD." What you do first is add the numbers of each of the letters of your message, together with numbers of the letters in the key to get a new number for each letter. So, if your first key string is WLBJK and your message is "HI BUD," the encryption is done as follows:

Key	22 (W)	11 (L)	1 (B)	9 (J)	10 (K)
Message	7 (H)	8 (I)	1 (B)	20 (U)	3 (D)
Key plus message	29	19	2	29	13

If a total for a column is larger than 25, you must subtract 26. In this example your first total, from the addition of the key-letter number (22) and the message-letter number (7), is 29. Subtract 26 and you get 3. Do the same with your fourth total (by chance, 29 again), and you get 3. Your final string of five numbers, together with their appropriate letter in brackets, is therefore 3 (D), 19 (T), 2 (C), 3 (D), and 13 (N). So this is the message you send: DTCDN. Don't forget to transmit with the text the serial number of the key page or your message will be impossible to decipher.

When he receives your message, your contact uses the key page with the matching serial number from his pad and reverses the process to decipher the text. He subtracts the key WLBJK from the coded message DTCDN, and adds 26 to the negative numbers.

Coded message received	(D) 3	(T) 19	(C) 2	(D) 3	(N) 13
Key	(W) 22	(L) 11	(B) 1	(J) 9	(K) 10
Coded message minus key	-19	8	1	-6	3
After adding 26 to negatives	7 (H)	8 (I)	1 (B)	20 (U)	3(D)

Try it yourself.

◎ *There are more than 60 million copies of* The Da Vinci Code *in print.* ◎

HOW TO
MAKE A GLASS HARMONICA

Benjamin Franklin obviously had too much time on his hands, because in 1761, while at a loose end, presumably, he invented the glass harmonica. This was a relatively complicated contraption that elicited music from a series of wineglasses. You can make your own, simpler version if you have eight small wineglasses to hand. I once heard a remarkable impromptu glass harmonica version of "Under Paris Skies" performed in a students' union bar by a wild-food scientist and his typographer assistant.

Required

- *8 small wineglasses*
- *Water*
- *Your fingers*

Method

The first thing you must do is learn to make the glasses ring. You achieve this by wetting your second finger and rubbing it smoothly around the rim.

To practice, half fill a glass and hold its foot with your left finger and thumb. Then dip your right middle finger into the water and rub it around the circumference, quickly and firmly. There's a knack to it but it shouldn't take you long to produce a sound. It's surprisingly loud and because there's no fundamental note there—just the harmonics—it has an ethereal quality. The technique is a bit like bicycle riding—once you've learned to do it, you hardly ever fall off.

When you have gained a bit of confidence, line up eight glasses and fill them carefully with varying amounts of water. This will give each a different pitch. The less water, the higher the note. Glasses vary in their properties so quite a lot of pouring in and out is required, but with eight glasses your first is usually nearly empty and your last nearly full. Tune them against pitch pipes, or a guitar or something, to make a major scale.

Practice a simple and slow tune, such as "Twinkle twinkle, little star" (see below). If you're one of those people who are bad with props, you might prefer to hit the glasses with a pencil. It's easier but not quite as impressive.

Do a bit of practice away from other people before you perform. It requires a strong constitution to listen to "The flight of the bumblebee" being incessantly butchered on a set of wineglasses.

Your first tune

Label your glasses 1 to 8, starting on the left with the lowest note. You can now use the numbers under the words below to play a famous tune.

Twinkle twinkle little star
| | | | | | |
1   1 5   5 6 6 5

How I wonder what you are
| | | | | | |
4   4 3 3 2   2 1

Up above the world so high
| || | | | |
5 54   4 3   3 2

Like a diamond in the sky
| | | | | | |
5   5 4 4   3 3 2

Twinkle twinkle little star
| | | | | | |
1   1 5   5 6 6 5

How I wonder what you are
| | | | | | |
4   4 3 3 2   2 1

◎ *Benjamin Franklin invented bifocals.* ◎

HOW TO
MAKE A CARTESIAN DIVER

René Descartes was famous for pretending he could prove he existed by saying: "I think, therefore I am." Bertrand Russell remarked that he had obviously got into an oven with his ideas and come out when they were only half baked. How this philosopher's name ever got attached to the Cartesian diver I don't know.

The Cartesian diver is one of those amusements that crop up in Victorian science books with endless pages of instructions involving semipermeable bladders, French retorts, alembics, and permanganate of potash. This is my own *quick* method for making one.

Required

- *A 2-liter plastic soda bottle*
- *A glass of water*
- *An eyedropper*

Method

1. Fill the plastic bottle with cold water, leaving a couple of inches of air space.
2. Empty the eyedropper of any residual oil.
3. To test the buoyancy of your eyedropper, put it into the glass of water. You want your diver to float upright, but he will probably lie drowned-man style. If he does, you must increase his weight by sucking a little water into the dropper. It shouldn't take you long to adjust matters so that he bobs on the surface in an upright position.
4. Transfer your diver into the bottle and screw on the cap. He will float there looking like a man wearing a derby hat, the crown visible just above the surface.
5. Squeeze the shoulders of the bottle. Alert physics students will tell you that although you can compress air, you cannot compress a

liquid—which is why brake cables are full of it. So when you squeeze the bottle, the air is squashed up a bit but, because the water can't be compressed, a small amount of it will instead be forced into the dropper making it slightly heavier. And it will sink.

You'll find that you can control the diver's rate of descent—and ascent—by varying the force of your squeeze.

You could probably work out a funny story, for when you show this to your friends.

◎ *Peter the Great of Russia was obsessed with dwarfs.* ◎

THE BRUSSELS SPROUT ON THE SHEET

Of the 1,001 party games that have been devised over the years, the Brussels sprout on the sheet is one of the most enjoyable and exhilarating. The rules are simple, the props always at hand, and any number above three can play. The game is suitable for children or childish grown-ups.

- Clear a big space and get two teams of around four or five to line up opposite each other. Hand out a laundered sheet and instruct everyone to grasp the long edge nearest them. When they all have hold, and the sheet is hanging between the opposing players in a loose *U*, throw a sprout into the middle.
- The aim of the game is for each team to snap the sheet so that the Brussels sprout is sent flying over the heads of the opposition, thus scoring a point. It's a lot more difficult than it sounds, and also more vigorous. Be sure to clear away your Ming pots, and take the Rembrandts down.
- In an emergency, or for very muscular players, a Champagne cork or ping-pong ball may be substituted for the sprout.

- A referee is essential—that's you.

Born in Brussels, Audrey Hepburn spoke Dutch, Flemish, French, and Italian.

THE HOMEMADE ORCHESTRA

There is no reason world-famous maestros should be the only ones allowed to have orchestras at their disposal. If you've always fancied yourself as a conductor (Toscanini-style, not choo-choo), then here's your chance to shine.

Required

- *A comb and a bit of wax paper*
- *Some tuned milk bottles*
- *A cookie tin and a few utensils*
- *A watering can*
- *Spoons*
- *A ruler*
- *A vacuum*
- *An empty wastepaper basket*
- *A few "musicians"*

Method

- Fill and tune your milk bottles à la the glass harmonica, described on page 194, then assign the instruments to the performers. Your melody instruments are the comb-and-paper, milk bottles (hit with a stick or spoon), and the watering can.
- The comb-and-paper is played by loosely wrapping the paper around the comb and humming against its teeth until a high, kazoo-like sound is produced.
- The watering can requires only a bilabial trill (raspberry) to be blown against its spout hole to produce a resonating mezzo forte baritone warble.

- Your percussion section consists of the cookie tin and the wastepaper basket, which may be struck with whisks, fingers, sticks, or a handful of dry spaghetti (for a "brushes" effect). And the spoons are played of course in the usual way, against the thigh.
- Special effects are possible with the vacuum (try blowing down the long tube) and the ruler, which makes a pleasing glissando *boing* when held against a tabletop at one end and twanged.
- The best way to perform is to play along to a record. In this way you can, with hardly any practice, give a performance that wouldn't discredit the London Philharmonic Orchestra. But make sure that pets are locked up.

◎ *"Karaoke" stems from the Japanese words for "empty" and "orchestra."* ◎

A RECORD-BEATING PAPER AIRPLANE IN A JIFFY

There is a balance to be struck between making a paper plane that can reliably transmit an illegal message such as "meet 4 cig behind bike sheds @ recess?" across the classroom, and one that will win a prize for speed, distance, or elegance.

The one described here beats all records for reliability. It is swift of flight, quick to make (with easy-to-remember folds) and robust. A dent in its nose will do little to mar its effectiveness.

Method

1. Take a sheet of paper and crease it once lengthwise (fig. 1).
2. Open it out and fold corners A and B against the crease, to form a point at the top of the sheet (fig. 2).
3. Turn the paper horizontally, its point to the left, and fold up the diagonal crease at the bottom so that it lies along the centerfold. The centerfold is to become your airplane's belly.

4 Mirror the action with the topmost diagonal (fig. 3).
5 You should now be looking at something definitely dart-like.
6 Close the paper along the centerfold, ending with the diagonal at the top.
7 Fold the top-right corner down so that it lies exactly over the bottom corner, and make a horizontal crease along the paper, parallel to the plane's belly (fig. 4).
8 Turn it over and do the same on the other side.
9 Finally, unbend the wings you have just made, so that they form an angle of 90 degrees with the body of the aircraft (fig. 5).

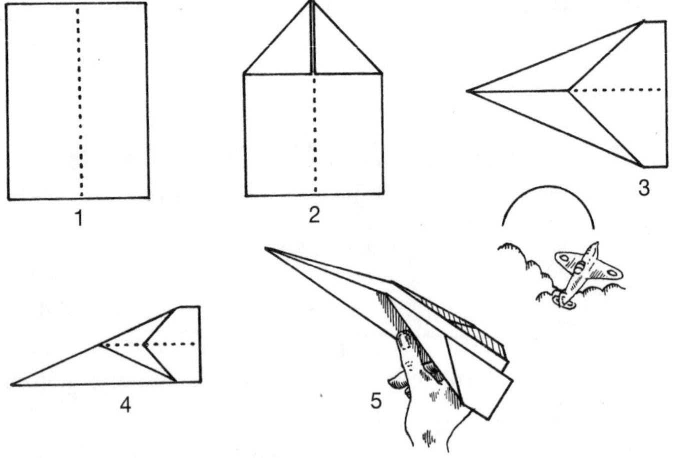

Launch

After launch the plane's flight is ballistic (powered only by gravity), so aim it high. It will remain stable even in a breeze—something that cannot be said of all paper aircraft.

◎ *Most air crashes happen during takeoff, climb, descent, or landing.* ◎

SOME UNUSUAL THINGS TO DO WITH A BALLOON

THE NEWSREADER'S HEADPHONES

Blow up a balloon, holding the opening of two paper cups against it on either side as you do so. The balloon will expand into the cups, making a firm seal, such that once you've tied it off, you can easily hold them suspended. It cuts down on the swearing if you can get someone to help you. If you draw a face on one side of the balloon with an indelible pen, you can make it look like a man wearing headphones. Say: "Here is the news and this is Walter Cronkite." Some (old) people may laugh.

THE PHANTOM "SCROTUM"

Inflate a balloon and allow it to subside three or four times until it goes all slack and wrinkly, then half fill it with tepid water and tie it off. Drop this sinister object into the pocket of the best man's jacket before his speech at some wedding or other. When, during his peroration, he idly slips his hand into his pocket his face will assume a fixed smile of disgust that's hard to reproduce.

THE ANTI-GRAVITY BALLOON

Rub an inflated balloon against your hair to produce a static charge. Hold it (the balloon) to the ceiling for a moment and when you let go it will cling there for ages. Children love this one.

THE "SOFT" NEEDLE

I first saw this trick described on a cereal box, and though it often crops up in books of beginners' tricks it is seldom performed. This is a waste, since it is highly mysterious.

1 Display two identical inflated balloons and hand one to a spectator.
2 Next, show him two needles and ask him to take either one. "I'm

glad you took *that* one," you say. "It's the *sharp* needle. You've left me the soft one—watch."

3 You now push your needle into the balloon, leaving it sticking out. When your spectator tries to do the same he bursts his balloon.

The secret is to put a square of Scotch tape secretly on to the side of your balloon before you start. Stick the needle into the tape and it will prevent the balloon from popping. It's a surprising trick.

Finish by displaying your balloon on the needle and burst it with your assistant's needle, thus getting rid of the evidence.

Martian invasion

Inflate a long, thin, green balloon and poke it through your neighbor's mail slot, shouting: "Look out! The Martians have landed." Thanks to Ken Dodd for this joke.

◎ *The Montgolfier brothers launched the first hot air balloon in 1783.* ◎

MAKE YOUR OWN BAROMETER

We all live at the bottom of a sea of air, and it presses down on us. You can demonstrate this by making a barometer.

Required

- *A straight-sided glass*
- *Masking tape*
- *A marker*
- *A plastic drinking straw*
- *Food coloring (optional)*
- *Chewing gum*

METHOD

1 Start chewing the gum.
2 Tape the straw inside the glass with its end about half an inch above the bottom.
3 Half fill the glass with water and stir in some food coloring.
4 Suck some water into the straw and when it's between the surface of the water and the top of the straw stop it by pinching the end. Make a permanent seal with the gum.
5 Mark the water level in the straw on a vertical strip of tape on the outside of the glass.
6 Carry your barometer up a local hill or, even better, take it into an elevator in a tall building and mark the changing water level as you go up and down.

It works because there is less air pressing the water into the straw when you are higher up, and more when you are lower down.

You can forecast the weather by leaving your barometer on a dark shelf. A fall in pressure (less water in the straw) presages wind and rain. Higher pressure and more water in the straw mean fair weather. Sometimes. It's not infallible. But it's about as reliable as that awful weather forecaster on the TV.

◎ *"When smoke descends, good weather ends": meteorological folk saying.* ◎

THE BEAST WITH FOUR FINGERS

Here's a quickie for frosty mornings. Secretly extract one of your digits from the finger (or thumb) of your glove and curl it into your palm. Extend the remaining digits and arrange the glove so that it looks normal. Now challenge your companion to say which finger doesn't contain a finger (if you see what I mean). It's very tricky.

By holding the fingers or thumb in an unusual angle, it is possible for accomplished players to fool the sharpest-eyed observer, who will usually plump for the "funny-looking" one.

You are allowed to bluff, by not removing any digits, or by removing two, three or more, to confuse things further.

This is a great game to play with philosophy students, whom you can bring back to earth with a thud.

◎ *Medical gloves (made from sheep's intestines) were first used in 1758.* ◎

HOW TO
MAKE A SWIMMING PAPER FISH

This charming diversion is just the trick if you find yourself suddenly surrounded by red-faced children who are looking for something expensive to break. If you sell it properly, everyone will soon be sitting quietly drawing and coloring and cutting.

Required

- *Paper*
- *Scissors*
- *A can of 3-in-1 oil*
- *A long shallow dish*

On a piece of ordinary writing paper, draw a fish like the one in the picture below. It should be about two inches in length. If you have young children helping you, you can spend some time getting them to draw and color fishes in competition with each other. An important element is the black circle in the middle connected to the tail by a black line.

Cut out the fish, including the circle and black line. Fill the dish with water and drop the fish carefully on to the surface, with its tail not too far from the edge, making sure that the top of the fish stays dry.

Now comes the magic part. Take the oil can and let a drop of oil fall into the hole in the middle of the fish. The oil will try to expand across the surface of the water. The quickest way for it to do this is to spread down the channel and out at the tail. As it does so the paper springs in the opposite direction, shooting rather quickly across the water. Everybody will be amazed.

◎ *Top oil-producing countries: Saudi Arabia, Russia, USA, Iran, China.* ◎

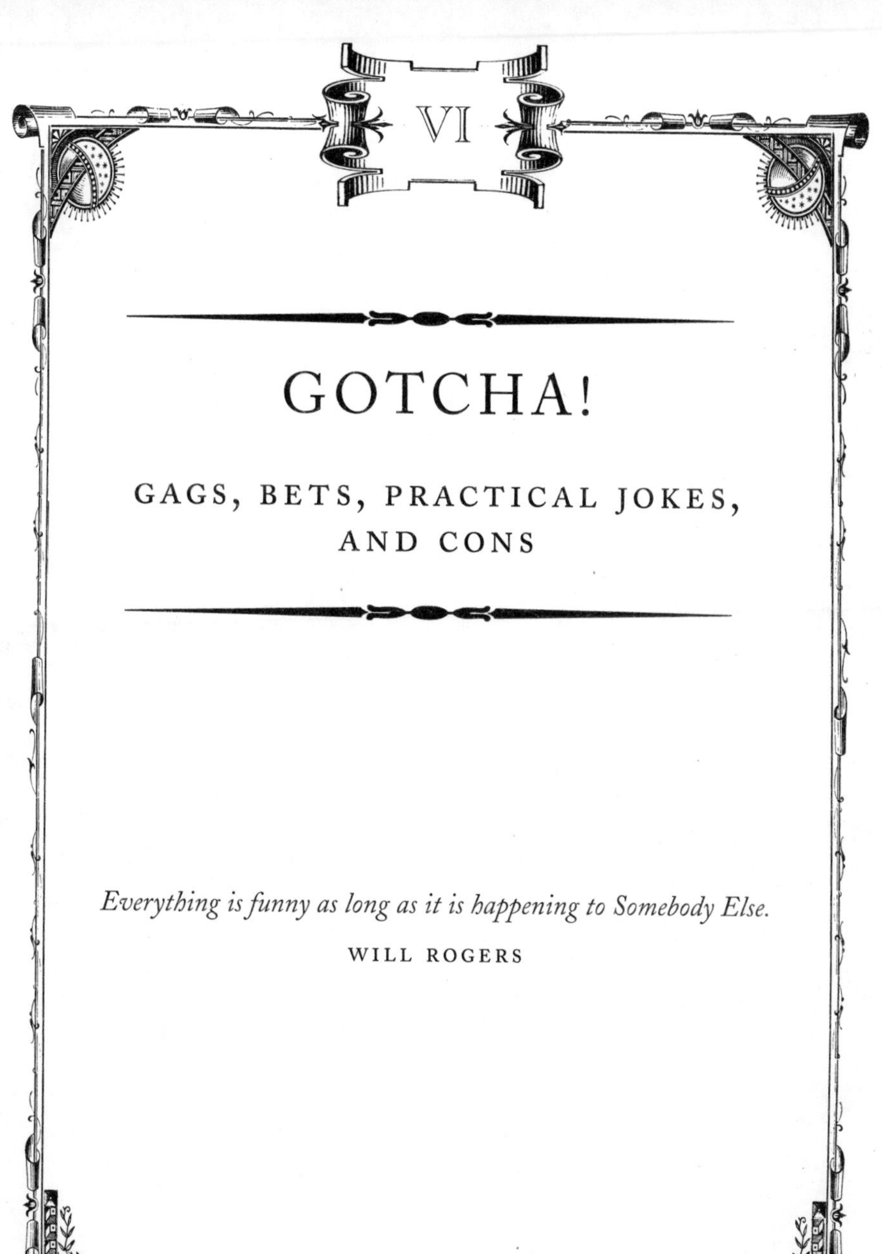

VI

GOTCHA!

GAGS, BETS, PRACTICAL JOKES, AND CONS

Everything is funny as long as it is happening to Somebody Else.

WILL ROGERS

THE EIGHT-INCH BEDQUAKE

Just imagine the effect: you've had a few beers with your buddies and retired happily to bed, where you've been sleeping the sleep of Rip Van Winkle. All of a sudden, a gigantic ogre shakes the world, the sky falls on your head, and your bed seems to crash to the floor with the noise of a thousand barrels rumbling down a grand staircase. As you sit up with a cry of "Wassamarrer?" and your heart in your mouth you notice that though the room is quiet and the door shut, your bed is at a crazy angle to the wall and the duvet has been thrown off violently. There is no sign of anyone about, but in the corner of the room, spinning eerily, are a couple of beer bottles. At this point you wish you had said your prayers when you were a child, and vow to give up your dissolute ways—starting tomorrow.

Although you don't know it, you have been the victim of "The eight-inch bedquake." This fiendish prank is especially suited to dorm rooms and sketchy hotels where a group of friends are staying for Spring Break. Here's how to accomplish it.

1. First identify your victim—often he will be self-selecting. You are looking for someone who has drunk enough to make himself sleepy but not so much that he won't wake up during the upheaval you are planning.
2. When the fellow has gone to bed, give him time to fall asleep and then go to his room with your accomplices (at least four strong men), taking along your apparatus—four empty beer bottles.
3. Once there you must work quickly and quietly, commando-style. Without rousing your victim, the four strongest of you lift the bed while the smallest and most agile carefully places an upright beer bottle under each bed leg. On his whispered command, you gently lower the bed on to the bottles and make your escape, closing the door softly behind you.

It's now just a question of when. At some indeterminate moment, as the poor chap turns over or shifts his weight, the bed will be flung with an almighty smash eight inches to the floor, firing bottles in every direction. This always produces a pleasingly musical effect, somewhat akin to a desk being thrown into the percussion section of an orchestra.

Rudely awakened in dark and unfamiliar surroundings, and aware only that the Last Judgment appears close at hand, even the most abstract thinker will be hard-pressed to work out what the hell has happened to him. Don't let on.

◎ *Ducks on the outer edges of a group sleep with one eye open. The rest shut both.* ◎

CLASSIC PRACTICAL JOKES

William Horace de Vere Cole (1881–1936) was the brother-in-law of Neville Chamberlain. He was also a notorious prankster, possessing the three essential personality traits of the successful practical joker: wild anarchism, utter fearlessness, and breathtaking opportunistic flair. A wealthy and well-connected aristocrat, Horace Cole delighted in embarrassing his famous friends by suddenly collapsing on the London pavement in a mock epileptic fit or having one of them publicly arrested for stealing a watch he had planted on him. Coming across some workmen one day, Cole directed them with great authority to excavate a gigantic trench in Piccadilly Circus while a helpful policeman redirected the traffic.

Here is one of Cole's best and simplest ideas—"The ball of string"—along with a few other classic tricks that you might like to adapt to suit yourself.

The ball of string

1 Get yourself a clipboard. A hard hat and high-visibility vest lend added authority, but aren't absolutely necessary.

2 Approach a mild-mannered gentleman on the corner of a busy

shopping thoroughfare and hand him the end of a ball of twine, asking him to please hold it for a moment.

3 Disappear around the corner, unwinding the string as you go.

4 Walk a fair distance and approach another friendly-looking person—nuns are good. Cut the twine and ask your victim if she will kindly hang on to the end while you get your "stramulator" from the van.

5 Stride off, ditch clipboard and costume, and creep back at a distance to watch developments.

People are astonishingly patient but after a time one of your suckers will follow the twine in search of you. It is enjoyable to witness the confusion on victims' faces as they meet, each brandishing one end of the same piece of string.

The fried egg in the pocket

This is best for formal occasions when people are dressed up, and the darkness of a concert hall or theater can help disguise your actions.

1 Fry a few eggs until they are well done—no soft yolks.

2 Cut the top off a thick zip-top bag so that it just fits into your side pocket and carefully drop two or three of the eggs sideways into the bag.

3 Once at your destination, sidle surreptitiously up behind a fancy-looking fellow and quietly slip an egg into the pocket of his dinner jacket.

4 This works with ladies' handbags too. The thunderstruck expressions as your anonymous gifts are discovered are gratifying.

The eternal thread

You need to be a jacket wearer for this to work.

1 Poke a broken pencil through the middle of a reel of white thread and wedge this into the inside pocket of your jacket so that it holds the reel and allows it to rotate freely.

2 Once it's secure in the pocket, draw out the thread and thread it on a needle. Poke this through the lining of your jacket at a point high on the shoulder.
3 Pull 4 or 5 inches through and take the needle off.

You now have what looks like a loose white thread on your jacket and people will be trying to pluck it off all day. When they do, yards of thread unwind embarrassingly.

The burst snowman

1 Fill a large manila envelope with shaving cream.
2 Slide the open end under the locked bedroom door of a good friend and stamp on the fat part. There's only one way the foam can go, and it does. Everything will be covered.

The gag should be done shortly before your victim gets back from wherever he's gone, so that the foam doesn't melt away or, alternatively, harden. Working out quite how that shaving cream got through the locked door will present your victim with a delightful puzzle.

The wet sneeze

You can perform this simple and disgusting practical joke for a friend or for someone you don't know. But if you do it for a stranger, have a friend with you.

1 Dip your fingers into a glass of water and walk up quietly behind your mark.
2 Make a loud gurgling-sneeze noise, at the same time flicking the water against your victim's neck.
3 Run like hell.
4 For extra realism, put a little guacamole in your left hand. When your subject turns around to hit you, he'll find you licking it off. Offer your hand and ask: "Like some?"

The impromptu rifle

A more impressive impromptu apparatus would be hard to find. In a matter of seconds, using only a sheet of paper, you can make a device that produces a crack loud enough to wake the dead.

1 Fold a sheet in half lengthwise and then unfold it again (fig. 1). Fold in the four corners diagonally so they lie against the centerfold (fig. 2).

2

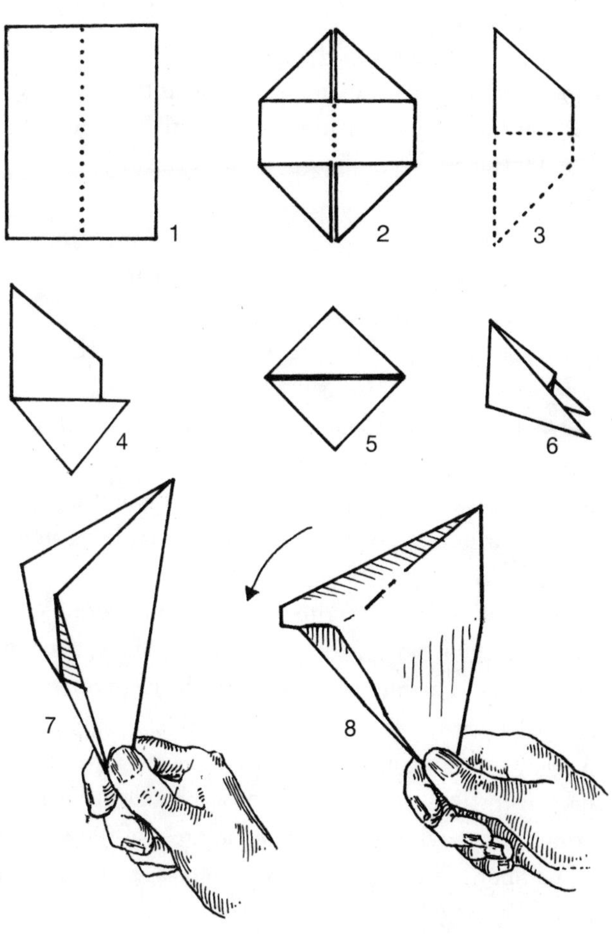

Making sure the points are pointing north and south, close the thing like a book and then fold the bottom point up against the top to make a horizontal crease. Unfold it again (fig. 3).

3 Fold the bottom half diagonally so its edge lies against the horizontal centerfold (fig. 4). Do the same with the top. You should now be looking at a diagonal square (fig. 5). Turn the whole thing over north to south and fold the bottom half up, to make a triangle (fig. 6).

4 Grasp the right corner, thumb on the bottom, first finger on top, and lift the apparatus vertically, with the slightly open corner pointing away from you (fig. 7).

5 Now, with a whip-cracking action, snap the contraption forward through the air and the interior flap will pop out with a clap like thunder (fig. 8).

The left leg

1 Get hold of a mannequin's leg (look, you are a responsible person who can sort out this kind of thing for yourself).

2 Put a sock and shoe on the end and secrete the leg under your coat—a long one, obviously.

3 Leave it in a movie theater, train, the lobby of a corporation or TV company, restaurant, pub, office building, and so on, then go back and claim it later. Ask, "Have you got the left leg I left?" It produces enormous amounts of fun and wastes long hours of people's valuable time.

- A good variation is to write the phone number of a local massage parlor on the inside of the thigh with indelible pen, and leave it in the back of a church. This causes the clergyman extra embarrassment.
- A lively sounding alternative, which I have never tried, is to pack some fish sticks into the leg and attach an official-looking printed label, with the name and address of some disagreeable acquaintance, along with the bold message: "REWARD! RETURN TO OWNER IMMEDIATELY."

BEN'S BREAD BOMB

1 Take a large, white, unsliced loaf and soak it overnight in a plastic bread bin, or sink full of water, making sure that the plug fits tight. In the morning the bread will have swollen grotesquely, having absorbed every last drop of liquid.
2 Carefully lift it out, carry it like a baby to a high window, and throw it down on to the pavement, where it will burst with a noise like someone doing a belly flop into a vat of custard, splattering white goo in every direction. It is possible to cover a whole sports car in this way.

THE AIR FORCE TEST-PILOTS TEST

This trick has been played on trainee waiters since the dawn of time.

1 Choose a self-important person from a group and explain that hand-eye coordination has been shown to be a sign of high intelligence. Tell him that Air Force test pilots have to pass the following test before they are allowed to fly.
2 Ask him to extend his hands in front of him, palms down, and tell him to keep them as still as he possibly can.
3 Now position a pint of beer on the extended fingers of each hand and explain that the test requires him to remove the glasses without soaking himself. Move away quickly.
4 With a straw in your top pocket and use of your teeth, it is possible to escape from this predicament. But it's touch and go.

PUTTING A POTATO IN A LADY'S HANDBAG

This trick works with any vegetable or fruit, including eggplants.

1 Conceal on your person a large potato, turnip, avocado, or banana.
2 When you're out with people in a dark concert hall, cloakroom, car, or dimly lit pub, choose your target. You are going to introduce your foreign object into her handbag, coat pocket, or glove compartment.

3 When you are satisfied that conditions are right, do the business. Don't be furtive about it—be bold.

Provided you do it early enough in the evening, you'll be able to enjoy her openmouthed astonishment as she reaches for her cigarette lighter, lipstick, or keys, and finds a turnip or kumquats. Don't let on that it was anything to do with you.

◎ *Ace prankster Alan Abel once called himself Stoidi Puekaw. Turn it around.* ◎

HOW TO
FLOAT AN EGG

Give your victim a glass of water and challenge him to choose an egg and float it on the surface. Demonstrate, using another egg and your own glass of water.

When your subject tries, he will fail. There's nothing wrong with the eggs: it's your water, which you have heavily salted beforehand, so that it's much denser.

◎ *The world's largest omelette was made in Madrid, using 5,000 eggs.* ◎

HOW TO
EAT A GOLDFISH

These days, people will do anything to get on TV but in the golden age of prehistoric television, things were less brash. There was a famous program then, full of innocent mischief, in which unsuspecting members of the public were secretly filmed having their legs gently pulled.

One of the most charming of those mild early-day gags was a stunt in which a man dipped his hand into a bowl of goldfish on a shop counter. Lifting one out, dripping and flapping, he ate it, to the disgust and outrage of the bystanders. Here's how to do it.

Required

- *A big carrot*

Preparation

If you know a doctor's office or somebody's house where there is a tank or bowl of goldfish, this is the trick for you.

- Get yourself a big carrot and, with a sharp knife, cut a thin oblong slice from the middle.
- Place this flat on the table and carefully cut out a goldfish-shaped silhouette. It's worth consulting a book to get an accurate profile. Make your "fish" as big as you reasonably can so that it will be easily visible.
- The next stage in the process has never been revealed before, as far as I am aware. You must soften the carrot by cooking it for a short time. You don't want to boil it to a mush but you do want to make it more flexible than it is when raw. Experiment with a few prototypes. When you have it right your "fish" will be quite flexible and you will be able to imbue it with life by holding its tail and shaking it a little. Drops of water will fly off and it will flap in a chillingly lifelike way.

Performance

- Secrete the carrot-fish in your palm and wander over to the tank or goldfish bowl. Create interest by staring intently into the water.
- When you have everybody's attention, quickly dip your closed hand into the water and withdraw it with the "fish" flapping between your fingers.
- Hold it by its tail so that everyone can see it fluttering for a moment and then pop it into your mouth. People's jaws will drop and now is the time to sell the trick by munching ostentatiously.

You can add a bit of color by taking a saltshaker from your pocket and sprinkling some on your catch before you eat it.

◎ *The climbing perch, a fish native to India, can walk on land.* ◎

NEVER ODD OR EVEN— THE PALINDROME CHALLENGE

A palindrome is a word or sentence that reads the same backward as forward. Coming up with a good one can be addictive, so it's the perfect distraction for those arid deserts of time during canceled flights, or while you're waiting to see the knee specialist.

Mom and *Otto* are palindromic words and *Ma is a nun, as I am* is a palindromic sentence. It's a challenge to make these sound tolerably convincing, especially if they are long. The following is 44 words long, but what can it possibly mean?

Do good? I? No! Evil anon I deliver. I maim nine more hero-men in Saginaw, sanitary sword a-tuck, Carol, I—lo!—rack, cut a drowsy rat in Aswan. I gas nine more hero-men in Miami. Reviled, I (Nona) live on. I do, O God!

British palindromist Leigh Mercer (1893–1977) was a master of the art. He was responsible not only for the apt: *Sums are not set as a test on Erasmus* and: *Straw? No, too stupid a fad; I put soot on warts*, but also for the beautiful: *A man, a plan, a canal—Panama!*

This is so good that it has spawned a number of waggish imitations, such as: *A man, a plan, a cat, a ham, a yak, a yam, a hat, a canal—Panama!* and the so-called near miss palindrome: *A man, a plan, a canal—Suez!*

The best palindromes tend to be short, like *Niagara, O roar again* or even *tit* and *boob*, and the economical narcoleptics' ditty gets a lot out of five little words.

We few,
We nap anew,
We nap and nap and nap anew.
We nap and nap and nap anew,
We nap anew,
We few.

So start thinking backward, and things like "Panama" being the mirror of "A man, a p" will soon start to leap out at you. You'll need a pencil and paper, of course, unless you're as brainy as Peter Hilton, who, during a lull in the breaking of the Enigma code in 1943, came up with the unusually long: *Doc, note, I dissent—a fast never prevents a fatness. I diet on cod.*

Here are some more palindromic classics to inspire your creativity.

- *Madam, I'm Adam*—The prelapsarian palindrome
- *Lewd did I live, & evil I did dwel*—John Taylor, 1614
- *Norma is as selfless as I am, Ron*—J. A. Lindon (another palindromist of the first order)
- *Draw pupil's lip upward*—Instruction to sadistic schoolmasters
- *Satan oscillate my metallic sonatas!*—For when you stub your toe, answering a wrong number at four in the morning

◎ *Finnish is the preeminent language for palindromes.* ◎

HOW TO

DEFORM YOUR NOSE—UNILATERALLY

Among the cleverest devices for imitating a broken nose or some lopsided nasal disfigurement, is the decapitated nipple of a baby's drinking bottle.

- To prepare your nose deformer, take the nipple and cut a small breathing hole in the very top with a pair of sharp nail scissors.
- Next, snip off the bulb and thrust it up your nostril of choice.
- Now comes the artistic bit: you must trim the excess. This won't take you long in front of a mirror with a pair of sharp scissors, but don't cut the pink thing—that's your nose.
- When you've finished, you will notice that your nostril is grotesquely distended. A smear of your girlfriend's skin-colored makeup, or a little fake blood will help disguise the mechanics and add nicely to the overall effect (*see* the blood recipe in Chapter 5).

Now all you have to do is sit on a park bench, and you will give everyone the absolute willies. Nobody ever asks what kind of horrible affliction you are suffering—that would be rude.

◎ *Jimmy Durante dropped out of school to be a full-time ragtime pianist.* ◎

THE COLD-BLOODED PAPER TEAR

Here's a great one for turning a victim's hair white. My friend Jed does this particularly well. You pick up what appears to be Grandpa's will, an original Picasso sketch, or some other paper document of value—and tear it in half. Though the joke lasts but a moment the look on your subject's face makes it very rewarding.

1. To practice, take a sheet of paper and suspend it in front of your face by one of the short edges. It should be held in the middle between the pinched thumb and first finger of each hand.
2. Imagine you are now going to tear it in half by pulling down and toward yourself with the right hand, while holding still with the left. If you actually do that now, you'll have the effect you are going to imitate.
3. But, instead of tearing the sheet, hold it firmly in the left hand, keeping right finger and thumb loosely pinched.
4. Quickly drag the nail of your first finger down the paper directly in front of your nose, at the same time making a sort of tearing-whooshing noise with your mouth, which is hidden from view.

The whole effect is horribly realistic for just a moment. Then your victim will realize what's happened and will either laugh or clock you with a glass ashtray—depending on his character.

◎ *It takes, on average, 17 trees to make 1 ton of paper.* ◎

THE TINKLING ESKIMO

Here's an amusingly vulgar effect for the Champagne bar or a church ladies' evening.

1 While nobody's looking grab a handful of ice cubes and hold them in your fist as secretly as you can, bearing in mind that they will quite quickly make your hand painfully cold, not to mention drip all over your pants.

2 At the appropriate moment, pick up an empty glass in your warm hand and say: "It must be a hard life being an Eskimo. Just imagine, you've got to empty your bladder, there's no toilet in the igloo, and it's a blizzard outside; you just have to take your courage in your hands and go for it."

3 You now stand up (if you were sitting) and lower the glass to the appropriate below-the-belt height, bringing your other hand over the vessel, in line with what I can only describe as your "gentleman's area."

4 Screw up your face, as if voiding into a -30 degrees F snowstorm, and make a whistling-blizzard sound through your teeth. With your cold hand in the garden-hose position, squeeze out the ice cubes in rapid succession, allowing them to tinkle into the glass, and say: "I've heard of a cold front but this is ridiculous."

◎ *In the summer, Eskimos live in tents, not igloos.* ◎

UNLOSABLE BETCHAS AND GOTCHAS

People are delighted to lose a bet if they are being entertained at the same time. Here are some bets you can't lose that will have them chuckling—even as they hand over their money.

THE GLASS MOUSETRAP

This ancient scam must be one of the easiest and most shameless ever. It is, nonetheless, seldom performed, for the simple reason that it's tricky to remember—especially if you were "tired" when you saw it done.

1 You need three glasses, which you place in a row on the table in front of you, the center glass mouth-down, the others mouth-up. In front of each glass, you place a nut, paper clip, olive, coin, or other suitable object.
2 When you're set, explain: "Look, I bet you can't catch these three mice under these three glass mousetraps in just two moves. To help you, I'll show you how it's done—watch."
3 You now lift glasses 1 and 2—one in each hand—and turn them both over, putting glass 1 over its mouse and replacing glass 2 (now mouth-up) in its original position *behind* its mouse. The glass mousetraps remain associated with their original mice throughout and can't hop about. You say: "One."
4 You then invert glasses 2 and 3, placing them both over their mice, saying: "Two." You have finished with each mouse under a mouth-down glass.
5 Once your victim grasps the rules, set up the glasses for him. It is at this point that the monkey business occurs.
6 What you appear to do is replace the glass mousetraps behind their mice in the start position, but what you really do is move all the glasses back but invert the middle glass so that it is *mouth-up*. This is the reverse of the original position where the middle glass

was *mouth-down*. No matter how hard your volunteer now tries, he cannot cover the mice without doing something that isn't allowed—even if he goes on all night.

The look on his face is wonderful to behold as he racks his brains and wonders what's gone wrong. Take the money and run.

The quick beer quaff

Your victim buys you both a round and, as your drinks arrive, you bet him $1 that you can drink his pint as well as yours before he can turn over five beer mats. Give him the mats to position wherever he likes. When he says go, you start drinking the beer, switching from glass to glass as he turns over the mats.

He will beat you hands down, but, as you finish the drinks, say, "Oh dear, I lose again," and pass him $1. At this point it will dawn on him that you've drunk his beer and done him out of a goodly sum. Tell him it's his round.

The impossible paper tear

Take a piece of paper and make two roughly vertical tears in it, about a third of the way from each end. These tears should finish a little short of the bottom edge. Now challenge some poor fool to hold the top corners A and B, and pull the sheet in three with a single tear.

I love this trick. It seems easy but is impossible. It's one of the many wonderful examples of the physics of the universe that I can't explain.

◎ *If you have 23 people in a room it's 50–50 that two will share a birthday.* ◎

HOW TO
POUR BEER INSIDE SOMEONE'S PANTS

You won't be able to pour beer inside a fellow's pants just by asking him nicely. Like all good confidence tricks, you must conceal your true purpose while persuading him to do some very odd things. You can accomplish this only by causing him to believe that there will be some sort of payoff at the end. Here's the way it works.

Method

1. First, secrete a plastic funnel behind a curtain close to a table in the school cafeteria, or at a busy wedding reception. Pool or dining tables are the ones to look out for.
2. Second, recruit three or four accomplices and brief them on their roles. Tell them they are to follow your instructions until you shout: "Knickerbocker Niagara!" At this point they must each pour the contents of their beer glasses into the funnel which your victim will have sticking out of his pants. They will probably object that nobody is going to stand there quietly while you push a funnel into his pants and pour beer into it. Tell them to wait and see.
3. Next, select a suitable subject for your prank. You are looking for one of those ghastly, competitive types who are very full of themselves. There is usually no shortage of this sort at parties or bars, so get one of your assistants to go over and lure him to the table, where the rest of you are chatting innocently.
4. As he arrives, you declare to the group: "So this is the deal: I will buy a drink for anyone who can lie on the table and hang on by just his heels while it's lifted off the floor at one end."
5. Your first enthusiastic stooge now bets you he can do it, and climbs into position. You instruct your friends to elevate the table at the foot end until it is at a very steep angle—almost vertical. Your plucky assistant has hooked his shoes over the end,

and is hanging on quite safely upside down, but will be unable to get down without hurting himself. After a round of applause, the table is lowered to the ground and there is much back slapping as you ostentatiously buy him a pint of beer. Another of your eager-beaver confederates says he'll try it too, and the stunt is repeated.

6 A crowd should have gathered by this time, and it is now that you encourage your mark to have a go, offering to hold his jacket and his drink. As he clambers up, do not allow your features to betray any feelings of self-satisfaction which you may be harboring, but instead offer him helpful advice. The table is again tilted, and, as it reaches its zenith, you call out: "Knickerbocker Niagara!" quickly inserting your plastic funnel into the bottom of one of the victim's pants legs.

7 One after the other, your assistants now decant their glasses and bottles into the funnel. There is no hurry, as the poor fellow is utterly helpless. It is tremendous fun to watch the variety of expressions that play across a guy's face as his pants fill up with beer. He will get good and wet and may start screaming blood-curdling threats. If he does, you'd be wise to make a quick exit, leaving your friends to do the explaining for you.

◎ *Average drying times: paper towel: 12 seconds, hot-air dryer: 43 seconds.* ◎

MASTER THE MOST FIENDISH TONGUE TWISTERS IN THE WORLD

The tongue twisters most people know are not particularly difficult. With a little practice almost everybody can manage "She sells seashells" or "Red leather, yellow leather." "The Leith police dismisseth us" is possibly the trickiest of the well-known ones.

Conversely, many an experienced newsreader has come a cropper with the simple-looking "Fog and frost," "Two United States twin-screw steel cruisers" or "The best West-Bankers on the West Bank." So if you can master a few hard ones, you'll be in the perfect position to impress train passengers and bored nephews with your fluency—not to mention all the bets you'll win down at the pub.

Commerce seems to have more than its share of the diabolically difficult.

- *Are these watch straps Swiss wristwatch straps?*
- *Pre-shrunk silk shirts (short-sleeved)*
- *Please pay promptly*
- *Freshly fried fresh flesh*

And there's a surreal yet practical slant to others.

- *Are our oars oak?*
- *Strange shredded Swiss cheese statistics*
- *Is this your sister's sixth zither, sir?*

Some, more notorious, have been designed to lure the innocent into profanity. These usually depend for their effect on repetition. Here's one from the playground.

One smart fellow, he felt smart
Two smart fellows, they felt smart
Three smart fellows, they felt smart

Others in this vein are printed below. The first is a classic of its type and the last must be familiar to English-speaking schoolboys the world over.

- *I slit the sheet; the sheet I slit; upon the slitted sheet I sit*
- *Mrs. Piggy-Wiggy has a square-cut punt*
- *I'm not a pheasant-plucker, I'm a pheasant-plucker's mate, I'm only pheasant-plucking cuz the pheasant-plucker's late*

Black Belt

Among the most challenging tongue twisters ever contrived are those reproduced below, numbered in ascending order of difficulty.

1 *Had Ed edited it?*
2 *Peggy Babcock's knapsack straps*
3 *A proper cup of coffee in a proper copper coffee cup*
4 *Billy broke a black bloke's back bike brake block*
5 *The sixth sick sheik's sixth sheep's sick*
6 *Stick these six thick thistle sticks in the sixth thick thistle stick stack*

Finally, here's a charming old poem a spooning couple might try getting their tongues around together.

You've no need to light a night-light
On a light night like tonight,
For a night-light's light's a slight light,
And tonight's a night that's light.
With a night's light like tonight's light,
It's really not quite right
To light night-lights with their slight lights
On a light night like tonight.

◎ *The tongue is the only human muscle to be attached at just one end.* ◎

THE DEVIOUS SHOT GLASS GOTCHA

Barroom wagers are a perennial favorite because the atmosphere is relaxed and your suckers' mental faculties are probably functioning somewhat worse than usual. The devious shot glass gotcha is best done in a busy bar, once everyone is in a convivial frame of mind. It works just as well at home with soda, or even milk.

Setup

1 Pour out (or order) two scotches or ryes or whatever your sucker is drinking, but make sure they come in shot glasses. Next, order (or pour) two glasses of beer for yourself. These should be large, say pint-size, glasses. *This is important.* Tell your victim that your speed of consumption is highly developed and bet him you can drink both of your big glasses of beer before he can down his two tiny glasses of liquor.

If he accepts the challenge explain the rules:

1 Neither of you is permitted to touch the glasses the other fellow is using (to avoid nefarious meddling).
2 Players may touch only one glass at a time (to avoid him trying to swallow his two drinks in one go—*or so you say*).
3 The loser will pay for the drinks.

Method

You need to be sitting at a bar or table where there is at least one empty glass (a *large one*). Say "go" and as he picks up his first drink, swiftly lift the empty pint glass and invert it over his second glass, trapping it like a fly under . . . well, under a glass. You may now casually drink your beers. That's all there is to it. If you've secreted a straw in your pocket you can even drink his second glass of liquor without breaking the rules: just lift and suck.

◎ *Under US law, rye whiskey must be made from a mash of at least 51 percent rye.* ◎

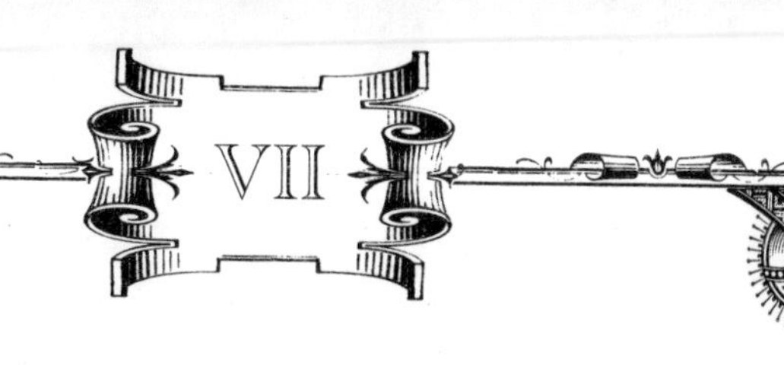

EXHIBITIONISTS' PARADE

UNUSUAL TRICKS AND PARTY PIECES FOR THE DISCERNING WIT

An old trick in a new dress is always a pleasant change.

HARRY HOUDINI

THE ONE-ARMED BUSKER

This impromptu gag is a speciality of London magician Terry Guyatt, who performs it with enormous comic panache. Even if you're no great shakes as a trickster, this piece of baloney can't fail to cause a stir.

"The one-armed busker" is a fine after-dinner party piece. So once the ladies have retired and the gentlemen are settling down to their cigars, demand attention and ask: "Whatever happened to that one-armed tin whistle player who used to entertain the crowds outside Lincoln Center [or some other posh venue]?"

People will prick up their ears at this, so continue: "Yes, he was terribly good but he had an awful problem." Your audience will demand to be told more, so, once the clamor dies down, say: "Let me show you what I mean."

Leave the room for a moment, to prepare. If there's a hat stand nearby, you can raid it for props. What you need is a jacket or short coat (if you're not already wearing one) and a hat of some description: the more ludicrous looking, the better. Put on the jacket with only the right arm in the sleeve, leaving the left sleeve hanging empty as if you were a one-armed man. Button it up and thrust your left arm down the waistband of your pants, your hand coming to rest directly over your "gentleman's area." This is all hidden beneath the jacket. Now, find a hat to put on. Failing a hat, a tea cozy or other ridiculous substitute may be pressed into service (see Chapter 5 for a 20-second paper hat).

Reenter the room, where you will be greeted by expectant murmurs, and demand a whisk, pencil, wooden spoon, or something similar to act as your tin whistle. Take this in your right hand and pretend to play it, asking for requests and dancing a little if that's your style. When the applause stops, say: "Yes, he was good all right, that one-armed busker. Of course, with only one arm, he had shocking trouble passing the hat around while he was playing, and never had so much as two pennies to rub together. But I think I've come up with a solution."

With a flourish, undo your fly with your right hand and push out the left forefinger, hooking it over the "whistle." There will be a gasp at this point. Now remove the hat with your right hand, and pass it around. It's a startling and hilarious finish.

◎ *Tin whistles are tuned diatonically.* ◎

HOW TO
GIVE A SPEECH

You've been asked to accept a prize, give a best man's speech, or talk about Aunt Mabel at her funeral. You've never spoken in public, you don't know where to start, and you're scared stiff. Here's a survival guide for you.

Background

Few people feel confident speaking in public—and that includes practiced speakers—but experienced speech-givers know that the secret of success is to exude an aura of confidence. Unless you appear to be in charge, your audience will become anxious and twitchy, so use your nervous energy to *fake* confidence; it's that simple. If there is a particular person you think oozes authority, say the Pope, or some past President, imitate his positive body language. Keep your head up, don't fidget, make eye contact, and speak decisively. It's what all the experts have learned to do.

Hints and tips

1 Don't be yourself when giving a speech. Instead, give a slightly exaggerated *performance* of yourself.

2 Don't learn your speech word for word, or read it from a sheet. Visualize it as a journey (see "How to develop a gigantic memory," Chapter 3). Design a well-shaped speech, with a beginning, middle, and end, and you'll be free to improvise. You must top and tail it properly,

though. A little research will turn up some suitably snappy openers and closers. Steal any that suit you. Producing a 12-foot newspaper tree as you walk on can make quite an impact too (see Chapter 5).

3 In question-and-answer sessions, begin with somebody sitting two-thirds of the way back, on your right, close to the aisle. Research shows that this is the area where "friends" sit. Avoid the front row on your immediate left. This is where your "enemies" will be lurking.

4 Never be apologetic, snotty, or foul-mouthed. If they aren't laughing at your hilarious remarks, carry on regardless. If they keep up the freeze, try this one: "Look, I know there are people out there because I can hear you breathing." Once they chuckle, you have them back onside. Whatever happens, keep looking confident.

5 Don't cry at a funeral while you're speaking.

6 If you get an unexpected roar of laughter, check your fly. To do this without being detected, rest your right palm against your belt buckle and slip the tip of your little finger behind the flap. If it's open, you'll just have to improvise.

7 If your mouth goes dry, bite the tip of your tongue and the saliva will flow.

8 This isn't the place for an essay on microphone technique but here are three tips:

   i. Grip the mic in one hand against your chest, and leave it there.
   ii. If it's on a stand, move it to your side and speak "across" it.
   iii. If it's on your lectern, talk over it.

9 Audiences prefer personal stories to a string of jokes, and there's usually something nice you can find to say about individuals. Mention their smile, their wit, or their kindness to animals. If you're really stuck, try: "Everyone said he was the rudest man on earth, but be fair—his brother was worse."

⊚ *Winston Churchill took up cigars in 1895, while in Cuba.* ⊚

HANDKERCHIEF FOLDING—THE MOUSE

A favorite of Lewis Carroll, "the mouse" is without question the finest hankie fold ever conceived. It's a first-class routine for small children, and should gain you quite a reputation as an entertainer.

REQUIRED

- *A gentleman's handkerchief*

METHOD

1 Place the hankie on the table in front of you, corners pointing north, south, east, and west (fig. 1).

2 Fold the south corner up to the north, making a triangle (fig. 2).

3 Fold the west and east corners into the center, to form a shape that looks roughly like an open envelope (fig. 3).

4 Roll up the hankie starting at the bottom and continuing away from you until roughly three inches of the north–south corner are showing. Pulling slightly on the ends of the roll as you go helps to stop everything unraveling (fig. 4).

5 Turn the hankie over right to left, so that the rolled portion is underneath.

6 Fold the ends of the roll into the center, as in the envelope move (3) above (fig. 5).

7 Roll the folded ends over once, toward the top corner. Now fold this corner back toward you, and tuck it into the fold at the top. Things are now delicately set and the next move often causes everything to fall apart. But with practice you should get the hang of it.

8 Poke your thumbs into the pocket facing you and turn the roll inside out—away from you (fig. 6). Keep on rolling and rolling

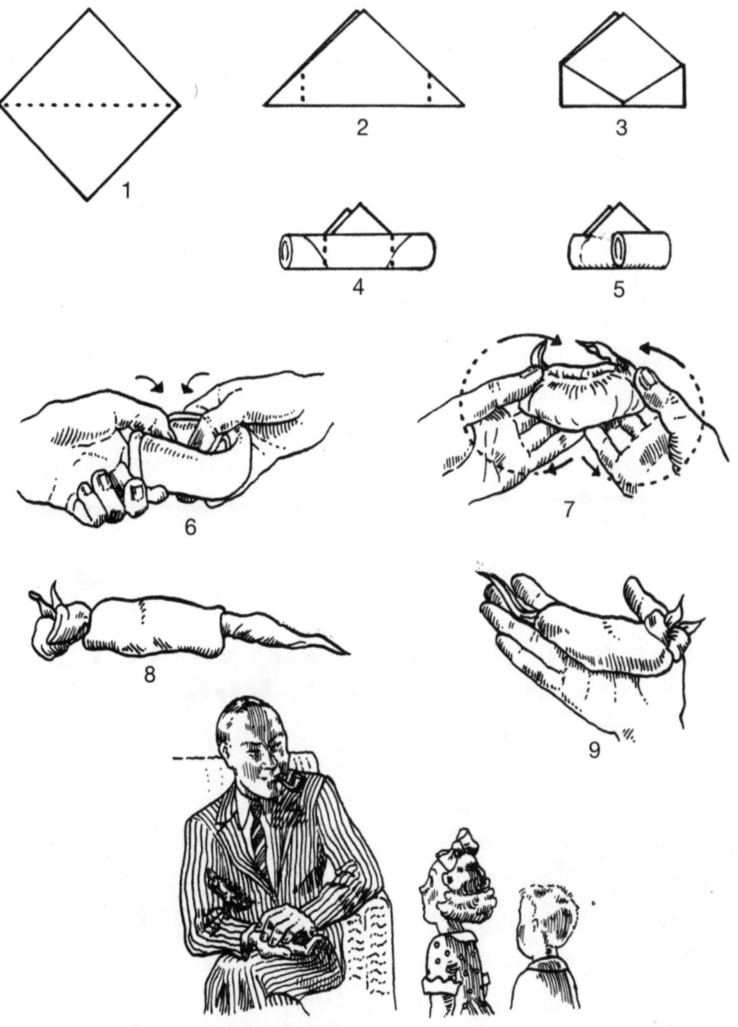

until you can't roll any more. You'll find that the hankie quickly begins to bind, and soon the two ends will become visible (fig. 7).

9 Hold on to the body, and cautiously draw out the ends, so that you get a thing that looks like a sort of long bonbon.

10 Tie a knot in one end to make the head (fig. 8). Fiddle with it a bit to give the appearance of ears, and you're ready for the acrobatics.

THE LEAP

1 Rest the mouse on your open right palm, its tail hanging over your middle finger, and its head on the base of your thumb. Your thumb and third finger steady it slightly (fig. 9).
2 Stroke the mouse down its back with your curved left hand, and as soon as the fingertips of your right hand are covered, snap your middle finger closed. This will propel the mouse up your right arm, sometimes right over your shoulder.

Children shriek with delight at this. Tell them he's on anabolic steroids.

◎ *Richard II is said to have "invented" the handkerchief.* ◎

HOW TO
DO A MIND READING ACT WITH YOUR DOG

As far as I know, the only performer ever to do a mind reading act with his dog is the urbane British magician Fergus Anckorn, who developed his unique show over many years. If you want to try a little mind reading with your own pooch, here are the basics, courtesy of Mr. Anckorn.

REQUIRED

- *A well-behaved, trainable dog*
- *A blackboard and chalk, or similar*

WHAT THE AUDIENCE SEES

The performer comes into the room with his dog, who sits obediently. He then asks for a volunteer to help him with an experiment in cross-species mind reading, and uncovers a blackboard or flip chart on which are written a number of commands such as:

- *Sit*
- *Lie down*
- *Bark*
- *Fetch the red ball/white ball/Frisbee/newspaper, etc.*

He explains that his volunteer is to circle any command, and the animal will detect the thought-waves, and obey. The performer points out that he will be standing well behind his dog so as to prevent any signaling. He also emphasizes that the dog has his back to the board to preclude any possibility that he might cheat by reading. This usually gets a laugh.

After a brief hush, the volunteer chooses a command and silently circles it on the board. No sooner has he begun the circling than the dog has obeyed and returned to his position. The assistant continues through the list while the performer stands or sits motionless, out of the animal's sight. When the commands have been exhausted, the performer and pooch take their bows.

Method

As everyone suspects, your dog does not really possess paranormal abilities. He has been trained to respond to a secret code that you are transmitting by nasal snorts. For example, one short snort might mean sit, one long followed by two short might mean pick up the newspaper. It is up to you to discover a system that works—and practice it.

After a little training with loud snorts, you'll find you can be very much quieter. It is surprising how sensitive a dog's ear is to the slightest sound—one that a human being cannot detect. Start with a single command and work on that, building gradually until you have three or four that your dog understands. The rest is showmanship. Mind reading with your dog is an intriguing puzzle rather than a magic trick and it is best presented in a witty, lighthearted, and easygoing style.

◎ *Publisher Henry Sleeper Harper fled the Titanic with his dog, Sun Yat Sen.* ◎

HOW TO JUGGLE ORANGES

The nice thing about juggling is that your audience can see that you are doing something skillful, and will therefore reward you with plenty of applause. When you are practicing, stand in front of your bedroom wall or your bed. This will prevent you from walking forward, which is a common problem for beginners. A bed makes a convenient fielder too.

The drop and recover

The first and most important move to learn is the drop. You will be making this move a lot. Take an orange and drop it on the floor. Now ask a friend to pick it up and toss it back to you. Say: "Thanks. Why should I do all the work?"

One orange

Begin practicing with just one orange, throwing it from the right hand into the left. Imagine you are facing a giant clock face. The right hand starts at 3 o'clock and lets go at about 2 o'clock, throwing the orange up toward 12 o'clock with just enough force that it describes a nice curve. Gravity and inertia will do the job for you; your hands stay pretty much where they are, facing the ceiling at all times. All their actions are "underarm." If you're doing it right, the orange should begin to fall at the top of its arc—about eye level or 12 o'clock, coming to the end of its curve just as you catch it in your left hand, at between 10 o'clock and 9 o'clock.

Two oranges

Start with an orange in each hand. Release the one in your right hand and, as it reaches the top of its arc, let the other go from your left, throwing it toward your right, as described. Catch the first in your left hand and then catch the second in your right. Repeat this routine, alternating your starting hands each time, until you can do it without thinking. It's left, right; left, right, like walking. Don't throw both oranges together.

Three oranges

Start with two oranges in your right hand (we'll call them Tom and Harry), and one orange (Dick) in the left. Begin by throwing the orange in your right fingertips (Tom) toward your left hand, as you've practiced.

When Tom reaches his zenith, throw Dick from your left hand in the usual way, and catch Tom, just as in the double-orange exercise above. When Dick reaches 12 o'clock, throw Harry from your right hand toward your left, catching Dick in your right. This is usually where the swearing starts, so try allowing Harry to roll on to your right fingertips before throwing him. When he reaches 12 o'clock, throw Tom from your left hand, and catch Harry. Concentrate on throwing Harry, Dick can look after himself. Throw the oranges evenly, and at eye level, otherwise you can get in a pickle, with oranges colliding in midair, and your timing going to the dogs.

◎ *W. C. Fields began his career as a superb comedy juggler.* ◎

HOW TO

DO A 10-MINUTE SHOW WITH NOTHING BUT A BOX OF MATCHES

Should you fancy yourself as a magician but be unable to afford all those costly doves and cabinets and things, here's a way you can entertain in the pub or at the table with just a box of matches. None of these tricks requires a top hat or a girl in a spandex bathing costume, and all are impromptu. Furthermore, the props can be carried in your pocket or bought for a few bucks almost anywhere.

Fundamental performance advice

A simple trick, like a fried egg, is much easier to do badly than well. Nobody relishes runny eggs on a grimy plate, and neither will your audience enjoy watching you fumble around dropping things, or forgetting what's supposed to happen next. So prepare properly, doing your *rehearsal in private* and only your *performance in public*. And remember, *fire is dangerous.* Use caution!

First, choose a trick from below, and practice it to yourself, over and over and over. Then try performing it for a critical friend, to get the lumps ironed out. Once you've mastered two or three effects, put them together in a short routine, ending with a big finish. It's also a good idea to write a simple script and learn it. Suggestions have been included to get you going but it is better to make up your own. Be imaginative; it's agony watching someone say, "I take a match out of the box. Now I close the box. Now I light the match. Now I put the box back on the table." Describing your physical actions is sensible only when performing for the blind.

The Natchez matches

This stunt works best in dimly lit intimate environments.

1 Start by removing four matches and wedging two of them between the drawer and the sides of the box. "The Natchez Indians

of Mississippi were a sophisticated people," you remark, "who used burning arrows to set fire to enemy villages."

2 As you say this, squeeze the third match tightly between the heads of the first two and go on: "They used to shoot them from beautiful hickory bows that looked something like this."

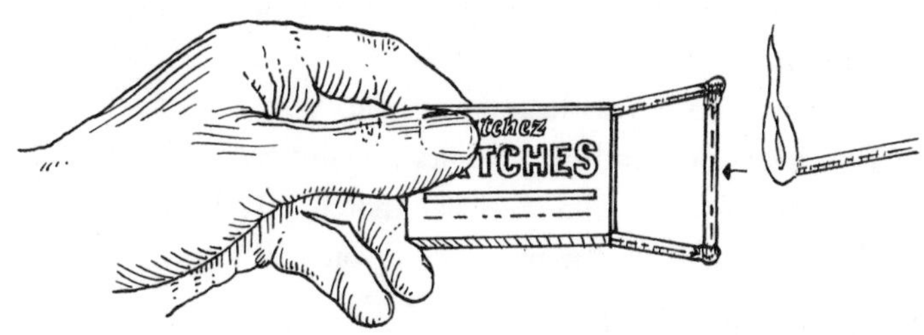

3 In fact, your arrangement looks nothing like a beautiful hickory bow, but since you are not under oath continue: "Now, these bows could send burning arrows a huge distance—watch."

4 Strike your fourth match and carefully light the middle one, dead center. It will burn for a moment until the tension of the other matches shoots it, still aflame, a short distance across the room. The trajectory is highly variable, so don't try this where there are expensive carpets or oil-soaked rags on the floor.

The handbag snatch

This beautiful little trick is particularly suitable for ladies, and deserves a polished presentation.

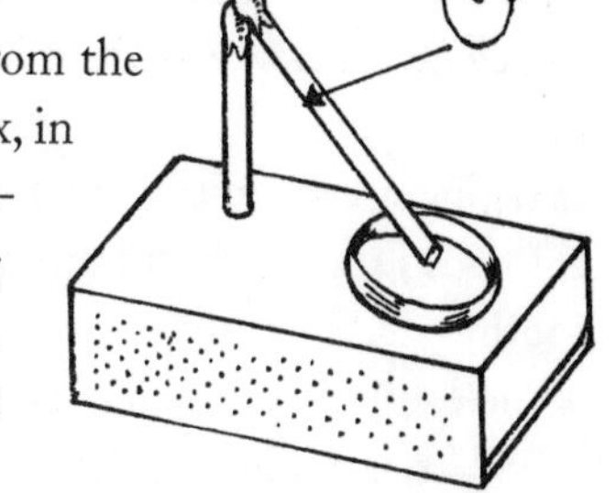

1 Begin by removing three matches from the box. Push one into the top of the box, in the position shown below, and request the loan of a thin lady's ring (that's a thin ring, not a thin lady). Good substitutes are a small elastic band, a paper clip, or even a coin.

2 Now begin your tale. "These canoodling couples should be more careful in busy places like this. A girl had her handbag nicked in here the other day by a guy standing right behind her, even though she'd put her leg through the handle, like this." Position the second match with its "foot" inside the ring (see page 243).

3 Continue: "She was leaning against 'Lover Boy,' all gooey, and he gave her a really *hot* kiss, like this." Strike the last match. Do this with a second matchbox or you will knock your "lady" over. Hold the flame under the diagonal match, about a quarter of the way down, until it catches light. The flame will creep up until both match heads suddenly ignite, causing them to bond. Shortly thereafter the female match will bend in the center, dramatically lifting her "leg" like a starlet being kissed something fierce.

4 Say, "That's when she lost her bag," and slip the ring out, returning it to its owner. Blow out the matches artistically while the ladies all go, "Oooh!"

Polar opposites

This fine trick starts as a puzzle and ends with a magical transportation.

First you must learn to hold a match secretly in your right hand. To do this, place it at the root of the second, third, and fourth fingers, which close loosely over it. The curled little finger can secure the match if necessary or it can be loosely pinched in the fold between palm and fingers. Although movement is restricted, the thumb and first finger can quite naturally pick up matches, or point at and poke things. Practice this for a day or two as you're lifting a cup, squeezing toothpaste, watching television, and going about your business. After a while everything will feel and look quite relaxed, which is important.

When you perform, it helps to make your hands appear innocent by having the left mirror the actions of the right and by allowing the thumb and forefinger of the guilty hand to hold a match between them whenever you can. Resting the loosely closed hand knuckles-down on the table when not in use is also disarming. Practice these moves before going on to rehearse the trick.

1 To perform, seat yourself opposite your spectator. You have a match hidden in your right hand, which is resting in the relaxed, knuckles-down position. Two matches are displayed in the left hand, at the base of the fingers.

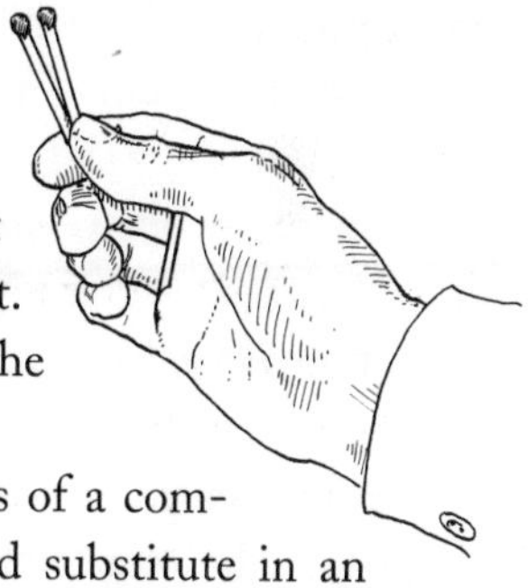

2 Press your left thumb on to their heads, to lever them up, and take them between the thumb and forefinger of the right hand. Display them as shown at right. This is the performer's view, revealing the hidden match.

3 Speak about the importance to explorers of a compass and say that matches make a good substitute in an emergency.

4 Ask a spectator to make a fist with each hand, and, taking one of the matches between your left thumb and forefinger, poke it head-up all the way into his *left* fist. Draw attention to this by saying: "This match is head-up—pointing due north."

5 With your right hand, display the second match and dramatically turn it head-down with the index finger of the left hand. With your right index finger, poke it into the spectator's *right* fist *head-down*. Say: "This one's head-down, pointing south."

6 Relax your hands into the knuckles-down position as you emphasize that the matches are pointing in opposite directions—one north, the other south. There is still a match hidden in your right hand.

7 Now tell the spectator to turn his hands palm-up without opening them (you can demonstrate this without revealing the hidden match) and, turning your own hands palm-down again, make a magic pass with the extended index fingers of *both* hands.

8 Relax again into the knuckles-down position and instruct him to open his hands. Both matches are revealed to be pointing in the same direction.

9 Ask: "Are you going north or south? Because your compasses are both pointing east, or is it west?" He may be surprised and puzzled but will probably recognize that the effect is automatic, and might try to let you know. So without more ado make fists of both your hands and put them on the table, close to the edge. Say, "Why not try it on me?"

10 From now on it is vital that you hold your hands exactly as described. Keeping the right fist motionless, advance the left for him to insert the head-up match. Say: "This is the *head-up* match—north—don't forget that."

11 Your next action is psychologically subtle and you are going to use it to conceal a secret move. What you do is advance your right fist just as the left is coming back to its original position on the table's edge. As the left is moving, relax the hand a little to allow the match it holds to fall to the bottom of the fist. This will be hidden by the larger movement of your arm. Say: "Now for the *head-down* match—south."

12 As he approaches your right fist with the match all attention will be focused there. Now look directly at your assistant and say: "Don't hurt me." This may get a small laugh, and it is exactly at this moment that you relax the fingers of your left hand just enough to allow its match to drop silently into your lap. It is vital that you keep all your attention on the other hand as you make this secret move. Do not look at your left hand or at your lap for any reason. *And keep your left hand still.* The position now is that you have no matches in your left hand and two in your right. Your audience believe there is one in each hand and they think you are about to do something sneaky to change the way they are pointing. In fact, all your cheating is finished and it's smooth sailing from here.

13 Stare straight at your spectator, even if he doesn't return your gaze, and slide the right fist back as the left comes forward. You

should aim to end with your hands at least eight inches apart and half-an-arm's-length from the table edge. Say, "I've forgotten which is north and which is south."

14 Turn your left fist palm-up and look at it as you move it forward slightly. Say: "What's that?" Whatever the answer, open your hand slowly to reveal an empty palm. Say: "That may be so, but it seems to have *gone* south."

15 Immediately turn your right fist palm-up and open it to reveal two matches. Say: "Well, they do say opposites attract." Drop the matches onto the table, saying: "Let me show you something else strange."

Balancing one match on another

This is a good one to follow the previous trick. As they are all clapping, absentmindedly suck your right thumb, leaving it wet. Pick up one of the dropped matches in your right hand and press its head against your wet thumb.

After a moment pick up the other match in your right hand and say that you have developed supernatural balance skills. Press the head of the second match onto the first, where the wetness will cause them to stick firmly. Now acting ability takes over as you let go with your left hand and apparently balance one on the other.

How to extinguish a match by blowing down the (wrong) sleeve

This piece of amusing by-play will be remembered long after your more grandiose tricks have been forgotten. It works best in a darkish room.

Secretly make a partial break in a wooden match about a quarter of the way down. Strike it, holding your fingers over the break and, as the flame takes hold, quickly press your thumb against the unbroken side, stealthily bending the top of the match toward you.

Display it, held at its tip between the thumb and forefinger of your right hand. Now ostentatiously blow into your left cuff, simultaneously giving the match a twist with your right thumb and finger. It will go out with a snap. No need to be subtle about it—everybody is looking at your left sleeve. They will see the match go out from the corner of their eyes. As they look directly at it, it will smoke attractively.

Another way is to flick the tail of an unbroken match with the nail of your second finger as you blow down the sleeve. Use the method that suits you best.

The cocktail glass

Arrange four matches in the shape of a cocktail glass as shown below, with the broken end of a match representing an olive. Tell your audience they must move two matches (only) so that the olive ends up outside the glass. They are not allowed to touch the olive or end up with a damaged-looking glass. The solution is illustrated here but it takes quite a bit of thinking out for the uninitiated. A lovely little puzzle.

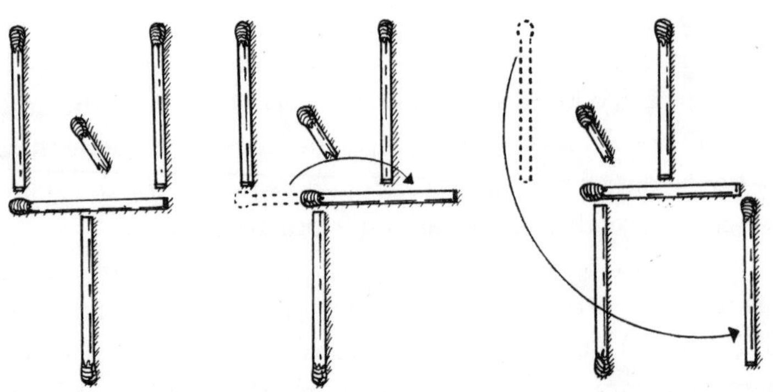

◎ *The phosphorous match was invented in France in 1831.* ◎

HOW TO
TRIP YOURSELF UP

A staple of the finest vaudevillians, tripping yourself up is a skill well worth cultivating. There's nothing more enjoyable for an audience in a formal setting than watching you stumble over your feet, especially if you are holding a tray full of wineglasses at the time. It's a good method, too, of upstaging the party bore just as he is coming to the punch line of his 19th joke. If you time it correctly, *you'll* get the laugh and he'll get the boot. The following instructions for tripping yourself up are rather like those for learning the steps to a waltz—only quicker.

Method

Although the trip is the inferior cousin of the pratfall, and correspondingly easy to do, it deserves to be practiced properly before you perform it in public.

To rehearse, stand in front of a full-length mirror in your shoes and take two steps forward, beginning with your left leg and ending with your right foot in front. This is the ordinary walking cycle, which you are about to mimic. What you are going to do is bring your right foot forward rather as you just did but instead of swinging it in parallel you are going to strike the back of your left foot, which is firmly planted on the ground.

If this happened by accident, you would probably lose your balance and flail your arms. So, as your right toe connects with the heel of your left shoe, mimic this by lunging forward with your upper body and arms, as if you had been pushed from behind. This is what stuntmen call "selling the move," and needs to be a somewhat exaggerated movement.

Rehearse the actions until you can do them without thinking. You are now ready to perform. To check its verisimilitude, try it first as you walk along with some friends. If you can fool them, it's time to move on to tripping yourself up behind an important or pompous person as he solemnly addresses a group. After the trip, flash the gathering a sickly grin and continue on your way. They will try to keep straight faces but it will be hard.

Once you have become confident in tripping yourself up, why not try it with a tray full of wineglasses held waiter-style? You can do this impromptu or you can make a terrific splash by secretly sticking the glasses down first with something like Fun-Tak. If they are all half full of wine, the effect, as you execute a little sideways dance on the balls of your feet, can be heart-stopping.

◎ *Christy Brown wrote* My Left Foot *in 1954.* ◎

HOW TO
STOP A TRAIN WITH YOUR BARE HANDS

Buster Keaton, clown of the old school, was a master of this inconsequential piece of nonsense. Imagine the scene: you have been waiting for your train and it is just pulling into the station. As it arrives on the platform, you reach out, grab hold of a handle, and with superhuman strength pull it to a stop. Catching a train in this way always gets a laugh but it's a stunt that could be extremely dangerous so you should *definitely not try this—leave it to the professionals.* Never touch the body of a moving train, and always stand behind the yellow line.

Method

Anyone who tried to stop a train just as it entered the station would be whisked smartly off his feet; stopping a train with bare hands doesn't work unless you are at the very front of the platform.

Once the train has slowed to a walking pace, and almost stopped, look out for a convenient handle. Then, facing the direction of travel, grab hold and pull against it as the carriages draw finally to a halt.

On old-fashioned steam railways there's always an embarrassment of knobs to get hold of. Newer trains, however, tend to be smooth, with very few bits and bobs sticking out. If this is the case, you must adapt your technique. Bracing yourself in a semi-crouch, feet rooted to the platform, press your flattened palms against the carriage and push hard against the direction of travel. As the train slows to a halt you will be shoved slowly backward, a foot or so along the platform, which, let's face it, adds to the overall effect.

The illusion that your actions are responsible for the stopping of a great big train is amazingly strong and is enhanced by such bonuses as screeching brakes, hissing compressors, and jets of steam. Once the train has stopped, clap your hands together and say: "Right, let's get on." This will provoke amused smiles from friends and fellow passengers, as well as nervous glances from the men in uniform.

An unfortunate side effect of this gag is that your hands will be unspeakably filthy afterward. But let's face facts, an artist always suffers for his art. Just don't shake anyone's hand.

◎ *The steam engine was invented in 1804 by Richard Trevithick.* ◎

10 THINGS TO DO AT THE RESTAURANT TABLE

Here are a few gags to perform in the restaurant—at a moment's notice. And there are no props to buy—terrific!

1 Table telepathy

Place the following eight items in front of a fellow diner, naming each one.

1 *Fork*
2 *Spoon*
3 *Bottle*

4 *Ashtray*
5 *Matchbox*
6 *Sugar cube*
7 *Saltshaker*
8 *Paper napkin*

Ask him to think of one and spell it to himself as you touch them, seemingly at random. When he gets to the last letter he is to call "stop." At this point you will be touching his thought-of object. This works because each object is spelled with one more letter than the one preceding it though you don't mention this. You can touch any article the first three times, but you must then touch them in order. You can go on to do a trick with whichever object has been chosen.

2 Fork

Place a fork on your left palm, with its handle pointing right. Close your fingers and turn the fork prongs up. Encircle your left wrist with the second, third, and fourth fingers of your right hand, secretly extending the right forefinger under the closed fingers of the left hand. By twiddling this finger you can make the fork rotate mysteriously, in answer to yes or no questions posed by fellow diners. Finally open the left fingers in a star to reveal the fork apparently stuck to your palm. Give it a couple of shakes, finally commanding it to drop to the table, accomplished by secretly releasing your forefinger's grip. Separate your hands briskly.

3 Spoon

Hand a spoon to someone at the table and say: "I'm going to turn away and I want you to take a spoonograph of one of the others. Just point it at their face and say, 'Click.'" When the picture has been taken, you turn back and examine the spoon closely, in due course naming the right person. The trick can be repeated during dull moments throughout the evening, with different spoonographers and subjects. You need a confederate to transmit the subject's identity by copying the position in which he or she is sitting.

4 Bottle

Rub a small, empty beer bottle rapidly up and down against the wall in a corner of the restaurant. With any luck, it will "stick" in the junction of the walls when you remove your hand. I am not sure quite how this works—though I suspect the heat generated by the friction does the trick. Plastic wallpaper seems to help. Eddie O'Shaughnessy, an Irish pub-magician of my acquaintance, does this just beautifully. If it doesn't work, call for a mop.

5 Ashtray

While waiting for your food, secretly pinch a coin between your first and second fingers as shown below and secrete two or three pieces of ice in your mouth.

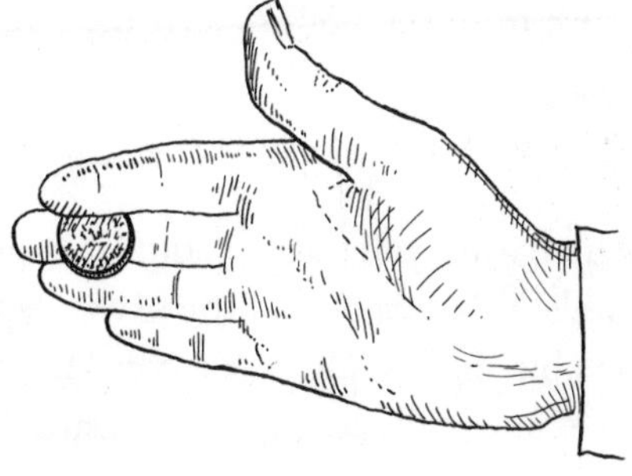

Lift the ashtray, which should be glass, saying "Mm, yum," as you pretend to bite into it. A loud snap is heard, made by clicking the coin sharply against the ashtray with your second finger. Remove the ashtray from your mouth and crunch the ice noisily, spitting out the occasional lump. I guarantee that people will remember you after this gag. They may not like you, but they *will* remember you.

6 Matchbox

Rattle a box of matches vigorously and say: "I bet nobody can guess exactly how many matches are in the box." Repeat the shake if they ask you to. You then open the box to reveal that it is completely empty: a big surprise. The secret is to have previously wedged a full box up your sleeve. You're going to have to remove it after the trick or you will rattle every time you move your hand, so take a trip to the cloakroom. Although this is a very simple trick, it is very effective.

7 Sugar cube

Secretly dip your finger into a full ashtray and transfer some ash on to a sugar cube as you pick it up. You can now set fire to and burn the whole cube. Nobody will be able to repeat the feat.

8 Saltshaker

Pour some salt on the table and place a glass of lager over it, then pick up the saltshaker and say: "This is a funny thing—the salt comes up from the bottom." Tap the saltshaker sharply on the rim of a glass. This will cause bubbles to rise from the bottom as if the salt is floating up through the drink.

9 Paper napkin

Drape a large paper napkin over your face, holding it in place with your glasses—or somebody else's. Now poke a little of the napkin into your mouth, and you'll resemble the invisible man. Say: "If it's the invisible man, tell him I can't see him." Silly but highly amusing.

10 Muddy shoe

For obvious reasons, this isn't on the list for table telepathy but there's nothing more delightfully surprising on a posh restaurant table than a muddy shoe, and it makes a terrific finale. Prepare for this by slipping off one of your shoes and secreting it in your lap. At the right moment attract everyone's attention and hold your left forearm in front of you, as if checking your watch. Drape a napkin over it. As your right hand comes down, grasp the shoe and as you move your left arm forward simply place the shoe on the table, where it will be hidden behind the napkin. Remove the napkin with an elegant flourish to reveal your filthy footwear on the beautiful table setting.

◎ *A new Beijing restaurant specializes in yak, donkey, and seal penises.* ◎

THE SEASICK ORANGE

The origins of this hilarious piece of table-nonsense have sunk below the surface of time's misty quagmire but it is well over 100 years old, and probably much older. There is something about this gag that makes people heave with laughter—possibly the combination of suggestive puppetry and a horribly realistic climax that everybody recognizes. Next time you find yourself seated at the captain's table on some interminable cruise, this is the one to do.

Required

- *A tumbler*
- *A juicy orange with a thin skin*
- *A napkin*
- *A sharp knife*

Take an orange and cut two narrow eyes and a large, downward-pointing "drunken" mouth. You don't need to be Michelangelo, indeed a crudely hacked blurry face adds to the effect—there's no need to bother with a nose if you don't want to. While you are cutting the mouth, surreptitiously dig around and loosen a few bits, which will help later on.

Next, drape a cloth napkin over the mouth of a tumbler, and place the orange on top. By holding the glass with one hand and pulling on the napkin from various points, you can get the face to swing around nauseously. You need to tell some sort of story, such as: "I never get seasick myself, but most other people seem to. It comes in three stages doesn't it? First you wave away your toast and eggs with a sickly smile; then you turn completely white and feel so horribly ill you think you must be dead; and finally you wish you were." During this you have been moving the head around in a queasy wobble, and people will be chuckling.

Finally, lift up the orange and drape the napkin around it like a cowl. Display it for a moment and then squeeze hard with both hands. Your orange will make some authentic noises and vomit realistically into the glass, even producing a few tears. You can embellish the sounds with your own retching effects if you like. Hold the dribbling fruit up for a moment, and then drink the juice with a flourish.

◎ *Best seasickness remedy: keep your eyes on the horizon ahead of the boat.* ◎

HOW TO
WALK INTO A DOOR

Walking into a door doesn't sound like much of a thing to do but the effect of this gag on spectators can be stupendous. What happens is that you approach a large door—glass ones are good—and, grabbing the handle, open it toward yourself with such force that it smashes you in the face with a loud crunch. There is usually a gasp of horror from the people behind you as you recoil from the shuddering door with your hand clutched over your nose.

Method

To practice this lovely stunt, walk briskly up to your kitchen door and grasp the handle in your right hand. For the purposes of these instructions, I am assuming that the hinge is on your right, although it works perfectly well with the hinge on your left: simply reverse your arms and legs accordingly.

As you stop briefly in front of the door, the position of your right foot is critical. It should be roughly its own length from the door and should hit the ground just as you grip the handle. There's a rhythm to it that comes with practice.

Pull the door smartly toward you and, as you do so, swing the upper body toward it slightly, in a continuation of your brisk forward movement. If everything's in the right place, the door will be stopped suddenly as it strikes your foot and, if it is a big glass one, will vibrate pleasingly. Your nose should be between two and four inches from the door, depending on how brave you are. There is a definite knack to putting your head in the right place and, though it should come naturally, confidence will be required in the early days.

The rest is showmanship. As the door strikes your right toe there will be an almighty thump and wobble. It is now that you must "sell" the gag. You do this by throwing your head back violently. The unexpected combination of actions is too much for people's brains to process quickly and they assume that you have received an almighty blow to the noggin. Whether you decide to grin or maintain the illusion by staggering around in mock agony depends on the circumstances, but I usually smile.

After performing this trick a few times you'll spot good-looking candidate doors in an instant. Broadway theaters, restaurants, and grand boutiques often have suitably imposing and ornate ones, though the stunt works fine with a boring local office or school door. If you do it going into the pub, you'll find people will want to reward you by buying you drinks.

◎ *"A day without laughter is a day wasted."—Charlie Chaplin* ◎

FOUR DIVERSIONS WITH A BANANA

There are many unexpected things you can do with a banana. Here are four that are especially out of the ordinary.

1 Take a ripe banana and poke a needle through a brown spot halfway down. By rotating it inside the skin, it is possible to cut the banana in half, without peeling it. Repeat the action from the opposite side. This will ensure that the top falls off when it's peeled. There will be some leakage of sticky juice, so prepare the banana a day in advance. You can leave it in the fruit bowl for an unsuspecting victim, or pretend to cut it with an invisible knife, before peeling it yourself. Children find this particularly mysterious.

2 A novel party game, guaranteed to send the introverts straight into the kitchen, is to blindfold two people, who then feed a banana to each other. This can be highly amusing, as you might suppose, and there are many interesting variations possible—which I will leave to your imagination.

3 For years it has been alleged that you can peel a banana by pushing it (already partly peeled) into the neck of a milk bottle into which you have just dropped a piece of burning paper. A reduction in air pressure inside the bottle is said to account for the effect. It is also supposed to be possible to suck a boiled egg into the bottle in this way, instead of a banana. But, in all my years of trying this interesting-sounding stunt, I have never made it work. The amount of energy required for the job is apparently just too great. Nevertheless in the spirit of scientific inquiry, you could try it yourself.

4 On a day out at a stately home, have a banana in your pocket. As you stroll around the gardens with your boring relations, secrete the banana in your hand, with the fibrous end pinched between thumb and fingers. This is not hard to conceal, since nobody is paying attention. Approach a small tree and grasp the tip of a young branch, your body screening the action from your audience. Cause the banana to swing out of your hand and press its tip against a twig. Keep hold of banana and branch, and turn sideways, allowing the fruit to be seen. With great seriousness, draw people's attention to it saying: "It's amazing what grows here now. It must be global warming." Pretend to tear the banana off, then peel it and eat it. Gets a laugh every time.

◎ *A 1982 law forbade jokes about Zimbabwean president Canaan Banana's name.* ◎

CAFÉ QUICKIES

Raisin the *Titanic*

Recount the story of the foundering of the mighty *Titanic* and describe the recent efforts to raise valuables from the deep. Drop a few raisins into a glass of clear lemonade or sparkling mineral water saying they are a team of salvage technicians who will be going down to the poop deck all night in search of pearl necklaces and silver plate. Suiting their behavior to your story, the raisins will rise and fall mesmerizingly throughout the evening. Don't absentmindedly drink the drink, it's too strange a sensation. There is an optimum raisin size for this and you might want to cut larger ones in half.

The regurgitant beverage

Drop two or three Smarties (or Mentos come highly recommended) into a newly opened can or bottle of soda. Before long the sweets speed the release of carbon dioxide, producing a prodigious amount of froth. It will keep on coming too, like a volcano spewing lava.

The boss everyone hates

This is another gag that works well with a group of office pals at a café table. I saw a version performed decades ago by Jay Marshall, a graceful and witty magician. You can vary the story to suit your own situation.

Pour a little water into a saucer and sprinkle some black pepper on to the surface. It works whether the pepper is freshly ground or from a shaker, but it must be black or you won't see it.

Tell a story about the people who work for your organization and describe how varied a bunch they are, but that there is one thing they all share: a hatred of the boss—or pick some other uniformly despised person.

Explain that the whole company was recently swimming in the local pool, having an enjoyable time, when the boss suddenly appeared in his tight DayGlo swimming trunks. As he lowered himself into the pool, you explain, everyone recoiled, giving him a wide berth. As you say this, dip your index finger into the water, at which moment the pepper will shrink from your digit, as if from some potent force field.

Of course, there is chicanery here, and the stunt especially suits the opportunistic performer. On a visit to the men's room, scrape your fingernail along the soap, collecting a goodly lump beneath the nail. It's the soap that does it.

How to re-light a candle from a distance

This is another of those things that works well in a gloomy place.

Theatrical time is "longer" than real time, and watching someone fiddling about trying to get a match out of a box can be excruciating for an audience. So, to prepare, open the drawer and pull a match partly out, closing the box so that just the head is sticking out. This is a dodge known to all actors who have had to strike a match on stage while trying to speak their lines.

Draw attention to the candle and blow it out with a staccato puff. Allow the smoke to rise and quickly strike the match. Hold the flame steadily against the smoke plume, a few inches above the wick. Candles differ in their properties, but, with a healthy wisp of smoke, a good candle will suddenly re-light itself with a pop.

What happens is that the flame travels down the smoke, which contains combustible materials. It is a charming and surprising trick for those who don't know it. In dark rooms where the smoke is almost invisible the effect appears truly magical.

The knife sharpener

Here's a wonderful optical illusion that gives the impression that your plate is a rotating knife sharpener.

While you are in a café waiting for the food to arrive pick up your knife and say to everyone: "This is completely blunt—no good at all." Now take your plate (it should be unpatterned) and rest its edge on your thigh so that the circumference remains partly visible above the table edge. The underside should be toward your body.

Holding it lightly with your left hand, grab the edge of the plate at 12 o'clock with your right fingers, a bit like a steering wheel. Now pretend to spin it clockwise two or three times, on an invisible axle running through its center.

Begin to jiggle your leg—or legs—up and down so that the plate bounces a little. Believe it or not, this is a very deceptive move—they will swear it's spinning.

Once its "up to speed" (some acting ability required, I'm afraid), lift the knife with your right hand and drag its blade lightly back across the plate's bouncing circumference. The illusion that the plate is a rotating grindstone is enhanced if the knife has a serrated edge, producing, as it does, sound effects of great verisimilitude.

Keep the leg-bounce going throughout. Naturally, you will occasionally have to give the plate the occasional pretend spin to "keep it going."

How to pull an "accordion" from your nose

Remove the paper sleeve from a plastic drinking straw, surreptitiously fold it into a tight zigzag, and thrust it up your favorite nostril with your thumb. At a moment of your choosing, pinch your nose gently with your left hand and smoothly draw out the accordion with your right finger and thumb. Say: "They always end up there, don't they."

The very annoying uncle trick

This trick was taught to me by a very annoying uncle. Tear a third of the length off the paper sleeve of a plastic drinking straw. Replace the sleeve, leaving half an inch of air space at the closed end. Put the straw into your mouth and aim it at somebody objectionable on the other side of the table. Now tilt it up a few degrees and blow firmly, with a staccato puff. The paper cover will be sent flying, striking your subject's forehead quite hard. Mildly amusing once, this is indescribably annoying done more than that. So keep going.

By dipping the end in ketchup it's possible to fire the papers at the ceiling and get them to stick there. With a team of two or three people you can create a dramatically stalactitic effect. It's also fun to launch half a dozen into the good seats during the dull bits of one of those Russian plays: harmless but gratifyingly annoying.

The wriggling water snake

Snip off the end of a plastic straw's paper wrapper. Holding the paper and straw at the closed end between the fingertips of your left hand, force the wrapper down the straw with the right. Compress the paper firmly, causing it to scrunch up on itself in a zigzag fold, like a sailor's squeezebox.

Put the thing down on the table and, with a cocktail stick or your finger, or something, allow just a drop of water to touch the scrunched up paper. You'll need to experiment beforehand to discover exactly how much to use. The paper will now unfold and the snake will insinuate itself across the table in a viperine slither. It's a mysterious and rather weird-looking trick.

Pea levitation

Snip a couple of inches off a drinking straw and, tilting your head back, put the short bit into your mouth. Take a pea from your plate and carefully place it on the tip of the straw. A rolled-up pellet of bread will also do. Blow gently and it will be lifted into the air. If you tilt your head slightly you can even suspend the pea at an angle. It looks as though it should fall but the higher air pressure outside the thin column that you are blowing through the straw pushes the pea back into place. A bit of practice helps. This is the Bernoulli effect again. It's the same thing that lifts an airplane off the ground. (See page 37 for more Bernoulli stuff.)

The invitation-to-leave trick

With your teeth, flatten about half an inch of a plastic drinking straw at the end. Now slit along the creases to make an oboe-like double reed. Pinch this "strawboe" between your lips and blow firmly. Loud "music" will come out. If you are an enthusiast, cut a few finger holes and try playing "Yankee Doodle."

It won't be long before you are surrounded by smiling staff and happy diners from all corners of the café, begging you to continue.

Instant Clangers

This trick is best with straws of a wide diameter.

Hold the straw vertically and pinch it closed near the bottom with the finger and thumb of your left hand. By sliding the pinched finger and thumb of your right hand up and down the straw as you blow across the hole, you can produce an agreeable slide-whistle sort of noise.

◎ *Baked beans resemble a Native American dish of beans cooked with bear fat.* ◎

TWO DIVERSIONS WITH A PULLOVER

Here are a couple of quickies for when you're dressed in a sweater. If you are a cardigan wearer you'll have to turn it around.

The owl

Remove your shoes and take your arms out of your sleeves. Now squat with your knees against your collarbones and pull the sweater down over your legs. Get a friend to drape the sleeves behind you, out of the way, while you grasp the hem with your toes. Push your hands out under the front with fingers spread and slightly curled, like an owl's feet gripping a branch. All you need to do now is turn your head 90 degrees, left and right, or all the way around if you can do it, blinking owlishly. Make hooting noises.

The arm transplant

While your arms are out of the sleeves, you can do an impression of a man who has had a strange operation. Simply cross your arms in front of you under the sweater and poke them all the way into the wrong sleeves. The effect is very strange, especially if you wave your hands up and down and shout about suing your arm transplant surgeon for being intoxicated.

◎ *The Smithsonian boasts a display of Mr. Rogers's cardigans.* ◎

THE ELASTIC HANDKERCHIEF

This truly startling bit of business makes a nice prelude to a few gags with a napkin or hankie. Ideal if you are master of ceremonies at a wedding reception.

Get yourself a large handkerchief or napkin and, holding its opposite corners, secretly gather two or three inches into each hand, drawing everything tight.

When you are ready, call attention to the handkerchief, which is stretched horizontally in front of you, with two corners hanging down in the middle and the other two scrunched in your hands. The illusion is that it is quite a bit smaller than it actually is.

By twirling it like a jump rope and gradually letting out a bit of material from each hand, you can make the thing "stretch" enormously. The moves are: twirl-stop, twirl-stop, twirl-stop, twirl-stop, letting out a bit out at each twirl.

It sounds unimpressive but is quite the reverse. Try it in front of a mirror and you'll fool yourself.

By way of patter, you could try the following: "This is one of those new stretchy hankies made by Gartons. You know Gartons, down by the river. They've got their name on a big sign—GARTONS—but they've decided to change it because someone noticed the reflection in the water reads 'SNOTRAG.' "

◎ *Spandex, invented in 1959 by DuPont, can stretch 500 percent without breaking.* ◎

THE MAGNETIC FINGERS

This old playground stunt holds a strange and mysterious attraction, and always provokes a laugh.

1 Ask your subject to interlock and close his fingers tightly.
2 He is then to extend his index fingers and hold them apart in a V, keeping the other fingers and thumbs tightly closed.
3 You now make a circling motion around his extended fingertips with your own finger, and his fingers will slowly close.

The effect is the result of involuntary relaxation of the muscles, coupled with a certain amount of suggestion from your good self.

◎ *Cows are fed "cow magnets" to attract any harmful metal objects they eat.* ◎

HOW TO "BOIL" AN UPSIDE-DOWN GLASS OF WATER

This is one to do near the sink. Failure in a restaurant would be embarrassing. A few practice tries will help you get it.

Fill a tumbler about three-quarters full of cold water. Place a wet hankie over the mouth of the glass and pull it taut, holding it firmly in place against the sides.

Poke the material into the glass with your left forefinger until it just touches the water. Now invert the glass with your right hand, holding the material tight against the sides (fig. 1). No water will penetrate and the concave dip can be gently touched by any spectator who wishes to do so. It feels a bit weird.

Keeping the glass inverted, twist the material at the closed end until it is as tight as a drum. Because there is a vacuum inside the glass, air

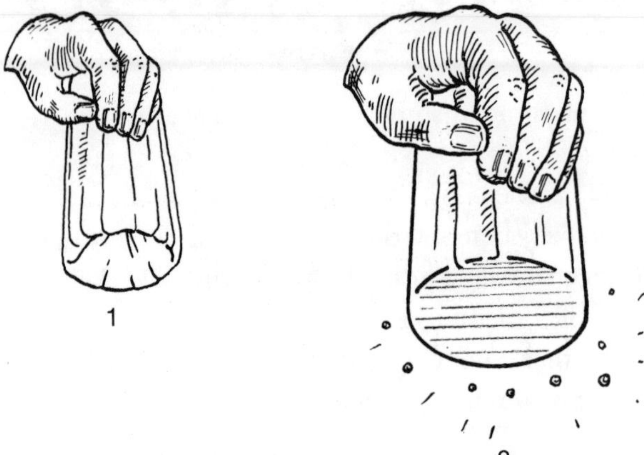

will penetrate the material, making tiny bubbling sounds as if the water is boiling (fig. 2).

You can spend ages playing around with this fascinating effect.

◎ *"In the end, everything is a gag."—Charlie Chaplin* ◎

VIII

MILITANT KITCHEN-CRAFT

BOLD CUISINE FOR CHEFS WITH ATTITUDE

It's nothing but a damned fried dough ball.

COLONEL HARLAND SANDERS

HOW TO
MAKE PICKLED EGGS

Sometimes described as the poor man's caviar, pickled eggs are cheap and extremely pleasing; if you've never tasted a pickled egg, you haven't lived. They make a tasty fat-free snack and once opened will last for ages without refrigeration. There are many recipes for pickling eggs, from oeufs ordinaire to spicy habenero killer eggs. There are bright yellow dill-pickled eggs, flustered eggs (beets), and even Aztec blue eggs (food coloring). This recipe is for Grandma's plain old-fashioned pickled eggs.

Required

- *12–16 large eggs*
- *A wide-mouthed pickling jar*
- *2 pints of ordinary brown vinegar*
- *A huge pinch of salt*
- *2 tablespoons of sugar*

Method

Using a large saucepan, completely immerse the eggs in cold water, adding a splash of vinegar to prevent the shells from cracking and improve peelability. Put a lid on and bring the water to a vigorous boil. As soon as it's boiling, turn off the heat, and let the eggs stand in the hot water for 15 minutes. Timing is vital. If you cook eggs for too long, or at too high a temperature, the whites shrivel and toughen, and the yolks become hard, taking on a glaucous tinge.

After 15 minutes, remove the lid, put the pan into the sink, and run the cold tap into the hot water, allowing it to overflow while you get on with something else for a few minutes.

To peel the eggs, tap them on the table, and crackle the shells between your hands. Peel them carefully under water, starting at the fat end. Try to get all the skin off but avoid damaging them. Wounded eggs look ugly. This part is mind-freezingly boring; get someone to help.

Pour the vinegar into a pan along with the salt and sugar, and bring to the boil. If you're making fancy eggs, now is the time to drop in chopped onion, cardamom seeds, chilies, garlic or whatever you like, and simmer until people start to complain about the unspeakable smell. Put the eggs into a very clean jar in the sink and pour the boiling vinegar mixture over them. After about five minutes put on the lid, making sure it's airtight.

Store the eggs somewhere dark and cool. They will be ready in a month or so. The longer you keep them, the rubberier they become, which is what the connoisseur prefers. The proper accompaniment is good beer.

◎ *The annual International Vinegar Festival is held in Roslyn, South Dakota.* ◎

HOW TO
COOK TASTY TESTICLES

Should the thought of tucking in to a plate of testicles have you crossing and uncrossing your legs, just think of the poor donor animal. Unless you live on a farm, the ingredients can, admittedly, be hard to come by and you will certainly receive a quizzical look if you ask the guy in the supermarket if he's got any testicles today. Nonetheless, this juicy recipe is ideal when entertaining your girlfriend's ex. Just watch him freeze with a piece of gravy-soaked bread halfway to his mouth, as you tell him what he's eating. "Rocky Mountain oysters" is the acme of testicle recipes and shows that there's more to cooking testicles than just throwing them onto a hot skillet until they explode.

Montana Rocky Mountain oysters

- *2 pounds bulls' testicles*
- *4 ounces flour*
- *1 ounce cornmeal*

- *A glass of red wine*
- *A glass of milk*
- *4 crushed garlic cloves*
- *Salt and pepper*
- *Hot chili sauce*
- *Cooking oil*

Method

1. Heat up your deep fryer.
2. With a sharp knife, split the tough membrane that surrounds each testicle. This job can be tricky but is made easier if the testicles are first blanched or frozen.
3. Put the testicles into a large pan, and cover with salted water. Leave them for an hour to allow some of the blood to ooze out.
4. While they are oozing, prepare your batter.

Cowboy Bill's old-time testicle batter

Mix the flour, cornmeal, and garlic in a bowl with a little salt and pepper. Pour the milk and chili sauce into another bowl and the wine into a third. That's it.

5. After an hour, drain and refill the testicle pan with just enough water for them to bob on the surface. Add several good splashes of vinegar.
6. Boil the testicles for three to four minutes, so they are partly cooked, then drain and rinse under the cold tap. Allow them to cool and slice into burger-thin patties with a sharp knife. Sprinkle with salt and pepper.
7. Dip the slices in the flour mixture and then in the milk and chili mixture. Re-coat in flour and dip quickly into the wine.
8. Lower into the deep fryer and cook until golden brown. They can easily become tough, so don't overcook.
9. Serve with chips and a sauce of your choice.

◎ *Montana's Testicle Festival feeds 2½ tons of meat to 15,000 visitors.* ◎

HOW TO
SPIT-ROAST A SUCKLING PIG

When it comes to barbecues, spit-roasted suckling pig is not the cheapest option but it is the most impressive. This recipe serves about ten hungry linebackers or 80 skinny people.

INGREDIENTS

- *An 8-pounds suckling pig*
- *4–5 apples*
- *3–4 onions*
- *A few garlic cloves*
- *A good tablespoonful of coriander seeds*
- *4 good handfuls of bread crumbs*
- *4 tablespoons of melted butter or oil*
- *A good handful of chopped parsley*
- *3 tender sage leaves*
- *Some ground ginger*
- *Salt and pepper*
- *A bottle of red table wine*
- *A black olive*

NOT FOR EATING

- *A spit and spit-turner*
- *A corncob*
- *Some thin string*
- *Hot coals*

METHOD

1 Give your pig a bath in a mild solution of bicarbonate of soda, not forgetting to wash behind the ears. There is no need to brush his teeth.
2 Drain the tub, rinse the pig, and fill the bath with fresh water. Stir

in a couple of handfuls of salt and let him soak for half an hour while you get your spit-turner set up, and your coals lit.

3 Drain the bath and drag your pig downstairs on a large towel. Lay him on the kitchen table and dry him with a clean cloth or hair dryer.

4 Remove the eyes but do not discard them; they are excellent for dropping into the pockets and handbags of people you dislike. Just watch their faces as they reach for their keys.

5 Crush up the herbs, ginger, and garlic, and stir them together. Add plenty of salt and pepper, and rub this preparation inside the pig.

6 Combine the bread crumbs, onions, chopped apples, parsley, and melted butter in a bowl and season with salt and pepper. Add enough wine to moisten the mixture.

7 Stuff the pig and sew up the cavity with some string.

8 Stretch out the legs and tie them neatly. Curl the tail, and fasten it in place with a metal skewer. Cover tail and ears with foil to prevent charring. Plug the mouth with a corncob to keep it open during cooking.

9 Put the pig on the spit, and baste with a little melted butter or oil. Finally, rub the skin with salt.

10 Now get someone to help you put your pig in front of—not over—the glowing coals. Start with the spit at least two feet from the coals or the skin will burn before the inside is done. Once the inside has cooked you can brown the skin by gradually moving the spit closer until it turns a warm bronze color (the skin, not the spit). Turn the pig regularly and baste with the fat drippings, which you can collect in a pan underneath.

11 When cooking outside, everything depends on the wind, weather, temperature of the coals, and other annoying variables. In an oven you'd need about 10–25 minutes per pound but you can test how things are doing on the spit by cutting into the deepest part of the meat and poking your finger in. It should feel too hot to bear. Look for plenty of steam. Pork must be piping hot before you eat it (about 165–170 degrees F). When it's done, remove the skewer,

foil, and corncob. Cut the olive in half lengthways and place the hemispheres into the eye sockets round side out. Stuff a spare apple into the mouth. You don't have to use an apple; a briar pipe can look rather distinguished too. Place the pig on a huge plate, surrounded by roast potatoes, sausages, and baked apples.

12 Slice and serve in crusty sandwiches or baguettes. Don't forget the applesauce.

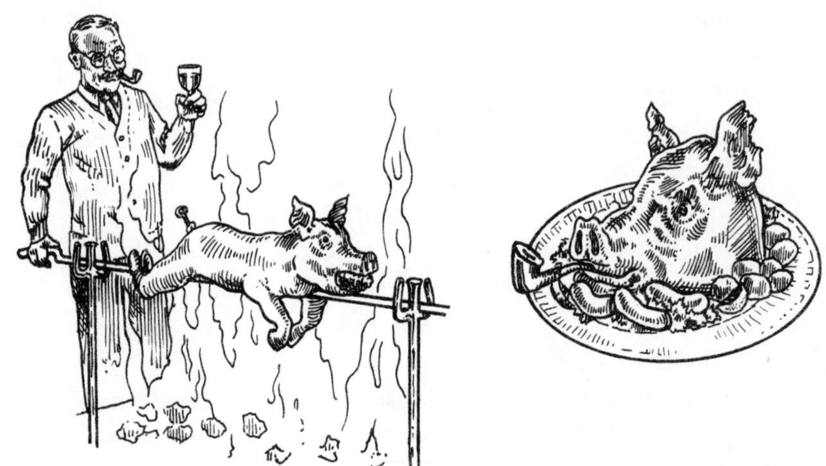

◎ *The* Babe *soundtrack includes the song "Anorexic Duck Pizzicati."* ◎

HOW TO
FLIP A PANCAKE

The vital factors in a good pancake flip are a nonstick pan, a smooth wrist-flick, and nerves of steel. The wrist-flick is essential to break the vacuum under the pancake, allowing it to slide out in an upward direction. The frying pan's curve is what initiates the flip, turning it as it exits.

The only way to master the technique is to practice. Make yourself a rehearsal pancake, using a plate to turn it so that it's cooked on both sides. Start with small unambitious flips. Only once you have a bit of confidence should you progress to the 3-foot flip—the average flip-height. Optimum flip-speed for a 3-footer is 10 miles an hour, the pancake attaining its zenith in less than half a second.

After some practice, try your hand at the dazzling ceiling-high "chandelier toss."

Pancake science

One of the world's foremost experts on the science of pancake flipping is Dr. Garry Tungate of the University of Birmingham. His research has revealed some startling statistics.

- ½ joule (energy) is required to propel your average pancake three feet into the air.
- Rogue pancakes (those you fail to catch) hit the floor in about 1.1 seconds (usually raw side down), slapping the linoleum at about 14 miles an hour.

If you're going to flip pancakes, you'll need to know how to make them. Here's a recipe that will yield 1,000 pancakes. That ought to keep you going for a while.

Mardi Gras pancakes

- *20 pounds plain flour*
- *33 pints milk*
- *12 pints water*
- *6 pounds butter*
- *166 eggs*
- *90 pinches salt*

Method

1. Sift the flour and salt into an aluminum mixing bowl.
2. Break the eggs into the center then whisk together with the flour.

3 Gradually add the milk and water, whisking continually to keep the mixture smooth and lump-free. The batter should resemble heavy cream when you've finished (takes about two hours).
4 Melt the butter in your frying pan. Not all of it, just a small pat—you're not making one huge pancake.
5 Put the pan over a medium heat, taking care not to burn the butter.
6 Pour enough batter into the pan for a thin pancake and distribute it evenly by rotating your wrist. It takes a bit of practice to get the right amount but after about 200 attempts you should be able to do it without thinking.
7 When the pancake starts to brown and you can loosen it from the pan by shaking, try your flip, following the instructions above.
8 Cook the other side—it takes just a few seconds.
9 Pile your pancakes on a plate and keep them in a hot oven.
10 Serve piled high with a pat of butter and the best syrup you can find.

◎ *The International Pancake Race takes place every Fat Tuesday.* ◎

HOW TO
MAKE OLD-FASHIONED GINGER BEER IN YOUR BATHROOM

Homemade ginger beer used to take ages, and the bottles always ended up viciously explosive. My 24-hour method is easy, glass-free, and can be done when confined to your bathroom. You'll forget you ever liked ginger ale.

Required

- *2 empty 2-liter plastic soda bottles, and 1 cap*
- *A large nodule of root ginger. Not ginger powder—that's cheating*
- *A big mugful of any old sugar you can find*
- *About a quarter of a teaspoon of dried yeast*
- *A cheese grater or something*
- *A lemon*
- *Nail scissors*

Method

1. In the shower, wash everything but the yeast and sugar.
2. With your scissors, cut the top half off one bottle and keep the bottom half in reserve. We'll call this piece B, for bottom.
3. Pour the sugar and yeast into the whole bottle, using the inverted top half of the other as a funnel.
4. Grate the ginger on to a mirror until you have about two tablespoons. Leave the skin on. A razor or abrasive foot scraper works well as a grater but take care of your knuckles: human skin adds nothing to the flavor.
5. Cut the lemon in half with your scissors and squeeze the juice into bottle-piece B. Then stir in the ginger with a nail file or something. Two tablespoons makes a mildly spicy drink so if you prefer it nose-clearingly pungent add more.

6 Top up with water and pour the brew into the uncut bottle through your improvised funnel, clearing any blockages with a toothbrush.
7 Rinse leftover bits and pieces into the bottle and top up with water leaving a couple of inches of air space for fizzing room. A bit of leakage is inevitable; put a towel down and don't fuss.
8 Screw the cap on tightly and shake the bottle until the sugar is dissolved. This is great fun and can be done to music if there's a radio around.
9 The bottle should now gently resist a squeeze, like a debutante's leg. Leave it somewhere warm such as on top of the radiator.
10 After about 24 hours (longer in cold weather) squeeze the bottle again. You know fermentation is complete when it feels hard, like a sailor's biceps. Do not leave it for longer than 48 hours or it will squirt big-time when you open it, or might even explode.
11 Serve chilled. If you dislike floating ginger shreds, strain it through a clean wash cloth or hankie before drinking.

◎ *Elizabeth I is credited with the invention of the gingerbread man.* ◎

HOW TO
SELECT, OPEN, AND EAT AN OYSTER

Somebody once described eating an oyster as swallowing snot off a tortoise. This is blasphemy since there is no shellfish more delicious. The most delicious oysters generally available in the United States are the pale and wrinkly rock or Pacific oyster. Rock oysters can be eaten at any time of the year, unlike the European oyster, which becomes unpalatable during the summer, and is best eaten only when there is an R in the month.

Selecting an oyster

Look for heavy, tightly closed oysters. When you have a few likely specimens, give them a tap. They should sound dense and full. Like other shellfish, dead oysters can be poisonous, so buy them from reputable suppliers and try to eat them the same day. You can store them in a bowl in the fridge, round side-down to retain the juice.

Shucking an oyster

Shucking oysters is a truly soul-crushing task but the job is easier if you put them in the freezer for 20 minutes first. When you're ready, give them a good scrub, to dislodge any grime. Assuming you don't have a metal oyster glove, wrap a tea towel around your oyster and hold it firmly.

With rock oysters, gently slide the tip of a short sharp knife into the hinge and slide it around—away from yourself—to loosen the shell. Try to avoid the soft tissue for the moment.

Should you get the chance to try European oysters, don't cut the hinge. Put it next to your thumb and cut around the opposite side with a long knife.

Open the oyster like a book, cut the flesh from the top shell, and drop it into the lower half. Discard the top and loosen the meat in the lower shell. Take care not to lose any of the liquor. Your oysters should be kept somewhere flat while you're working—not on top of the TV, for example.

How to eat an oyster

Hold the oyster in your left hand and squeeze a little lemon juice on to the flesh. That's all you need. Switch hands, grasping the opposite edges of the shell from beneath. Bring the oyster to your mouth and tip it all in. Whether you chew is up to you.

◎ *Oysters can—and do—change sex.* ◎

HOW TO
MAKE A CLUB SANDWICH

The club sandwich is a quintessentially American food, served at lunch counters across the country. It dates back at least to the 19th century and consists of cooked chicken or turkey breast, crispy bacon, tomato, and crunchy lettuce, between layers of toasted white bread enlivened with mayonnaise. Arguments rage about the merits of chicken over turkey and although the club sandwich is almost always made with three slices of bread, held together by the now emblematic toothpick, this "double-decker" version is considered low-brow eating among some sandwich snobs.

Nobody knows where the name came from.

Ingredients

- *2 ounces cooked turkey or chicken breast*
- *3 pieces thin-sliced white bread*
- *Mayonnaise*
- *A crunchy lettuce leaf*
- *A small ripe tomato*
- *2 slices crispy bacon*
- *4 toothpicks*
- *A sharp knife*

Method

1. Thinly slice the turkey/chicken and tomato.
2. Toast the bread and spread it with mayonnaise—one side only.
3. Drop half a lettuce leaf on to one slice of the toasted bread and add the turkey.
4. Place the second slice, mayonnaise-up, on top of the meat.
5. Next add the other half of the lettuce leaf, a slice or two of tomato, and cram on the bacon. (My mouth's watering already.)

6 Finish with the final piece of bread, mayonnaise-down (obviously).
7 Cut the sandwich into four triangles, impaling each with a toothpick to stop everything from falling apart.
8 Get your laughing gear around it. (One does not eat the toothpick.)

◎ *When Duke Richelieu took Port Mayon in 1756 his chef created "Mayonnaise."* ◎

HOW TO POP A CHAMPAGNE BOTTLE LIKE A PRO

There I was at a fancy reception in Washington, DC, soaking in the ambiance of class and social graces, when an oleaginous man in a tuxedo offered to open the Champagne for our hesitant hostess. He wrenched off the foil, tore away the wire cage, and began pushing violently at the cork with this thumbs, doubled over in a most unattractive posture and grimacing as if in agony. At length he began an undignified low cursing, causing dismayed guests to put down their empty flutes and wander away. Suddenly, in a fit of rage, he gave the bottle a violent shake, as if wringing its neck, thrusting it finally between his thighs. All at once there was a crack like a rifle, followed by a sickening tinkle as the speeding cork struck the face of a valuable-looking mantel clock. Our man shot backward in a jet of froth, upsetting a Ming vase and banging his head smartly against an unsmiling bust of Abraham Lincoln. "Funny fellow," muttered a distinguished-looking gentleman in a cumberbund.

Look, it needn't be this difficult. The proper method is as follows:

1. Chill the bottle. Warm Champagne will froth everywhere. The bottle should feel *very* cold just before you open it. Let it sit in the ice bucket for 20 minutes.

2. Dry the bottle with a napkin or linen cloth to provide friction, but don't drape it like a cloak. This practice was begun to conceal inferior labels.
3. Remove the foil *neatly.* This should appear artistic not just utilitarian.
4. Loosen the wire, counterclockwise, until it is free of the glass, and take it off. It is said that if you can do it in five and a half twists, you have in your hands a top-quality bottle.
5. Point the bottle away from yourself (and others): the pressure in the bottle is 90 SUV tires. Grip the neck and grasp the cork with your right hand. Slowly twist the bottom of the bottle with your left hand. (*It's hold the cork and twist the bottle. Not the other way.*) You'll soon feel it give, but go slowly; you are not attempting to fire it across the room, nor do you want a deafening pop—like the noise you get in the movies. Continue to apply torque until the stopper is released with a quiet pop or sigh. Put it down on the table. The Champagne may produce a wisp of "smoke" but it should not gush from the neck in an uncontrollable froth unless you have handled the bottle carelessly or it's warm.
6. Pour a little into each glass in turn and wait for the mousse to dissipate. Top up to two-thirds full so that the Champagne doesn't pour down the sides in a Strombolian lava flow. Use tall fluted glasses not those bowl-shape goblets. It's better for the bubbles (*and you spill less*).
7. Occasionally you'll get a very tight cork. Don't fight it with your bare hands, use a lever, such as nutcrackers or pliers. Best do this out of the way of guests, it's not very pretty. Or do it with your sword (*see* Chapter 3).

◎ *There are reportedly 58 million bubbles in one bottle of Champagne.* ◎

HOW TO
MAKE A BACKYARD SMOKEHOUSE OUT OF AN OLD FRIDGE

My grandma, putting down her knitting, once told me that she had just two remaining ambitions. One was to punch someone in the face and the other was to be shut inside an old fridge. I remember thinking that this must be the first sign that she was slowly going bananas. She was at that time being kept alive on a heroic regime of different colored pills for everything from bad feet to itchy teeth, and I thought they might be interacting poorly. But apparently she wasn't losing it: these were indeed long-held desires. Of course, her fridge suggestion was a dangerous one, so my brother-in-law Pete instead made her a smokehouse out of an old refrigerator, later cold-smoking some of the most succulent trout I've ever eaten. Here's how to make the "smokerator" electric smoker.

Your smokerator consists of a smoke/heat source in the bottom and somewhere to put the meat. It's that simple. Vents at the top and bottom control the airflow, regulating the temperature and smoke.

Required

- *An old fridge (metal shelves* not *plastic)*
- *A small cast-iron skillet*
- *A can of your favorite beer*
- *A single-burner electric hot plate*
- *A hammer and chisel or old screwdriver*
- *Scissors*
- *Self-tapping screws*
- *Proprietary smoking wood sawdust, chunks or pellets*

Method

1. Remove all the innards from your refrigerator. Don't leave *any* plastic in there. There should already be a couple of holes in the

back and bottom of the fridge, where the wires and pipes used to emerge but you need one more. Using a chisel or an old screwdriver, or something, whack a hole in the top, about 1½ inches in diameter. *Watch your fingers.*

2 Drink the beer.

3 Cut the can into smallish pieces with scissors (not those devilishly small nail scissors). These will act as movable flaps to let you control the flow of air through your smokerator. Screw one into place over each hole with some self-tapping screws.

4 Mount the hot plate in the bottom of the fridge and position the skillet on top (on top of the hot plate, obviously, not on top of the fridge).

5 Run the cord out of one of the holes in the back and plug it in. Turn it on medium-low and fill the skillet with the sawdust, following the instructions on the pack.

6 Place your properly prepared meat on the metal shelves and close the door. (Get out first.)

7 Refill the skillet every 3–4 hours until the meat is well smoked. It takes between 12 and 24 hours, depending on what you're smoking.

8 "Cold smoking" is smoking at a temperature lower than 100 degrees F. For cold smoke you need a smoke source outside the unit, so cut a 4-inch hole in the side of the fridge, toward the bottom and use an old woodstove connected to the smokerator via a 4-inch metal stovepipe. The length of the pipe will determine the temperature of the smoke.

9 Get smoking.

◎ *President Lyndon Johnson smoked 3 packs of cigarettes a day.* ◎

MEXICAN POTATO SOUP

The following recipe is amazingly cheap and quick, which is ideal if you are, say, a broke and idle student.

INGREDIENTS

- *2–3 stock cubes*
- *A few small potatoes*
- *1 scallion stalk*
- *Some very hot chilies*

METHOD

1 Cut a few small potatoes into ugly lumps and boil them in enough water for two generous bowls of soup. Don't allow them to go soft—a 10-minute simmer is usually plenty.

2 Sprinkle in two or three vegetable stock cubes. A really good way to make this soup is to include a stock cube that contains chili, but beware—they mean business.

3 Chop your hot chilies and throw them in.

4 Chop your scallion into rings and throw them in.

5 Serve.

In Latin America it is said that nursing mothers rub chili oil around their nipples to accustom their infants to the spicy food they will encounter as they grow up. Nonetheless, you should avoid rubbing your eyes or answering the call of nature after handling hot chilies. The residue can play merry hell with your mucous membranes.

Whole milk, wine, beer or spirits are an antidote to the fiery capsicum. Bread works too, but not water, which intensifies the agony.

◎ *The world's hottest chili is India's Naga Jolokia.* ◎

HOW TO
PREPARE A GOOSE FOR THE OVEN

METHOD

1 Catch your goose.

2 Pluck it. There's *nothing to this*, just pull out the feathers in the direction they grow, looking out for shot holes as you go. Dig out the pellets with a small pointy knife, which you can also use to pull out the pinfeathers. Remove the hairs and down by holding the bird over some burning paper and singeing it all over.

3 Behead the bird.

4 Cut through the skin around the leg 1½ inches below the knee, without severing the tendons. Place the leg over edge of your table and press down to snap the bone. (The bones of properly reared geese are brittle and sharp. Rubbishy supermarket birds have crumbly soft bones. Avoid.) Take the foot in your right hand, grasp the body securely in your left, and pull the foot off. The tendons should come trailing along with it. In older geese, you'll have to dig them out with a skewer—they get hard and cartilaginous during cooking if you leave them in.

5 Cut into the body below the breastbone, so you can just get your hand in and drag out the entrails. While you are about it, pull out the gizzard, heart, and liver (the giblets). Goose liver is delicious, sautéed in a little butter and served with toast. Lying under the liver is the gallbladder. Don't break this or you'll leak bile all over the meat, imparting a non-delicious bitter nastiness.

6 The spongy red things surrounded by the ribs are the lungs. Take them out along with the kidneys, which you can't miss. They're lurking there, by the backbone.

7 Slip your first two fingers under the skin by the neck, where you'll find the trachea. Pull it out.

8 Remove the bird's stomach (the crop), which kind of clings to the skin by the breast.

9 Now draw back the skin of the neck, and cut the neck off, close to the body, leaving a long trailing piece of skin to fasten under the back, nice and tidy.

10 Remove the uropygial gland, sometimes called the "oil bag" or "preen gland," and wash the bird by running cold water through it. Give it a pat dry and check that you haven't left anything in there—especially money.

11 Cook your goose.

◎ Contes de ma Mère l'Oye (Mother Goose Tales) *first appeared in 1697.* ◎

HOW TO
MAKE GOOGLY EYES

Every young man should know how to prepare a novelty meal or two, and googly eyes have the advantage that they are quick and cheap, as well as unexpected. They are the perfect breakfast for young nephews and nieces who have turned up their noses at the suggestion of scrambled eggs on toast. Indeed, they are likely to be so popular that you will find yourself woken during the early hours for years to come by children demanding their production.

Required

- *Sliced bread*
- *Butter*
- *Eggs*

Method

1 Place a slice of bread on the table and press the mouth of a glass into the center hard enough to cut out a disc. Rotate the glass slightly to loosen the circle and lift it out. Reserve it.

2 Sizzle a pat of butter in a frying pan over a medium heat. Take care not to let it burn.
3 Butter the bread on both sides and drop it into the pan.
4 Carefully break an egg into the hole and allow it to fry. After a while, flip over the slice with a spatula and allow the other side to cook.
5 Once the bread is golden-brown and the egg is cooked through, turn the googly eye onto a plate. Children find ketchup the perfect accompaniment.
6 If you are making a number of googly eyes, you can use the circles cut from the middle to make fried or toasted "holes." For some reason, children who have sneeringly rejected buttered toast will tuck into toasted holes with enthusiasm. You can make a face on a "hole" by pushing in a few raisins.

◎ *Causes of bulging eyes include thyroid problems, thrombosis, and glaucoma.* ◎

HOW TO
COOK FOR A GIRL

Sausage, eggs, and toast is great served up in a greasy spoon café for a bunch of taxi drivers, but it is no meal to present a girl you are trying to impress. Ladies like fuss, frills and that kind of stuff, so what you need is some fancy concoction that looks like it required much more skill than it did, and cost a lot more than it did. Here is a recipe that should fit the bill. Some may object that spaghetti, like corn on the cob, is messy to handle. However, this actually puts you in a subtle position of power and gives you a great excuse for getting up close to the lady. So, be ready to leap in with the old napkin.

Pasta rapida con crema, basilico, aglio, e pancetta affumicata

Ingredients

- *A packet of fresh spaghetti*
- *½ pint half-and-half*
- *Some streaky bacon (smoked)*
- *2 cloves garlic*
- *Some fresh basil leaves*
- *Olive oil*
- *Butter*
- *Salt*
- *Freshly ground black pepper*

Any of these items that you can't filch can be bought at the supermarket.

Method

1. Put a large pan of water on to boil and warm a serving dish and two plates in the oven.
2. While it's all heating up, chop a dozen slices of bacon and fry them briefly in ½ teaspoon olive oil, stirring frequently.
3. Bring down the heat and add a pat of butter and two cloves of crushed garlic. The best way to crush garlic is to put the unpeeled clove under a broad-bladed knife and smash it with your closed fist. The skin then comes off effortlessly. *Warning:* garlic and butter both burn easily, so cook them slowly over a low heat.
4. Once the garlic has softened, stir in a tablespoonful of olive oil and pour in the half-and-half. Season to taste.
5. Keeping the heat low, stir it around briskly until hot, then cover with a lid.
6. Tip the pasta into the boiling water. Follow the instructions on the packet religiously. Fresh spaghetti cooks fast so you must stand there and watch it. Chop the basil while you do.
7. As soon as the pasta is cooked, strain it and transfer to the serving

bowl. Do this carefully because fresh spaghetti is more fragile than dried. Pour the creamy, bacony, garlicy gumbo on top and sprinkle with the chopped basil. Try to make it look pretty, for goodness' sake. The garlic, smoked bacon, and basil produce a delicious aroma, and the cream, bacon fat, oil, and butter make the meal delicious, as well as filling. Serve at once on hot plates.

For an economical appetizer, try a can of consommé and pretend you made it yourself. If you are totally broke, two stock cubes with boiling water in a nice bowl make a delicious light soup. Do it in secret obviously. Properly presented, this works like a dream. If you can add three drops of scotch, you'll turn it into a feast. For dessert, a fudgy chocolate bar melted all over some cheap ice cream looks and smells magnificent. Pretend the recipe is an old family secret.

A flower in a vase (plucked from the park or someone's garden) lends a suggestion of class to a guy's table. Add a candle: a nice one. Tea lights will do—ladies like them.

Et voilà!

◎ *The correct singular form of "candelabra" is "candelabrum."* ◎

NOVEL RECIPES FOR THE JADED PALATE

Among the delicious recipes included by Prosper Montagne in his *Larousse Gastronomique* is one for a dish named *Entrecote à la Bordelaise.* This sounds delicious until you realize it is "grilled rats, Bordeaux style." This specialty requires the catching, skinning, and gutting of a few alcoholic rats of the type that live in French wine cellars (I'm not making this up). The boozy rodents are then brushed with a viscous dressing of olive oil and crushed scallions, before being grilled over a fire of broken wine barrels.

Both brown rats and roof rats have been enthusiastically eaten by hungry Parisians over the years, while the ancient Romans particularly enjoyed sewn-up fish-and-nut-stuffed dormice, baked to perfection. The litany of quirky chow down the ages also includes horse, witchetty grubs, pig's nose, and mashed brains, as well as the now rather commonplace frogs and snails. So, for the man who has had enough of chicken, steak, and ice cream, here are a few novelty meals that will make your guests sit up and pay attention.

Souris à la crème (Mice in cream)

This is a pretty good one to start off with. It's accompanied by an interesting salad and followed by a novel dessert, so you could serve the whole thing as a three-course meal, maybe with a liquidized Spam and anchovy shake to finish. Here's what you need for the mousey element:

Ingredients

- *A few fat mice*
- *A hunk of salt pork or sowbelly*
- *A bottle of industrial-strength vodka*
- *3 ounces Grand Marnier*
- *A few cloves*
- *½ pound all-purpose flour*
- *Salt and pepper*

Method

1. Skin, eviscerate, and wash the mice but leave the heads on. If you don't like the reproachful look in their eyes, tie an old sock over their faces.
2. Marinate in vodka for two hours (the mice, not you).
3. While you wait, dice the pork belly and render the fat by cooking slowly for several hours.
4. Drain the mice (be careful—that vodka is flammable).
5. Dredge them thoroughly in the flour, seasoned well with salt and pepper.

6 Sauté in the pork fat for five minutes.
7 Add ½ cup vodka, the Grand Marnier, and a pinch of cloves.
8 Simmer covered for 15 minutes.
9 Prepare a Béchamel cream sauce (an old cookbook will show you how if you don't know) and transfer the hot, succulent, and orangey mice into it.
10 Warm for about 10 minutes.
11 Serve.

Spider side salad

In addition to tarantulas, you should include spiders of as many different kinds as you can find, depending on where you live. Don't go anywhere near the poisonous ones, *obviously*.

Method

1 Steam your spiders live, like crab, to maintain crispness.
2 Amputate the legs from larger specimens, and quarter them.
3 Make a bed of romaine lettuce, parsley, chopped portobello mushrooms, radishes, and scallions. Toss in 1 cup chopped spiders and a generous squirt of extra-virgin olive oil, vinegar, lemon juice, and fresh ground pepper. Sliced jalapeño chili pepper adds an extra kick (since you won't get one from the spider legs).

Cow udder eclairs

Ingredients

- *12 fresh cow udders*
- *1 pint heavy cream*
- *1 can artichoke hearts*
- *1 filleted smelt (small)*
- *1 cup brown sugar*
- *1 stick butter*
- *Food processor*

- *Skillet*
- *1 can depilatory cream (such as Nair)*

1 Soak the udders in depilatory cream to remove the hair. Repeat as necessary until bald (until *the udders* are bald). Shaving won't do it; it leaves a nasty stubble.
2 To remove milk traces, soak the udders in lukewarm water for 2–4 hours while you go and make a periscope or something.
3 Rinse.
4 Melt a stick of butter in a warm skillet and add the udders. Fry until golden.
5 Finely chop the artichoke hearts and smelt.
6 In a food processor, gently whip the cream, sugar, artichokes, and smelt. Remove the udders from the pan when creamy and slit down the side of each. Spread the pudding mixture into the slits and serve cold. A majestic dessert.

◎ *Spiders come in just under 40,000 varieties.* ◎

HOW TO MAKE THE PERFECT AMERICAN HAMBURGER

German snacks, like the frankfurter, are often named after their place of origin. The origin of the name "hamburger" is, unsurprisingly, Hamburg, where ground meat was traditionally served in a bread roll, called a *Brötchen*.

The origin of the American hamburger is, however, contentious, with the burghers of Connecticut, Texas, and Missouri, all claiming first-burger status. The putative date of introduction hovers very roughly around the cusp of the 20th century.

Hamburgers are now a staple of the American diet, but the kind you get in a restaurant differs in important respects from the kind you grill yourself in the backyard. One leading burger is reported to contain, in addition to beef, the following delectable ingredients: calcium lactate, benzoic acid, dextrose, mono- and diacetyltartaric acid esters of glycerides of fatty acids, water, mono- and diglycerides of fatty acids, soy, saccharose, sodium stearoyl-2-lactylate, calcium sulphate, ascorbic acid, sodium acetates (i) sodium acetate (ii) sodium hydrogen acetate (sodium diacetate), and salt. If you'd rather make your own perfect American hamburger, here is the last word on the subject.

1 Choose the right meat. Coarse grind is what to look out for. Finely ground meat can become mushy and hard to work. High fat is the key to a delicious burger (but not necessarily to heart health). Lean beef, like sirloin or 7 percent fat meat, makes a dry burger. The more fat, the more succulent the meat—but the more it will shrink during cooking, with 30 percent fat beef dwindling by as much as 25 percent. Try 20 percent fat beef, but make the patties a bit wider than your buns to allow for shrinkage.
2 Mix the meat with coarse ground black pepper, a little olive oil, and some minced garlic. But no salt yet. Adding salt to the mixture has a deliquescent effect, sucking the moisture out of the meat, and producing burgers as dry as crumbled plaster. Instead sprinkle salt on the patties just before you put them on the grill. You need plenty; sorry about your blood pressure.
3 Form into patties, pressing your thumb into the center of each, so that you have a ring-shaped thing with a dent. This will stop the burgers becoming almost entirely spherical as they cook.
4 Heat an oiled grill until it's too hot to hold your hand over, position the patties on the grill, salt them extravagantly, and swiftly close the lid.
5 Wait for 2–3 minutes.
6 Try lifting a patty with a spatula. If it sticks, keep grilling until the moment it comes free, and then flip all the patties.
7 Close the lid and grill for another 2–3 minutes.

8 Check the patties again and as soon as they are free of the grate, flip once more.
9 Grill until the juices run clear and the burgers feel firm and solid.
10 Remove from the grill and check for doneness by piercing with a fork. If the meat looks too pink, grill for another minute or so.
11 Serve on good buns with fried onions, horseradish, condiments, and fixings to taste. But not a great big Dagwood sandwich full of everything. There's no need to be a slob.

◎ *Felix Mendelssohn (1809–1847) was born in Hamburg.* ◎

HOW TO
COOK A PROPER SUPER BOWL CHILI

Super Bowl Sunday has achieved, informally, the status of a national holiday and surely counts as a true *festival of the people*, along the lines of the celebrated Rio de Janeiro Carnival or Cup-of-Tea-Saturday, the famous holiday when the English put on their derbies, stand politely in line—sipping tea through bad teeth out of fancy cups and saucers—and chat to each other in rhyming slang about the wet weather, warm beer, and the Queen's stuck-up family, before indulging in a soccer riot with rolled umbrellas. No, I made that one up; there's no such holiday.

But it's certainly true that the Super Bowl, which has only been going since 1967, is now a phenomenon rather like Thanksgiving, in which whole families—not only football lovers and their buddies—get together to enjoy themselves in one of the biggest party days of the year, with betting and football and the party and gambling and the football and beer and the TV commercials and the gambling.

And, of course, there's the food.

My friend Mike Chaussee not only loves Super Bowl Sunday but knows how to make the party go with a swing. And what he doesn't know about Super Bowl chow isn't worth knowing. I am indebted to him for the recipe ideas that follow.

When I asked Mike what was his favorite Super Bowl food, he assumed a faraway look and said in a dreamy voice: "Chips, dips, beer, pop, potato salad, beer, Lit'l Smokies in a Crock-Pot with barbeque sauce and Tabasco, big big sandwiches, beer, seven-layer bean dip, salsa, chips, beer, pizza, burgers. And *chili* . . ." I suggested that all this might not be good for one's arteries but he couldn't hear me; he was far, far away.

Of course, if families or girlfriends or wives are present they will most likely do the salads and sandwiches and dips and all the non-guy stuff. Because, let me tell you, they aren't gonna be watching the football. This is good because the last thing you want is people who don't know what they're talking about either asking questions, or worse, cheering during the game. The true desire of the True Man is to have True Football Fans present. And not others.

But it's during the halftime show that you can come into your own on the culinary front. That show has to be just for the ladies. For most of my football buddies it's just terribly long and annoying, although the 2004 halftime show was moderately interesting, I seem to remember. That was Super Bowl XXXVIII in Houston, when there was a "wardrobe malfunction" and the nation was treated to more of Janet Jackson's charms than maybe they were expecting.

Chili

There are two sorts of food: the kind a guy can make and the kind he can't. Spun sugar, tiny roses made out of marzipan, and soufflé are things of the sort that tend to crash and burn if a man is attempting them, while steak, hamburger, and hot dogs are all on the man-can-do-this list. Chili is on the list too, which is good, as it is a pretty universal menu item at Super Bowl parties.

The true origins of chili are lost in history, with cowboys, Texas prisoners, and Spanish Conquistadors, who brought the dish to Mexico, being variously cited as the originators of the meal. The original Spanish name, *chile con carne* means "chili with meat" and the earliest role of the chili peppers was to tenderize or disguise inferior meat. In 1828 J. C. Clopper noticed people in San Antonio chopping the little meat they had and cooking it with chili so as to stretch the meal. Garlic and beans are both 20th-century additions.

Nowadays there's plenty of good meat, and a vast range of chilies from the mildest and sweetest to tiny, innocuous-looking things that will blow your eardrums out and melt your clothes. Choose the sort that suit you, but don't forget that other people have to eat the stuff too.

Perfect Super Bowl Halftime Chili

This recipe will easily provide enough chili for 16 people. If you suddenly find there are more people than you think you can feed, stir in some more chopped jalapeño. That will slow them down a bit. Obviously, start it long before the game and serve it up during the halftime show.

Ingredients

- *4 tablespoons olive oil*
- *4 medium onions (chopped)*
- *2 medium green peppers (chopped)*
- *8 pounds ground beef*
- *1 6-ounce can tomato paste*
- *2 1-pound cans stewed tomatoes*
- *2 1-pound cans tomato sauce*
- *1 7-ounce can chili salsa (OK, it's cheating, but you're pressed for time)*
- *6 cloves garlic (crushed)*
- *3 ounces chili powder*
- *1 jalapeño pepper (seeded, de-veined, and chopped. Do not touch your eyes!)*
- *2 tablespoons salt*
- *1 tablespoon oregano*
- *2 tablespoons garlic powder (or as much as your friends will put up with)*
- *1 tablespoon ground black pepper*

Method

1. Fry the meat in large skillet. There's a lot of it so it may take two goes. Once it's browned, drain the juice.
2. Heat the oil in a huge pot over a medium heat. Sauté the onions, peppers, and crushed garlic until soft. Do not burn.
3. Add the meat, tomato paste, stewed tomatoes, and tomato sauce. (This is not a good meal if you are allergic to tomatoes.)
4. Stir in the garlic powder, salt, pepper, oregano, chili powder, chili salsa, and jalapeño.
5. Turn down to low and simmer for 3 hours, stirring every 15 minutes. Yes, it's boring.
6. Halfway through cooking (stir number 6) season with salt and pepper (and additional chili if underperforming. This is not a skin-peelingly hot chili. If you like it really hot, just use hotter chilies and more of them).
7. Serve with grated cheese, onions, and tortilla chips for dipping.

Vegetarian halftime chili

You might wonder why a vegetarian would wish to eat a meal of chili. After all, it's basically a meat dish. But I have this friend who says he's a vegetarian not because he respects animals but because he hates plants. For a person like him, substitute kidney beans, extra onions, and more tomato paste for the meat (weight for weight). A little butter is sometimes required to replace the meat fats. It is amazingly good and even unreconstructed carnivores will dig in.

Now you can dash back in with your plate piled high and another cold beer in your hand, to watch the latest car commercials before the deciding half kicks off. I can barely control my excitement.

◎ *Tabasco is the official hot sauce of the U.S. space shuttle.* ◎

HOW TO
MAKE A DECENT BREAKFAST

Breakfast is often said to be the most important meal of the day. Regardless of whether that's true, it's useful to know how to prepare it.

Eggs over easy

Eggs over easy is the breakfast of choice for those who like a runny yolk but not slimy albumen. In a skillet over medium heat, cook as for sunny-side up, then flip for 15 seconds. Don't flip too soon.

Hash browns

Hash browns are fried shredded-potato cakes. They should be crisp, but are often disappointingly soft. The secret is to remove as much water as you can before frying. This water-light recipe will serve two hungry people.

Ingredients

- *½ pound grated potatoes*
- *A generous splash of vegetable oil*
- *Salt and pepper*

Required

- *A big frying pan*
- *A cheese grater*
- *A collander*

Method

1. Put the grated potatoes into your collander and squeeze out as much water as possible. *You'll be surprised.* Without a collander, you can improvize using a couple of baking sheets with a fat man or a car on top.

2 Heat the oil over a fairly high heat. When it's about to smoke put the spuds into the pan in a thin even layer, and season.
3 When they are golden brown flip them with a spatula (or see How to flip a pancake, in this chapter). Fry the other side to a similar color, and serve.

Cinnamon French toast (serves 2)

A breakfast classic for which you will need:

Ingredients

- *4 slices white bread*
- *½ can evaporated milk*
- *1 small egg*
- *1 shake vanilla extract*
- *Powdered cinnamon to taste*
- *1 pinch salt*
- *A big pat of butter*

Method

1 Blend everything but the bread and butter in a bowl.
2 Melt the butter in a hottish frying pan while you coat your bread with the mixture.
3 Fry for about 3 minutes on each side until nicely brown.
4 A little sprinkled powdered sugar adds an authentic touch, especially if you're having this with sausage or something else aggressively savory.

◎ *It is said that French toast was invented in upstate New York.* ◎

HOW TO
COOK FOR GUESTS WHILE YOUR KITCHEN IS BEING REPAIRED

Suppose you are expecting illustrious company for dinner but have forgotten that there are repairmen meddling with your oven and the floors are torn up. Don't worry, *it's happened to all of us* and if you have the right ingredients there's no reason you can't entertain your guests. Here are the emergency procedures, along with suggested menu items.

Hors d'oeuvres

- *Eggs mayonnaise*
- *Mulligatawny soup with warm breads*

Main course

- *Fresh mixed salad with vinaigrette*
- *Fillet of steamed salmon with new potatoes, green beans, vine tomatoes, and parsley sauce.*

Dessert

- *Crème caramel*
- *Blanched almonds with honeycomb*

To finish

- *Homemade cappuccino*

Method

1. Before you begin cooking, start the car and allow it to warm up.
2. Put your white wine into the toilet tank to chill (leave it in the bottle, obviously: you don't want to be flushing every time someone asks for a glass of Chablis).

3 Warm the bread over the vents at the back of your television, but turn the sound down so conversation can take place unhindered. Pita bread warms nicely with an iron.

4 Clean your potatoes with a power washer or garden hose and put them on to boil on the stove. Chuck in the beans toward the end.

5 Prepare the eggs by boiling for a good five minutes in your foot spa.

6 Pour your soup into a hot water bottle and run it under a very hot tap in the bathroom sink. Mulligatawny is a good choice, disguising, as it does, the astringent rubber taste. Try not to serve it from the hot water bottle; it's poor salesmanship.

7 Start the salad by putting your lettuce through the document shredder. Then combine with the remaining salad ingredients.

8 For the dressing, mix up the vinaigrette, which you can either serve from a liquid soap dispenser at the table or toss into the salad in the washing machine, set to "spin." Slivers shaved off a lump of Parmesan with an old razor look rather classy on top.

9 For the main course, first skin your tomatoes. This takes just seconds with a powerful wallpaper stripper.

10 Wrap your salmon pieces in foil and either steam them in the dishwasher on "energy saver" or pack them around your car radiator and get someone to take the jalopy out for a spin. Either method will cook the fish to perfection. Here's a tip: before serving the fish, warm your plates with a hair dryer.

11 Begin the white sauce by clarifying a chopped onion in a little oil on a good hot iron—set to "cotton." Scrape this into a pan with a little cut parsley, and season well. Mix together with flour, milk, and cream over a hot car engine.

12 For dessert, crème caramel is a snap with your paint stripper on full blast.

13 If you are doing the almonds, dip your nuts into scalding water to remove their skin just before serving.

14 For a really good frothy cappuccino, try using an electric toothbrush.

◎ *At their conclusion many French films bring up the word* Fin *(the end).* ◎

INDEX

C

D

E

Y